the seasonal BAKER

the seasonal BAKER

EASY RECIPES FROM MY HOME KITCHEN TO MAKE YEAR-ROUND

JOHN BARRICELLI

Owner of the SoNo Baking Company

CLARKSON POTTER/PUBLISHERS

NEW YORK

Published in the United States by Clarkson Potter/Publishers, an imprint of the Crown Publishing Group, a division of Random House, Inc., New York.
www.crownpublishing.com
www.clarksonpotter.com

CLARKSON POTTER is a trademark and POTTER with colophon is a registered trademark of Random House, Inc.

Library of Congress Cataloging-in-Publication Data
Barricelli, John.
The Seasonal Baker /John Barricelli. —1st ed.
p. cm.
1. Cooking (Fruit) 2. Cooking (Vegetables) 3. Baking. I. SoNo Baking Company & Café (South Norwalk, Conn.) II. Title.
TX811.B36 2012
641.6'4—dc23 2011027042

978-0-307-95187-8

Printed in China

Book design by Ashley Tucker based on an original design by Jennifer K. Beal Davis
Jacket design by Ashley Tucker
Jacket photography by Ben Fink

10 9 8 7 6 5 4 3 2 1

First Edition

To my biggest fan . . .
We miss you, brother Michael.
Watch over us.

Contents

Introduction

I have two great passions: baking and family. The first is probably genetic. My great-grandfather Giuseppe Barricelli was a baker from the Italian city of Nola, in the Campania region south of Naples. He settled with his family in Williamsburg, Brooklyn, at the turn of the twentieth century. He opened a *panetteria* there, making breads and desserts in a coal-fired brick oven to sell from his sidewalk cart. My grandfather Anthony worked in the bakery before giving up the business to become an electrician. My dad was an electrician like his father, but he knew his way around a kitchen, too.

I grew up in Valley Stream, Long Island, number six of eight brothers. It took me a while to find my way to baking, but I was always interested in food. There isn't anything I won't eat: anchovies, okra, you name it. I loved pizza as a kid. (I still do.) I used to sneak up the street to Mario's, the neighborhood pizza place, to watch them make their doughs. And I have fond memories of stealing sacks of Mario's flour for flour fights with the neighborhood kids.

My mom died the summer after third grade. My dad and my grandmother taught me to cook. I used to help my dad prepare dinners, prepping for him after school while he was working. And every Sunday, for as long as I can remember, we had dinner at my grandparents' house.

My grandparents Anthony and Julia lived in Williamsburg in a four-story house stuffed with three generations of Barricellis. What a scene. The family's kitchen and dining room were in the basement. Sundays at one o'clock, the whole clan—aunts, uncles, nephews, nieces, and cousins—would descend into the basement for dinner. We didn't surface until six o'clock in the evening. My dad always gave us the option of staying home, but I don't remember missing one Sunday dinner there. I used to look forward to it all week long.

The dining room table was probably about twenty feet long, but it seemed endless. It seated twenty to thirty family members and a rotating cast of characters. Side tables were set up for the kids. My grandmother and Aunt Ida were at the stove and they cooked and fed the never-ending stream of people all day long. There was

always a pot of "gravy" (our term for tomato sauce) on the stove. Julia and Ida made everything: roasted chicken, eggplant dishes, lasagne, baked ziti, my grandmother's escarole pie. Aunt Ida's fried chicken was incredible. One of the dishes I remember most clearly though was my grandmother's antipasto, a simple dish with great roasted peppers, dried meats, provolone cheese, and olives. She always finished it with a good olive oil. To this day, every time I have an antipasto at a restaurant, I think of her.

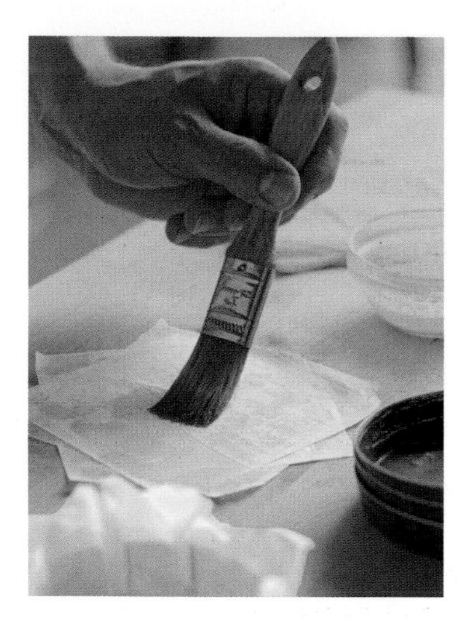

Squares of store-bought filo dough are brushed with butter for Banana–Macadamia Nut Tartlets (page 134).

Desserts at Sunday dinner were seasonal. In the summer, we enjoyed my grandfather Tony's sliced peaches marinated in red wine. For Easter, he made a traditional Neapolitan pie filled with a sweetened ricotta–wheat berry mixture. And there was always a selection of biscotti.

After dinner, my grandmother would load up our car with trays of more food to get my dad through the week. She included sandwiches to get us through the thirty-minute ride home—yes, by the time we got in the car, we were already hungry again!

When my dad died during my senior year of high school, I took over the cooking for my brothers. I made the dishes I'd learned to cook: the meatballs and gravy, the meatloaf, the tuna salad, and the mac-and-cheese.

I don't know whether my parents were watching out for me from above or I've just been lucky. But people have always been there to offer help when I needed it. I got my start in restaurants with Rick Steffann, the chef at River Café in Brooklyn. I got my first taste of baking there, too. I loved the kitchen so much that I applied and was accepted to the Culinary Institute of America in Hyde Park, New York. From there, a friend of the family helped me get an externship at the Louis XVI restaurant in New Orleans, one of the most elegant restaurants in the French Quarter. I drove there alone from Long Island, with a life-size stuffed animal in the passenger seat for company. I was eighteen years old (and looked about twelve).

In New Orleans, I met a young French woman, Babette, who later introduced me to the delights of French pastry when I visited her in Paris. I explored the outdoor markets in the morning and spent my days shopping, cooking, and eating. Paris is where I tasted my first éclair, raspberry tart, tarte Tatin, and apple charlotte.

I honed my pastry technique at some of the best places in New York, including the Helmsley Palace Hotel, the Pierre Hotel, the Four Seasons Hotel, and the restaurant Le Bernardin. I returned to Europe several times to expand my pastry skills and take classes at La Varenne and Le Cordon Bleu cooking schools. I studied Italian cuisine and bread-baking in Italy and fell in love with the street food of Bologna. I've owned and operated several bakeries of my own since then, including my current bakery, SoNo Baking Company, in Norwalk, Connecticut.

Along the way I married and had kids. I love kids. And like my own father, I'm now a single dad with visiting children. Sometimes I'm feeding one child, sometimes two or three. I spend the most time with my youngest, Peter, who is four. He appears often in this book because he's the best eater. He likes sitting in the grocery cart while we shop and he's pleased to eat almost everything, including broccoli and asparagus. My elementary-school-age daughter Nola visits regularly too. Already a good athlete, she has lately become interested in cooking. (I just bought her her first knife—a five-inch Japanese santoku.) When we're lucky, my grown-up son, Nik, drops by to make us a family of four. He loves to play in his own kitchen in Brooklyn, as well as with me, Peter, and Nola in mine.

My son Peter loves to cut out cookie shapes.

My work doesn't leave much time for family and friends. My day starts by three o'clock in the morning, often earlier. When I start at five a.m., I consider it a day off. But I try to spend as much time with my itinerant family as I can. Baking and cooking with them is a rewarding way to do what I love while giving my kids the rich experience of food and family that I grew up with.

The sweet and savory recipes in this book are conceived with family—mine and yours—in mind. I love working with produce—there's such incredible diversity and it keeps me connected to the seasons. My recipes offer new ways to use much of what you find in the produce aisle of your supermarket, with options for every season. With the exception of some of the more complicated, special-occasion pies and layer cakes, the recipes are geared to everyday baking. I've simplified techniques and recipes from my professional career wherever possible so that most of the recipes are practical for beginning bakers. Experienced bakers will enjoy the challenge of more complex recipes. As in my first book, technique tips give you the best possible advice for anticipating and solving problems. For dedicated bakers, a standing mixer is a must, but for most of these recipes, a handheld mixer and

food processor will offer as much mechanical help as you'll need.

These recipes will entice children to enjoy fruit and vegetables for the rest of their lives. I encourage you to get the kids involved in the cooking, whatever their age. They are a blast to teach and they like to help. Nik and I used to make gelato together on the weekends when he was a boy. With supervision, Nola can now make many of the recipes in this book. Peter is too young to do much but eat, but he does help with pizza dough, which he likes to punch down and stretch out.

ABOVE: I buy locally grown herbs and produce whenever possible.

OPPOSITE: My daughter Nola helps make her favorite Grilled Pizza Margherita (page 269).

This is not a farmers'-market cookbook, although I think it's good for the soul to visit a market when you can. Shopping there is a slower, inspirational experience. The markets give the SoNo Baking Company access to excellent seasonal produce. But when I'm baking at home, I'm shopping at supermarkets more often than not, and the recipes in this book assume that you will be, too. A shopping guide on page 18 offers recommendations on how to buy, store, and prepare the fruit and vegetables you'll come across in this book.

My baking is based on my philosophy of excellence. As I discovered with my grandmother's antipasto, if you start with tried-and-true cooking techniques and the best ingredients you can get hold of, you can't help but produce the best possible results. The goal of this book is to bring that philosophy into your home. I don't use anything in my bakery that you wouldn't use at home; we make everything by hand, and from scratch, with produce that is readily available. I don't have the equipment at home that we have at the bakery. I adjust for my home kitchen and I'll show you how to adjust for yours. (Even in the bakery, I tell my staff that a pair of clean hands often suffices.)

Thirty-five years' experience in commercial kitchens adapted to your home is what this book will give you. I hope these recipes sweeten your home life as much as they do mine.

Ingredient Checklist

If you keep the following ingredients on hand, you'll be able to jump into many of the recipes in this book without a special trip to the grocery store. I recommend buying small quantities and replacing them often. Leaveners such as baking powder and baking soda lose their potency over time and should certainly be replaced every two to three months. Other seemingly indestructible dry ingredients such as flour, sugar, and oats will absorb moisture over time; store them in airtight containers. With the exception of refrigerated dairy, of which I only list buttermilk because of its long shelf life, ingredients should be stored in a cool, dark place unless otherwise specified.

A note about measuring: Dry ingredients should be spooned into the cup and leveled with the back of a knife for precise measuring.

- BAKING POWDER
- BAKING SODA
- BUTTER (always unsalted)
- BUTTERMILK
- CHOCOLATE (good quality bittersweet, milk, and white chocolate chips; mini semisweet chocolate chips; dark chocolate chunks; bittersweet and semisweet bars)
- COCOA POWDER (Dutch-processed)
- CORN SYRUP
- CORNMEAL (coarse yellow: refrigerate for up to four months or freeze for up to several months)
- CORNSTARCH
- DRIED FRUIT (raisins, golden raisins, currants, dried cherries, dried cranberries, dates)
- EGGS (large)
- EXTRACTS (vanilla, orange, lemon, almond)
- FLOUR (most recipes call for all-purpose; buy bread, whole wheat, and cake flours as needed)
- HONEY
- MAPLE SYRUP (never imitation: refrigerate after opening)
- MOLASSES (unsulfered)
- NUTELLA HAZELNUT SPREAD
- NUTS (blanched whole; sliced almonds, hazelnuts, walnuts, pecans; shelled pistachios and pine nuts: freeze for up to several months)
- OLD-FASHIONED ROLLED OATS (never instant)
- OIL (vegetable and extra-virgin olive)
- PUMPKIN PUREE (canned)
- SALT (coarse, as in kosher salt)
- SEEDS (pumpkin, sunflower: freeze for up to several months)
- SHREDDED COCONUT (unsweetened and sweetened angel flake: refrigerate after opening)
- SPICES (ground cinnamon, ginger, allspice, cloves; whole nutmeg)
- SUGARS (granulated, light brown, confectioners', sanding sugar)
- VANILLA PASTE (see sidebar on page 212) and extract (never imitation)
- VEGETABLE COOKING SPRAY

Equipment Checklist

Cooks typically accumulate baking equipment as the need arises, and the variety and quantity will depend on the size of your kitchen and how much and what you like to bake. If you don't like Lemony Madeleines (page 86) or Banana–Chocolate Chip Kugelhopf (page 154), for example, or don't ever plan to make ice cream, you won't need to clutter your cupboards with a Madeleine pan, Kugelhopf mold, or ice cream machine. This is a list of equipment that I have in my kitchen at home and just about everything you need to make all the recipes in this book.

Pans, Molds, Baking Dishes, and Sheets

- BAKING DISHES (8-by-8-inch square Pyrex, 9-by-13-inch rectangular Pyrex, 10-by-14-inch rectangular ceramic, 12-by-9-inch or 14-by-10-inch oval ceramic, 9½- or 10-inch round ceramic)
- BAKING SHEETS (17 by 12-inch rimmed and rimless, 12¼ by 8¼ by 1¼-inch rimmed)
- CAKE PANS (Two 9-by-2-inch round aluminum)
- COOLING RACKS
- KUGELHOPF MOLD (6½-cup: 8 inches in diameter and 3½ inches tall)
- LOAF PANS (glass or ceramic: 8½ by 4½-inch and 9 by 5-inch pans may be used interchangeably)
- MADELEINE PAN
- MUFFIN PANS (standard, jumbo, mini)
- PIE PLATES (9-inch Pyrex, 9½-inch deep-dish Pyrex, 10-inch Pyrex)
- RAMEKINS (4-ounce) and Pyrex custard cups (6-ounce)
- TART AND TARTLET PANS (9-inch and 10-inch aluminum tart pans with removable bottoms, 3½-inch and 4-inch tartlet pans)
- TUBE PAN (7-inch and 10-inch with removable bottom)

Utensils and Small Equipment

- BOX GRATER (for cheese, vegetables, and zest)
- CITRUS REAMER (metal, plastic, or wood)
- COOKIE CUTTERS AND BISCUIT CUTTERS
- KNIVES (3½-inch paring, 8-inch offset serrated, 8-inch or larger chef's, 12-inch serrated)
- MELON BALLER
- METAL TONGS
- MICROPLANE GRATER (for hard cheese, chocolate, and citrus zest)
- MIXING BOWLS (varying sizes in glass, stainless steel, plastic, or ceramic)
- NONSTICK SILICONE BAKING MATS OR PARCHMENT PAPER
- PASTRY BAG AND FITTED TIPS (I recommend Ateco brand)
- PASTRY BRUSH
- PASTRY OR BENCH SCRAPER (plastic or metal blade)
- PIE WEIGHTS (metal)
- PIZZA WHEEL
- ROLLING PIN (I prefer a "French" wooden rolling pin shaped like one long baton, without handles)
- SIEVE OR STRAINER (fine-mesh)

- SHEARS
- SPATULAS (flexible metal, offset metal, rubber, and flexible silicone heat-proof)
- SPOONS (wooden)
- WHISK

Large Equipment

- FOOD PROCESSOR (12-cup or 16-cup bowl)
- ICE CREAM MACHINE (electric or nonelectric: see page 230)
- MIXER (hand or standing mixer)

Measuring Tools

- MEASURING CUPS (metal, straight-sided for dry ingredients; 1-, 2-, and 4-cup glass or plastic, with a lip, for liquid)
- MEASURING SPOONS (1 tablespoon, 1 teaspoon, ½ teaspoon, ¼ teaspoon, ⅛ teaspoon)
- OVEN THERMOMETER
- RULER (metal is preferable to plastic)
- TIMER

Shopping Guide to Fruits and Vegetables

Nothing beats local produce in season. Fruit that is sold locally is picked at its peak because it doesn't have far to travel. Locally grown, seasonal produce almost always offers the best flavor, but depending on where you live, buying locally is not always practical. In the Northeast, for example, we have plenty of apples, pears, and tomatoes in season, but you'll never see local citrus fruit or pineapple in Connecticut.

Good produce is currently available year-round from around the country and around the world. Some of the best strawberries I buy in the middle of winter are from Florida and Australia. Some melons from South America are fantastic and most grapes sold in the Northeast are grown in South America. We live in a global economy and it makes sense to take advantage of it.

This section is geared to help you choose the very best produce, wherever it's from and wherever you shop. I'll tell you the best season to buy it and how to store it. I'll tell you the best ways to ripen bananas and stone fruits such as peaches, plums, and nectarines, which are usually purchased unripe. Some basic instructions that are not included in the recipes (how to wash mushrooms and berries, for example, or cut the peel from pineapple) are included in this section.

A few general rules apply to all produce. Fresh produce usually feels heavy for its size because as it ages, juices diminish and produce loses weight. A good rule of thumb is to buy what you need and use it as soon as possible. That's the way it's done in Europe, where people shop daily. All fruits and vegetables should be stored out of direct sunlight. Do not store produce in plastic. It needs to breathe! If you like, cover produce stored at room temperature with a fine netting to avoid fruit flies.

A note about frozen fruit: I use fresh fruit as much as possible. But frozen fruit can be of very good quality. Fruit for freezing is picked and processed at its peak because it needn't be protected from damage during transport. Freezing ruptures the cell walls in fruit so once thawed, frozen fruit will be softer than fresh and it will give off juices. Some fruit freezes well in a home freezer, and I've given freezing instructions for those fruits. Otherwise, I don't recommend it.

FRUIT

Apples

Many varieties of apples are available year-round but the best time to buy is late summer and through the fall while they're in season.

BUY: Choose apples that are very firm and heavy for their size. For all of the recipes in this book, I prefer to use baking apples such as Rome, Granny Smith, and Cortland because they hold their shape well during cooking.

STORE: Keep apples in open air at room temperature for about three days, or in the crisper drawer of the refrigerator for up to one week. In the winter, apples are held in cold storage. While they store well, they will no longer be at their peak.

PREPARE: Most of the recipes in this book call for peeling and coring apples. Wash, then peel with a vegetable peeler. To core, cut the apple in half and scoop out the core from each half with a melon baller. Or quarter the apple and cut out the core from each quarter with a paring knife.

Avocado

AVOCADOS are technically a fruit. Several varieties are grown in California. The Haas variety, grown year-round in California, accounts for a huge percentage of the avocado crop there. You may also see them imported from Mexico and Chile. The thick, pebbly textured skin is green on the unripe fruit, turning to purplish-black when ripe. Avocados are eaten raw, and some recipes call for them to be warmed in the oven.

BUY: Buy avocados under-ripe. They should be hard, or give slightly to pressure, with no bruising or soft spots. Avocados should feel heavy for their size.

STORE: Ripen at room temperature for one to three days. Then refrigerate for up to three days.

PREPARE: Avocados contain a large pit in the center. Cut the avocado in half lengthwise and twist to release one half. Then carefully whack the seed with the blade of a large knife. Twist the knife gently to free and remove the pit. The light green flesh will brown quickly once exposed to air; use as soon as possible.

Bananas

Imported from the tropics, bananas are available year-round.

BUY: I prefer to buy bananas under-ripe and ripen them at home under optimal conditions. (At the supermarket, ripe bananas may already be bruised.) Choose bananas that are just turning from green to yellow and show no bruising.

STORE: Ripen bananas at room temperature for one to two days. Bananas placed on a hard surface will develop soft spots and bruises so I recommend ripening on banana hangers. Or, store the banana "hands" so that the curve of the bananas faces up (like a curved bridge) and the ends support the weight of the bananas. Once they ripen, it's best to use them immediately. But if necessary, store them in the crisper drawer of the refrigerator to slow their ripening. (Note that refrigeration will firm the texture of the fruit; they will lose some sweetness and eventually turn mealy.) Once refrigerated, use within one or two days.

Berries: Blueberries, Blackberries, Strawberries, and Raspberries

Good-quality berries are available from somewhere around the world, year-round.

BUY: Blueberries, blackberries, strawberries, and raspberries are sold in dry quarts, pints, or half-pints. I turn the covered plastic box upside down and take a peek at the berries on the bottom: They should not be molded or flattened, they should be firm with skins intact, and the berries should not be bleeding (which indicates age). The bottoms of berry baskets are usually lined with an absorbent tissue to catch any juices, so make sure the tissue is not soaked.

STORE: Keep berries in the crisper drawer of the refrigerator for up to three days. Bring to room temperature before eating.

PREPARE: Do not wash blackberries or raspberries; even gentle wiping will break the skins. Wipe strawberries with a damp towel, only if necessary. Blueberries may be washed because the skins are firm.

FREEZE: Berries and cherries freeze well in a home freezer and can be used for pie fillings if the juices are bound with cornstarch (see Winter Blueberry Streusel Pie on page 128). Place the berries in a single layer on a paper-towel-lined baking sheet. Place the baking sheet in the freezer and freeze until the berries are frozen solid, four to six hours. Gather the frozen berries, transfer to resealable plastic freezer bags, and freeze for up to two months. Except where noted, unthawed berries can be used in all of the recipes in this book.

Cranberries

Cranberries are harvested in the United States in September and October. They are traditionally available fresh through the winter holidays, frozen the rest of the year.

BUY: Fresh cranberries should be uniform in color, size, and firmness.

STORE: Refrigerate fresh cranberries in the vegetable drawer of the refrigerator for up to one week.

PREPARE: Stem and rinse cranberries in a large bowl of water. Ripe, fresh cranberries will float. Discard any old ones that fall to the bottom of the bowl.

FREEZE: Cranberries freeze well. Buy several bags of fresh fruit at a time and put the bags in the freezer for up to two months. Frozen unthawed cranberries can be used in all of the recipes in this book.

Citrus Fruits: Lemons, Limes, and Oranges

Citrus fruits are grown principally in California and southern states including Texas, Louisiana, and Florida. Citrus season in the United States is late winter and early spring, but good-quality citrus fruits are available somewhere in the world year-round.

BUY: All citrus should be very firm with bright-colored flesh and no soft spots. They should be uniform in color and heavy for their size. When you scratch the skin with your nail, oils should bead up on the skin.

STORE: Keep in the vegetable drawer of the refrigerator for about one week.

PREPARE: Many recipes call for citrus zest but no juice. Even if you have no immediate need for it, I recommend zesting the skin of citrus fruits before juicing. Wrap the grated zest in a paper towel, enclose in a resealable plastic bag, and freeze.

Dried Fruits: Dates, Figs, Cranberries, Raisins, Golden Raisins, Currants, Cherries, and Apricots

Dried fruits have been sun-dried or dehydrated to remove most of their water content, resulting in fruit that is very sweet, with a concentrated flavor and a soft, leathery texture. Most dried fruits are processed with the chemical compound sulfur dioxide to preserve color and flavor. Fruits that are not preserved with sulfur dioxide are dark colored, even black.

BUY: Dried fruit should be soft.

STORE: Store dried fruit at room temperature in an airtight container.

PREPARE: Dried fruit should be plumped before baking. Otherwise, the heat of the oven will dry it further and make it unpleasantly hard. Plumping is also useful for dried fruit that has dried and hardened with age.

To plump dried fruit: Place the dried fruit in a heat-proof bowl. Bring 1 cup water (or enough to cover the dried fruit) to a boil. Pour the boiling water over the dried fruit and let stand for ten minutes. Drain and pat dry on paper towels.

Figs

There are hundreds of varieties of figs ranging in color from yellow to brown to purple to black. I use two popular varieties: Brown Turkey and Mission figs. Depending on where they're grown in the United States, figs are in season from mid-spring to the fall, and sometimes up until Christmas.

BUY: Whatever their color, figs should be firm and plump with smooth skin. The stem should be intact.

STORE: Keep figs in the crisper drawer of the refrigerator for up to three days. Serve at room temperature.

PREPARE: Do not wash. Wipe figs with a damp cloth or paper towel, if absolutely necessary. The skins are edible, so figs needn't be peeled.

Mangos

Mangos are cultivated in many parts of the world, including California and Florida, where they are in season from May to September.

BUY: Ripe mangos may be green, orange, yellow, or red. Choose mangos as if you're choosing an avocado: They should be firm, with no bruises, and should give slightly when pressed. I prefer large mangos because there is more flesh to them.

STORE: Buy under-ripe mangos to ripen at room temperature in the open air for one to three days.

PREPARE: Mangos have a large, flat seed in the center. The skin is not edible; peel with a vegetable peeler. To pit the mango, stand it on one end and cut off one half, working around the pit. Then cut the other half off the pit. Cube or slice the mango as desired. Another easy way to cut a mango into cubes is to leave the peel intact and cut the two halves off the pit as described above. Score the flesh of each half all the way down to the skin, first lengthwise and then widthwise, to make squares.

Turn the mango half inside out so that the squares "pop" out, and cut the mango squares off the skin.

Melons: Honeydew, Cantaloupe, and Watermelon

While there are many varieties of melons, the most common, and those used in my recipes, are honeydew, cantaloupe, and watermelon. They are available year-round from Mexico and South America but are best during the summer and early fall. Cantaloupe and honeydew are grown domestically in California, Arizona, and Texas; watermelon in California, Florida, Texas, and Georgia.

BUY: Ripe melons should be heavy for their size and uniform in color. They should be firm (once soft, they're overripe). Look for an indentation at one end of a cantaloupe or honeydew. This is the blossom end. It should give slightly on a ripe cantaloupe or honeydew when pressed with a finger. It's very difficult to gauge the ripeness of a watermelon.

STORE: Keep at room temperature in the open air for up to three days.

PREPARE: Wash, then cut the melon in half. For cantaloupe and honeydew, scrape out the seeds with a spoon. Cut the melon into thick slices and slice off the rind with a large knife. Then cut as desired.

Stone Fruits: Cherries, Peaches, Nectarines, Apricots, and Plums

Stone fruits are grown all over the United States, including the Northeast, California, Texas, and Georgia. Their season is summer. There are many varieties of plums and you can use any in my recipes. I especially like the oval, deep-purple Italian prune plums that are in season in the Northeast from late summer through early fall. There are several varieties of cherries, as well. I prefer sweet, dark red Bing cherries in my baking. Bing cherries are available in the Northeast, Midwest, and Pacific Northwest (Washington in particular) from late spring through summer, but they're imported year-round from South America.

BUY: Unless they are local, peaches, nectarines, apricots, and plums are usually sold under-ripe. (You know when stone fruit is ripe: The smell is wonderful.) Look for unbruised fruit with firm skin and uniform color. Cherries should be purchased ripe. Look for firm flesh and bright color. Refrigerate for up to three days.

STORE: Ripen peaches, nectarines, apricots, and plums in the open air, at room temperature, in a single layer. Once ripened, use immediately, or store briefly in the crisper drawer in the refrigerator.

PREPARE: To pit peaches, nectarines, apricots, and plums, cut the fruit in half through the stem ends. Twist to free one half. Remove pit with your fingers or a knife. Unripe fruit is difficult to pit. Pit cherries with a cherry pitter.

To skin peaches and apricots: Bring a large saucepan of water to a boil. In a large bowl, combine water and ice for an ice bath. Score an X in the skin at the bottom of each peach. Add the fruit to the boiling water and cook just until the skin peels off easily. Depending on the ripeness of the fruit, this will take between thirty seconds and about two

minutes. Transfer the fruit to the ice bath with a skimmer or slotted spoon.

FREEZE: Cherries freeze well. Wash, stem, and pit; freeze as for berries on page 21.

Pears

Many varieties of pears are available during the late summer and early fall, including Anjou, Bartlett, and Bosc. I use these three varieties in my recipes, but you can use whatever looks good. Bosc are especially nice for poaching whole because their shape is so beautiful and their crisp texture holds up well to cooking. Bartletts have a lovely buttery texture.

BUY: Even if you're buying pears locally grown, they will usually be very firm when you buy them and need a little ripening. Choose fruit without bruises, and of consistent color.

STORE: Ripen pears in the open air at room temperature for one to three days. Then store in the crisper drawer of the refrigerator and eat as soon as possible. Ripe pears should be juicy, but still crisp.

PREPARE: Peels are edible. Wash, and remove with a vegetable peeler, if desired. Core whole pears with a melon baller, through the bottom end, or cut the pears in half and core with a melon baller.

Persimmons

You may see two varieties of persimmons at your supermarket: Fuyu and Hachiya. I prefer the large, heart-shaped Hachiya variety because it contains more flesh. Its season is October through February.

BUY: Choose persimmons with bright, smooth skin. They are sold under-ripe. They should be plump and firm, not squishy.

STORE: Although they ripen to a beautiful, tangy sweet flavor, an unripe persimmon is incredibly, mouth-puckeringly tart. Ripen at warmish room temperature for at least one to two weeks, depending on how ripe they are when purchased. A ripe persimmon will feel very soft, like an under-filled water balloon. (At the SoNo Baking Company, we buy the fruit in early November for our Christmas puddings. We allow them to ripen for several weeks until the flesh turns to puree. When the bottom end is cut, the soft fruit squeezes right out.)

PREPARE: Peel and eat out of hand, or cut as desired.

Pineapple

Imported from Central and South America, the Philippines, and Hawaii, pineapples are available year round in the United States.

BUY: Buy pineapples as ripe as possible. The color should just be turning from greenish to golden yellow. A ripe pineapple will be firm with a slight give and a rich smell. The leaves should be green (not brown). Soft, dark areas on pineapples are a sign of overripeness.

STORE: Keep in the open air at room temperature for one to two days.

PREPARE: The thick, prickly skin and spiky "eyes" must be removed before eating. Using a large knife, cut off the top and bottom ends of the pineapple. Stand the pineapple on its base and slice off the peel, cutting deeply to remove all of the prickly "eyes." Cut crosswise into rounds and cut out the center core, or quarter lengthwise into wedges and cut off the core.

VEGETABLES AND FRESH HERBS

Asparagus

In the United States, asparagus is in season, depending on where you live, from February through May or June. It comes in green, white, and purple varieties. Green asparagus, the most common variety, is sold in three thicknesses: jumbo, medium, and pencil. All of my recipes use medium green asparagus. Asparagus is usually cooked.

BUY: Green asparagus stalks should be bright green in color, crisp, and firm. The heads should be closed and tight. Neither stems nor heads should look wilted. Uniform size makes timing for cooking easier.

STORE: Keep asparagus in the refrigerator as you would a bunch of flowers, stems down in a jar of water.

PREPARE: Trim the woody ends. Medium and pencil asparagus needn't be peeled but I peel the bottom half of jumbo asparagus stalks with a vegetable peeler because the peel is tough.

Corn

We have lots of sweet corn in Connecticut and the Northeast starting in early summer. Florida corn is typically available from January through midsummer. California corn is in the market from May through early fall. Corn is eaten cooked or raw.

BUY: Corn is sold in and out of the husk. Husks should look tight, not wilted. I often buy husked corn for convenience at home.

STORE: In a word, don't. The sugars in corn turn quickly to starch, changing a sweet, delicious treat into starchy, bland kernels. Store in the refrigerator, but eat as soon as possible.

PREPARE: To remove the kernels from an ear of corn, place the ear upright on a cutting board, wide end down. Slice down the cob with a large, sharp knife to cut off several rows of kernels. Continue cutting, rotating the ear as you go, until all of the kernels have been removed.

Eggplant

Eggplant is available year-round. If you shop at farmers' markets in the summer or fall, you'll see many shapes, colors, and sizes, including the slender Japanese eggplant without seeds. I suggest experimenting! Eggplant is always cooked.

BUY: Eggplant should be firm, feel heavy for its size, and have no bruising. I prefer small eggplant because the larger they are, the more bitter seeds they contain.

STORE: Keep in a cool place at room temperature for one to two days. After that, refrigerate and use as soon as possible.

PREPARE: The flesh of eggplant will brown once it is exposed to air, so cut it just before cooking. The skin is edible but slightly bitter, so I prefer to remove it with a vegetable peeler. If you decide not to peel, wash the eggplant.

Fennel

Fennel is a bulb, round or flattened in shape, topped with several long stems and delicate fronds. Fennel is available year-round, but the quality is better during fall and winter months. Fennel may be eaten raw or cooked.

BUY: Buy bulbs that feel heavy for their size.

The flesh should be bright, greenish white, and crisp.

STORE: Keep in the crisper drawer of the refrigerator for up to three days.

PREPARE: Cut off the stalks and discard. (The fronds may be used for seasoning; use as you would fresh dill.) Remove outer layers if browned, tough, or wilted. Cut the bulb in half and use a large knife to cut out the woody core in a triangle shape. Wash and cut as desired.

Leafy Greens: Escarole, Arugula, and Spinach

These greens are available year-round.

BUY: Greens should be crisp and fresh looking. Make sure that the tips of the leaves aren't dry or browning and that the leaves aren't soft or blackening. The stems should be crisp. Arugula should be dark green, with a slightly peppery taste. Baby arugula now sold in most supermarkets is more tender and less peppery than the larger leaves. It is also packaged clean, which makes it convenient. The same goes for baby spinach, which I so often use. Greens may be eaten raw or cooked.

STORE: Keep greens in the crisper drawer of the refrigerator for up to three days.

PREPARE: Wash greens and spin dry in a salad spinner. Escarole is almost always very dirty. To wash it, put chopped leaves in the sink and fill with cold water. Jostle the leaves to release the dirt, then lift the escarole out of the sink into a colander. Repeat with fresh water until the water remaining in the sink is clean. Use a salad spinner to remove as much water as possible before cooking.

Leeks

Leeks, which look like big, thick scallions, belong to the onion family. They have a lovely, subtle onion flavor. They are available year-round. They are almost always cooked.

BUY: The leaves should be firm, crisp, brightly colored, and tightly wrapped. There should be no discoloration or browning of the white stalks or dark green tops.

STORE: Keep in the crisper drawer of the refrigerator for up to five days.

PREPARE: Leeks are typically dirty and must be washed well. Trim the root end, cut the leek in half lengthwise, and rinse well under cold water, pulling the leaves apart to allow the water to get in between the leaves. Or, halve the leek lengthwise, slice, and rinse well as you would escarole (see above).

Mushrooms

At farmers' markets, you'll find a wonderful variety of foraged and cultivated mushrooms, all with different flavors and textures. My supermarket always carries white button, cremini, shiitake, and portobello mushrooms. (Portobello mushrooms are a large version of creminis.) Specialty stores in my area often carry oyster mushrooms, chanterelles, and hen of the woods. Button and cremini mushrooms may be eaten raw; other varieties are cooked.

BUY: Look for firm, plump mushrooms with no sign of softening, blackening, drying, or decay. The caps on cremini and button mushrooms should be tightly closed.

STORE: Keep mushrooms in the refrigerator for up to two days.

PREPARE: Mushrooms absorb water readily, so the best way to clean them is gently, with a damp paper towel. (Cultivated mushrooms are likely to be much cleaner than foraged varieties. If you don't have the patience, rinse them quickly and dry them well.) Trim stems of all mushrooms except shiitakes; their stems are tough and should be discarded. For other mushrooms, check that the stems are not soft and spongy. If so, the mushrooms are old; pull off the stems and discard. Mushrooms shrink enormously during cooking: One pound will shrink to about one cup.

Onions, Garlic, and Shallots

Most supermarkets carry red, white, and yellow onions, as well as some sweet specialty onions such as Vidalia or Maui. Red onions tend to be sweeter than the white and yellow varieties. You can use any variety in my recipes. Onions, shallots, and garlic are eaten raw and cooked.

BUY: Onions, shallots, and garlic should be very firm with tight skin and no browning, soft spots, or bruising. They should feel heavy for their size.

STORE: Keep at room temperature or in a cool dark spot for up to seven days. If exposed to light, onions and shallots will sprout.

PREPARE GARLIC: Squeeze the head with one hand to break the cloves apart. Then peel the cloves individually, or place on a cutting board and smash with the side of a large knife blade to loosen the peel. Fresh garlic peels more easily than older garlic.

PREPARE ONIONS AND SHALLOTS: Trim the hairy root ends and peel off the papery skins. Cut in half through the root ends. Slice or chop as indicated in the recipe.

Peppers: Bell Peppers and Jalapeños

Peppers are bountiful in the summer, but you'll find them year-round. They grow in any warm climate, all over the United States. They are eaten raw or cooked.

BUY: Red and green bell peppers are most common, but at my supermarket, I have the choice of yellow and orange as well. Red, yellow, and orange all taste about the same and are sweeter than green peppers. The beautiful, thick-fleshed, regular-size Red Holland peppers are more uniform and more expensive, but domestic peppers taste as good. The heavier the pepper, the thicker the flesh. For both bell peppers and jalapeños, look for firm peppers with smooth, unwrinkled skin. Wrinkled skin is the mark of age. As the pepper ages and loses moisture, the skin pulls away from the flesh.

STORE: Keep in the crisper drawer of the refrigerator for up to three days.

PREPARE: Cut off the tops. Cut the peppers in half lengthwise and pull out the seeds and ribs. (That's where you'll find the heat in a jalapeño. Leave in the ribs if you want some spice; add some seeds if you want even more.)

Potatoes: White- and Yellow-Fleshed Potatoes; Sweet Potatoes, and "Yams"

At my supermarket, potatoes come in all shapes and sizes. White- and yellow-fleshed potatoes can be divided into three categories: starchy (such as white-fleshed Idaho potatoes);

all-purpose (yellow-fleshed Yukon Golds); and low-starch (red- or white-skinned white-fleshed "new" potatoes). Starchy potatoes are great when you want baked or mashed potatoes; lower-starch potatoes fall apart less readily during cooking and are excellent boiled or roasted. I like fingerling potatoes for their tender skins and creamy, low-starch flesh and short cooking time.

Vegetables sold as "yams" in the supermarket are actually a variety of sweet potato. (You probably won't come across true yams unless you're shopping at an ethnic supermarket.) Sweet potatoes and so-called yams may be used interchangeably. Potatoes and sweet potatoes are always cooked.

BUY: Choose potatoes that are very firm with no blemishes, cuts, soft or green spots, or sprouts.

STORE: Keep in the open air in a cool, dark place for at least one week. Fingerling potatoes may be refrigerated for up to three days.

PREPARE: I never peel white- and yellow-fleshed potatoes. I like the fact that you can eat the whole thing and there's no waste. (I particularly like fingerling potatoes because the skin is thin and delicate and their long, skinny, irregular shape provides for a lot of skin relative to the flesh.) Scrub if dirty. If you do peel, keep them submerged in a bowl of cold water to prevent the flesh from blackening. Peel sweet potatoes before using.

Rhubarb

Technically a vegetable, rhubarb is used as a fruit in sweetened preparations. Its flavor is very tart. Only the stalks are edible; the leaves can be toxic. Rhubarb is unusual in that the reddish-pink, celery-like stalks are both field- and hothouse-grown. Field-grown rhubarb is in season from late winter through early summer, peaking from April through June. Hothouse rhubarb is available year-round.

BUY: Choose crisp, slender young stalks with no blemishes; the thinner stalks are less woody than larger ones (and the strings are thinner). Field-grown rhubarb should be bright red. Hothouse rhubarb is lighter in color.

STORE: Keep in the crisper drawer of the refrigerator and use within two to three days.

PREPARE: Although some people peel rhubarb, I never do; I buy slender stalks and cut them crosswise into small pieces.

Summer Squash: Zucchini and Yellow Crookneck

Different varieties of yellow and green squash are grown all over the United States and are available year-round.

BUY: Regardless of color or shape, the squash should be very firm with uniform color and no cuts or bruising. Medium or small sizes are best; larger squash contain longer seeds, and their texture is woody. Summer squash is eaten raw and cooked.

STORE: Keep in the crisper drawer of the refrigerator for up to three days.

PREPARE: Summer squash often benefit from a good scrubbing, as sand gets caught in the skin. The skin is edible. Trim the ends, cut as desired, and eat raw or cooked.

Tomatoes

The best tomatoes have been ripened on the vine. During tomato season in the late summer and fall, you can find some ripe, fabulous heirloom tomatoes at farmers' markets. They're likely to be expensive, but they're worth it. Hothouse tomatoes never quite develop the same flavor.

BUY: Tomatoes come in all shapes, sizes, and colors. Look for tomatoes that are uniform in color, heavy for their size, firm, and free of blemishes.

STORE: Tomatoes will continue to ripen after picking. Ripen in a single layer in the open air at room temperature in a warm place for one to two days. A ripe tomato is still firm but gives slightly to the touch. Once ripened, keep tomatoes at room temperature. Above all, don't refrigerate a beautiful tomato—it mars the flavor.

PREPARE: Tomatoes may be skinned just like a peach (page 23), but I rarely do that. Raw tomatoes should be eaten at room temperature. For cooking, I recommend a good-quality canned tomato.

Winter Squash: Butternut and Pumpkin

There are many varieties of winter squash. I like butternut squash for its bright color and sweet flavor. The large Halloween pumpkins at the supermarket are too watery to be practical for cooking, so when a recipe calls for pumpkin, I use a good-quality canned puree. Look on the label: Pumpkin should be the only ingredient. Winter squash is grown throughout the United States during warm months and harvested in September and October. Winter squash is always cooked.

BUY: Choose squash that is heavy for its size, firm, with no cuts or blemishes. Butternut squash is also sold halved, quartered, or packaged in large dice. Make sure the flesh looks firm and dry. Refrigerate and use as soon as possible.

STORE: Keep in the open air in a cool, dark area for up to two weeks.

PREPARE: Cut butternut squash in half lengthwise and scrape out the seeds. Cut the halves into smaller, more manageable pieces and peel with a vegetable peeler or a sharp knife. Cut as indicated in the recipe.

Fresh Herbs

Herbs can be divided into two categories: soft herbs (parsley, cilantro, basil, and tarragon) and woody herbs (rosemary, thyme, oregano, and marjoram). Herbs may be eaten raw or cooked, but I prefer rosemary cooked.

BUY: Look for herbs that are brightly colored and do not look wilted. Test the freshness of woody herbs such as rosemary and thyme the way you'd test a Christmas tree: Run your fingers along the stem. If the tree (or herb) is old, the needles (or leaves) will fall off.

STORE: Wash herbs by holding the bunch by the stems and swishing the leaves in a bowl of cold water to get rid of any sand. Spin dry in a salad spinner. Wrap in paper towels, place in a resealable plastic bag, and refrigerate for up to one week.

PREPARE: Remove the leaves from the stems and chop. Slender cilantro stems can be chopped and used along with the leaves.

1
Muffins, Quick Breads, Buns, and Other Breakfast Treats

Glorious Morning Muffins

Apple-Walnut Muffins

Cranberry-Pumpkin Muffins

Bran Muffins with Golden Raisins

Citrus-Almond Loaf with Olive Oil

Date-Walnut Bread

Nola's Five-Fruit Granola

Strawberry-Pecan Coffee Cake

SoNo Buttermilk Pancakes with Bananas

Pumpkin-Spiced Pancakes with Cranberry Compote

Cousin John's Café Belgian Waffles

Buttermilk-Pecan Waffles with Blueberry Maple Syrup

Brioche French Toast with Vanilla Filling

Chelsea Buns with Currants

Acadia Popovers with Strawberry Jam

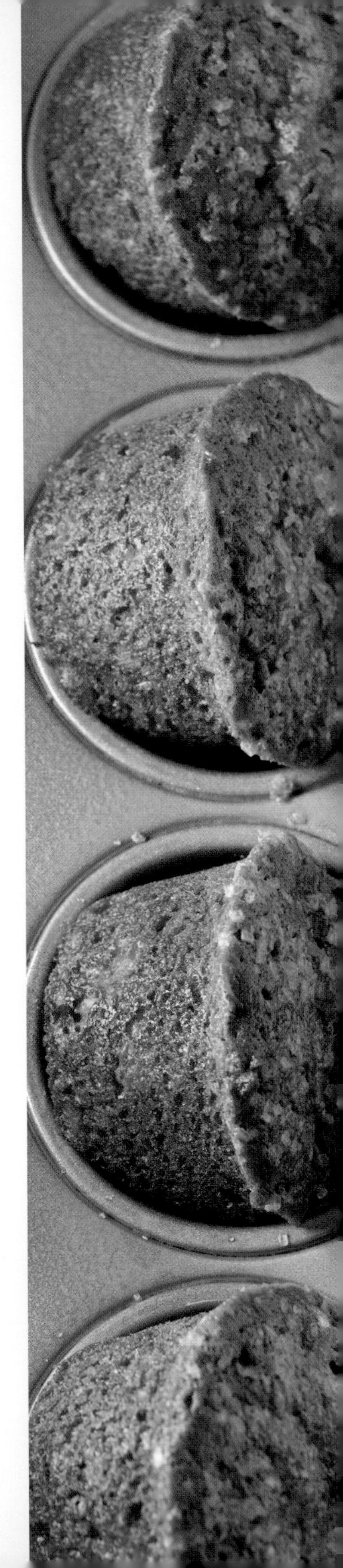

Fruit is popular at the start of the day. Simple recipes for muffins, pancakes, waffles, and quick breads are all a little more tempting with the addition of fresh or dried fruit. These recipes are quick to make and easy enough that the whole family can help.

Sunday was the big breakfast day for my family when my mother was alive. We'd sit down to her scrambled eggs, pounds of bacon, breakfast breads from the local bakery, and a *lot* of orange juice. With eight boys, it was all about volume.

But I had the best breakfast of my life in the 1980s, at Campton Place Hotel in San Francisco. Bradley Ogden was the chef at the restaurant there. Pumpkin pancakes with cranberry compote and candied pecans, topped with cinnamon whipped cream. I wrote down the menu on a piece of paper so I'd never forget it. I still have that paper.

You will find my version of these Campton Place pumpkin pancakes on page 45. You can also make my basic pancakes, two varieties of waffles, and a range of fruit-flavored muffins and quick breads. I finish the chapter with the best recipe I know for popovers—discovered in a café in Maine's Acadia National Park—served with strawberry jam.

In my first cookbook, *The SoNo Baking Company Cookbook,* I noted that all muffin recipes could also be baked as jumbo muffins, or in loaf or Bundt pans. For this book, I've mixed things up with standard and jumbo muffin tins, loaf pans, and an 8 by 8-inch baking dish. But these quick-bread recipes can all be baked as muffins. As a rule of thumb, muffins bake at 375°F because they cook relatively quickly; longer-cooking loaves and coffee cakes are baked at 350°F so that the exterior won't overcook by the time the interior is cooked through. If you like, a sprinkle of sanding sugar before they go in the oven will give your baked goods a nice sheen and a professional look.

Except for Cousin John's Café Belgian Waffles (page 46) and the Chelsea Buns with Currants (page 52), all of these recipes can be made with a whisk, a rubber spatula, and a couple of bowls. With the exception of the Chelsea Buns, all can be made in under one hour.

Store breakfast pastries is in a sealed plastic container or covered cake stand at room temperature for up to three days. Store granola in an airtight container for up to two weeks.

By the way, all of the batters for my muffins and quick breads may be made in advance. They'll hold in an airtight container for about one week in the refrigerator. That way, you can make batter when you have a moment, and have muffins in about 35 minutes flat (55 to 65 minutes for a loaf of quick bread), any morning of the week.

Whether you're cooking for a big Sunday breakfast or for a weekday grab-and-go, this chapter offers quite a selection.

Glorious Morning Muffins

This is my version of the popular Morning Glory muffin, created in the 1970s at a Nantucket restaurant of the same name. I've been making them at home for years. The original recipe is made with pineapple, coconut, cinnamon, and grated carrot and apple. I add whole wheat flour for a sturdier muffin, and I omit the pineapple for the sake of simplicity. Grated apple keeps these muffins very moist. They're my personal favorite for the bakery because they travel so well. At home, they're great breakfast or snack food. They're one of Peter's favorites because he thinks he's eating a cupcake.

MAKES 18 MUFFINS

½ cup pecan pieces
1¾ cups all-purpose flour
¼ cup whole wheat flour
2 teaspoons baking soda
1½ teaspoons ground cinnamon
1 teaspoon coarse salt
1 cup granulated sugar
¼ cup firmly packed light brown sugar
1 cup vegetable oil
3 large eggs
1½ teaspoons pure vanilla extract
½ cup peeled, cored, and coarsely grated Granny Smith apple
½ cup grated carrot
½ cup sweetened angel flake coconut
½ cup golden raisins
Sanding sugar (optional)

1 Set the oven rack in the lower third of the oven. Preheat the oven to 375°F. Spray 18 standard muffin cups with nonstick cooking spray, or generously butter with softened butter; set aside.

2 Spread the pecans on a rimmed baking sheet. Toast until fragrant, 5 to 7 minutes. Remove from the oven and let cool.

3 In a large bowl, whisk together the all-purpose and whole wheat flours, baking soda, cinnamon, and salt; set aside.

4 In a medium bowl, whisk together the granulated and brown sugars and the oil until blended. Add the eggs and vanilla and whisk well to blend. Stir in the apple and carrot with a rubber spatula. Add to the bowl with the dry ingredients and stir with the spatula just until the flour has been absorbed. Do not overmix. Fold in the coconut, raisins, and pecans.

5 Divide the batter evenly among the prepared muffin cups. Sprinkle the tops of the muffins with the sanding sugar, if using.

6 Place the muffin pan on a baking sheet and bake, rotating the sheet about two-thirds of the way through the baking time, until the muffins are golden brown, the tops spring back when touched, and a cake tester inserted in the center of a muffin comes out clean, 22 to 25 minutes.

7 Transfer the muffin pan to a cooking rack and let stand for 10 minutes. Then remove the muffins from the pan and let cool entirely on the rack.

TIP I always place muffin pans on a baking sheet before baking. A baking sheet catches spills and is much easier to maneuver than a muffin pan. This way, the pan can be removed from the oven without damaging the muffins.

Bran Muffins with Golden Raisins (page 38)

Glorious Morning Muffins (opposite)

Apple-Walnut Muffins (page 36)

Cranberry-Pumpkin Muffins (page 37)

Apple-Walnut Muffins

This is a great fall item, packed with sweet diced apple and fragrant with cinnamon. I keep the nuts coarse when I chop them because I like to taste the walnuts in my apple-walnut muffin. The apples are sautéed quickly with a little sugar to bring out the flavor of the fruit. Topped with cream cheese frosting (page 99), these are a healthier alternative to most cupcakes.

MAKES 12 MUFFINS

- **2 tablespoons unsalted butter**
- **2 cups peeled, cored, and diced (½ inch) baking apples, such as Rome, Cortland, or Granny Smith**
- **1 tablespoon plus ¾ cup granulated sugar**
- **¾ cup chopped walnuts, plus 12 walnut halves for garnish**
- **2 cups all-purpose flour**
- **1 teaspoon coarse salt**
- **2 teaspoons baking powder**
- **½ teaspoon baking soda**
- **½ teaspoon ground cinnamon**
- **½ cup vegetable oil**
- **2 large eggs**
- **¾ cup whole milk**
- **2 teaspoons pure vanilla extract**
- **Sanding sugar (optional)**

TIP You can use butter or vegetable cooking spray to grease pans and baking sheets. If you do use butter, make sure it's softened, not melted: melting separates the butterfat from the water in butter, so the butter coats less efficiently. Vegetable cooking spray is as effective as butter and is very convenient. Inexpensive, flavorless, and odorless, it lasts practically forever in a cool, dark place.

1 Heat the butter in a 9- or 10-inch skillet over medium heat. Add the diced apple and 1 tablespoon of the granulated sugar, and cook until the apples are tender but not mushy, 5 to 7 minutes; set aside to cool.

2 Set the oven rack in the lower third of the oven. Preheat the oven to 375°F. Spray a standard 12-cup muffin pan with nonstick cooking spray, or generously butter with softened butter; set aside.

3 Spread the chopped walnuts on a rimmed baking sheet. Toast until fragrant, 5 to 7 minutes. Remove from the oven and let cool.

4 In a large bowl, whisk together the flour, salt, baking powder, baking soda, and cinnamon; set aside.

5 In a medium bowl, whisk together the remaining ¾ cup granulated sugar and the oil to blend. Add the eggs, milk, and vanilla and whisk to blend. Add to the bowl with the dry ingredients and stir with a rubber spatula just until the flour has been absorbed. Gently fold in the cooked apple and chopped walnuts.

6 Divide the batter among the prepared muffin cups. Sprinkle the tops with sanding sugar, if using, and top each with a walnut half.

7 Place the muffin pan on a baking sheet and bake, rotating the sheet about two-thirds of the way through the baking time, until the muffins are golden brown, the tops spring back when touched, and a cake tester inserted in the center of a muffin comes out clean, 24 to 27 minutes.

8 Transfer the muffin pan to a cooling rack and let stand 10 minutes. Then remove the muffins from the pan and let cool entirely on the rack.

Cranberry-Pumpkin Muffins

This recipe is a variation on the pumpkin muffin we make at the bakery. Great for the fall, it has everything going for it: It's sweet, with a very tender crumb, and the cranberry is nice and tart against the sweet pumpkin. Pumpkin seeds (also called pepitas—available at gourmet food stores, health food stores, and some supermarkets) add a little crunch. You'll only need half of a 15-ounce can of pumpkin puree for these muffins. Refrigerate the rest for the Pumpkin-Spiced Pancakes with Cranberry Compote (page 45), Pumpkin Roulade (page 188), or Pumpkin Whoopie Pies (page 194); the puree will last about ten days in an airtight container in the refrigerator. Use either fresh or frozen cranberries; the frozen cranberries can go straight in, without thawing.

MAKES 10 JUMBO MUFFINS

- **1½ cups all-purpose flour**
- **1½ teaspoons coarse salt**
- **1 teaspoon baking soda**
- **½ teaspoon ground cinnamon**
- **½ teaspoon ground ginger**
- **¼ teaspoon ground cloves**
- **¼ teaspoon grated nutmeg**
- **1¼ cups granulated sugar**
- **½ cup (1 stick) unsalted butter, melted**
- **2 large eggs**
- **1 cup canned pumpkin puree**
- **¼ cup applesauce**
- **2 cups whole fresh or frozen cranberries**
- **¼ cup pumpkin seeds**
- **Sanding sugar (optional)**

1. Set the oven rack in the lower third of the oven. Preheat the oven to 375°F. Spray 10 jumbo muffin cups with nonstick cooking spray, or generously butter with softened butter; set aside.
2. In a large bowl, whisk together the flour, salt, baking soda, cinnamon, ginger, cloves, and nutmeg; set aside.
3. In a medium bowl, whisk together the granulated sugar and butter to blend. Add the eggs, pumpkin puree, and applesauce. Add to the dry ingredients and stir with a rubber spatula just until the flour has been absorbed. Do not overmix. Gently fold in the cranberries.
4. Divide the batter among the prepared muffin cups. Sprinkle the top of each with 1 rounded teaspoon of pumpkin seeds, and then with sanding sugar, if using.
5. Place on a baking sheet and bake, rotating the pan about two-thirds of the way through the baking time, until the muffins are golden brown, the tops spring back when touched, and a cake tester inserted in the center of a muffin comes out clean, 23 to 26 minutes.
6. Transfer the muffin pan to a cooling rack and let stand for 10 minutes. Then remove the muffins from the pan and let cool entirely on the rack.

Bran Muffins with Golden Raisins

If you're used to the old-style bran muffins that could double for doorstops, you'll be delighted with these buttery cakes. They're incredibly light and moist, particularly for a muffin that's part whole wheat flour. Buttermilk is a wonderful medium: it's low in fat, and the acid hinders the development of gluten (see sidebar, page 174) to create a tender bite. Serve these right out of the oven with a little pat of butter, or split and toast them on the griddle, cut sides down.

MAKES 12 MUFFINS

1¼ cups all-purpose flour
1¼ cups whole wheat flour
1½ cups wheat bran
2 tablespoons baking powder
2 teaspoons coarse salt
½ cup sour cream
½ cup buttermilk
2 tablespoons honey
Grated zest of 1 orange
1 teaspoon pure orange extract
10 tablespoons (1 stick plus 2 tablespoons) unsalted butter
½ cup firmly packed light brown sugar
½ cup granulated sugar
4 large eggs
1 cup golden raisins, plumped in boiling water (see page 22) and drained
Sanding sugar (optional)

1 Set the oven rack in the lower third of the oven. Preheat the oven to 375°F. Spray a 12-cup standard muffin pan with non-stick cooking spray, or generously butter with softened butter; set aside.

2 In a medium bowl, whisk together the all-purpose and whole wheat flours, wheat bran, baking powder, and salt. In another medium bowl, whisk together the sour cream, buttermilk, honey, orange zest, and orange extract until smooth; set aside.

3 In a large bowl, cream the butter, brown sugar, and granulated sugar with a whisk until light and fluffy. Whisk in the eggs, one at a time, scraping down the sides of the bowl, and whisking until each egg is completely incorporated before adding the next. With a rubber spatula, stir in the dry ingredients in three batches, alternating with the wet ingredients, beginning and ending with the dry ingredients, just until absorbed. Do not overmix. Gently fold in the raisins.

4 Divide the batter among the prepared muffin cups (use about ½ cup batter per cup). Sprinkle with the sanding sugar, if using.

5 Place the muffin pan on a baking sheet and bake, rotating the sheet about two-thirds of the way through the baking time, until the tops of the muffins spring back when touched and a cake tester inserted into the center of a muffin comes out clean, 30 to 35 minutes.

6 Transfer the muffin pan to a cooling rack and let stand for 10 minutes. Then remove the muffins from the pan and let cool entirely on the rack.

Citrus-Almond Loaf with Olive Oil

This is one of our best sellers at the New Haven farmers' market, where we sell it both as a small loaf and as a big muffin. The bread doesn't actually taste like olive oil at all, but the oil adds a depth of flavor that seems to go particularly well with the bright taste of the citrus. Flecked with bits of orange and lemon zest, and topped with crisp, sliced almonds, this tender all-season loaf is ultra-moist and perfect for breakfast, snack, or teatime.

MAKES ONE 8½ BY 4-INCH LOAF

2 tablespoons plus 1 cup extra-virgin olive oil
1½ cups all-purpose flour
1½ teaspoons coarse salt
¼ teaspoon baking soda
¼ teaspoon baking powder
1 cup plus 2 tablespoons granulated sugar
3 large eggs
1 cup plus 2 tablespoons whole milk
2 teaspoons finely grated lemon zest
2 teaspoons finely grated orange zest
¼ cup sliced blanched almonds
Sanding sugar (optional)

TIP Here's a trick to prevent quick breads from doming unevenly. When the bread has been baking for 20 minutes, insert a knife about 1 inch deep into the batter, and run it down the length of the batter in the pan.

1 Set the oven rack in the lower third of the oven. Preheat the oven to 350°F. Spray an 8½ by 4½-inch bread pan with nonstick spray, or generously butter with softened butter. Pour 2 tablespoons of the olive oil into the pan and tilt the pan to coat the bottom evenly. Place the pan on a baking sheet.

2 In a medium bowl, whisk together the flour, salt, baking soda, and baking powder; set aside.

3 In a large bowl, whisk together the granulated sugar and the remaining 1 cup oil to blend. Whisk in the eggs, milk, and grated lemon and orange zest. Slowly whisk in the dry ingredients until the flour is absorbed and the batter is smooth.

4 Pour the batter into the prepared pan. Sprinkle with the sliced almonds and the sanding sugar, if using. Bake, rotating the sheet about two-thirds of the way through the baking, until a cake tester inserted in the center of the loaf comes out clean and the top is mounded and golden brown, 55 to 65 minutes.

5 Cool on a wire rack for 20 minutes. Turn the cake out and let cool on the rack.

Date-Walnut Bread

I was first introduced to date-nut bread at a teahouse in London, where afternoon tea was served as a buffet with a selection of tea sandwiches, crumpets, scones, and some type of tea cake such as banana bread, lemon cake, or date-nut bread. Dates plumped in hot water supply the moisture for my chunky, orange-scented date-walnut bread. Try it toasted and spread with jam (or you might like a little cream cheese instead) for breakfast, teatime, or in a lunch box (and yes, kids like it too!).

MAKES ONE 8½ BY 4½-INCH LOAF

1 cup boiling water
1 cup chopped dates (about 5 ounces)
1 cup very coarsely chopped walnuts
1½ cups all-purpose flour
1½ teaspoons baking powder
1 teaspoon coarse salt
1 cup sugar
2 large eggs
Finely grated zest of 1 orange

TIP Let quick breads cool for about 20 minutes in the pan before turning them out to cool completely. This will ensure that the bread holds its shape.

1 Set the oven rack in the lower third of the oven. Preheat the oven to 350°F. Spray an 8½ by 4½-inch loaf pan with nonstick spray, or coat with softened butter; set aside.

2 In a large bowl, pour the boiling water over the dates and let stand until the dates soften, about 5 minutes.

3 Spread the walnuts on a rimmed baking sheet. Toast until fragrant, 5 to 7 minutes. Remove from the oven and let cool.

4 In a medium bowl, whisk together the flour, baking powder, and salt; set aside.

5 Whisk the sugar, eggs, and orange zest into the date-and-water mixture. Add the dry ingredients and stir with a rubber spatula just until the flour is absorbed. Do not overmix. Gently fold in the walnuts.

6 Pour the batter into the prepared pan, place on a baking sheet, and bake, rotating the sheet about two-thirds of the way through baking, until a tester inserted in the center of the cake comes out clean and the top is mounded and lightly browned—55 to 60 minutes.

7 Cool on a wire rack for 20 minutes. Turn the bread out and let cool on the rack.

Nola's Five-Fruit Granola

This recipe is inspired by one given to me by Ronit, an avid farmers'-market shopper, good friend, and former co-worker at Martha Stewart Living Television. My daughter Nola and I put together the mix of nuts and dried fruit based on her preferences, but you can substitute any of your favorites and leave out what you don't like. The dried fruit and coconut are tossed with the granola when it's completely cooled so that the fruit doesn't dry out from the heat of the oven. It will keep for two weeks.

MAKES ABOUT 10 CUPS

- **½ cup vegetable, safflower, or soybean oil, plus extra for the baking sheet**
- **½ cup pure maple syrup**
- **¼ cup honey**
- **½ teaspoon coarse salt**
- **1 vanilla bean, split and scraped**
- **4 cups rolled oats (not instant)**
- **1 cup sliced blanched almonds**
- **2 tablespoons sesame seeds**
- **1 teaspoon ground cinnamon**
- **½ cup raisins, plumped in boiling water (see page 22) and drained**
- **½ cup golden raisins, plumped in boiling water and drained**
- **½ cup dried cranberries, plumped in boiling water and drained**
- **½ cup currants, plumped in boiling water and drained**
- **½ cup dried cherries, plumped in boiling water and drained**
- **½ cup sweetened, shredded coconut**

1. In a medium saucepan, heat the oil, maple syrup, honey, salt, and vanilla bean until hot. Remove from the heat and let steep for 10 minutes.
2. Set the oven rack in the lower third of the oven. Preheat the oven to 350°F. Line a rimmed baking sheet with a nonstick silicone mat, or coat lightly with oil (but don't use parchment paper or the granola will stick).
3. In a large bowl, combine the oats, almonds, sesame seeds, and cinnamon. Pour the oil mixture over the dry ingredients, and toss with your hands or a spoon to thoroughly coat. Spread the mixture over the prepared baking sheet and bake, tossing every 10 minutes with a spatula and rotating the sheet pan two-thirds of the way through the baking, until the granola is golden brown, 25 to 30 minutes.
4. Remove from the oven and let cool completely. Toss in all the fruit and the coconut.

Strawberry-Pecan Coffee Cake

Fresh strawberries are incredibly sweet when cooked into this buttery, streusel-topped coffee cake. This recipe was inspired by a strawberry-pecan muffin that I tasted at a sandwich shop while bike riding in Nantucket one summer. It's based on the same premise as a banana cake, using mashed strawberries instead of banana. This is a great brunch bread, and it tastes even better the day after it's made. If I have time, I pour some of the sugar from the batter over the strawberries and macerate for an hour, so the strawberries release and soften in their own juices, making them easier to mash.

MAKES NINE 2½-INCH SQUARES

Streusel Topping

- **½ cup all-purpose flour**
- **½ cup firmly packed light brown sugar**
- **¼ teaspoon coarse salt**
- **⅛ teaspoon ground cinnamon**
- **¼ cup (½ stick) cold unsalted butter, cut into ¼-inch cubes**

Cake

- **1 cup pecans, coarsely chopped**
- **2 cups all-purpose flour**
- **1 teaspoon baking powder**
- **1 teaspoon baking soda**
- **2 teaspoons coarse salt**
- **½ cup (1 stick) unsalted butter, melted**
- **½ cup firmly packed light brown sugar**
- **½ cup granulated sugar**
- **½ cup buttermilk**
- **1 teaspoon pure vanilla extract**
- **2 cups mashed, hulled strawberries (about 1 pint strawberries, mashed with a fork or potato masher)**
- **1 tablespoon confectioners' sugar, for dusting**

1. To make the streusel: In a medium bowl, use a fork to stir together the flour, brown sugar, salt, and cinnamon. Add the butter and, using your fingertips, quickly work it into the dry ingredients until pea-size crumbs form; set aside in the refrigerator.
2. Set the oven rack in the lower third of the oven. Preheat the oven to 375°F. Spray an 8 by 8-inch Pyrex baking dish with nonstick spray, or coat with softened butter. Place the baking dish on a baking sheet; set aside.
3. To make the cake: Spread the pecans on a rimmed baking sheet and toast in the oven until fragrant, 5 to 7 minutes; set aside.
4. In a large bowl, whisk together the flour, baking powder, baking soda, and salt; set aside. In a medium bowl, whisk together the melted butter, brown sugar, and granulated sugar to blend. Whisk in the buttermilk and vanilla. Add to the dry ingredients and stir with a rubber spatula just until the flour is absorbed. Gently fold in the mashed strawberries and the pecans.
5. Transfer to the prepared baking dish, and smooth the top. Sprinkle with the streusel topping, bunching the crumbs together to make large crumbs and give the topping texture.
6. Bake, rotating the sheet about two-thirds of the way through the cooking time, until a tester comes out clean and the top is nicely browned, 45 to 50 minutes.
7. Let cool completely. Dust with confectioners' sugar before cutting into squares.

SoNo Buttermilk Pancakes with Bananas

This is the basic pancake batter we serve at the bakery. The pancakes are a great canvas for any fruit—berries in the summer, sautéed apples in the fall—spooned on top. But at home, my kids like them best with sliced banana, pressed into the batter while the pancakes cook. I recommend an electric griddle because it's the easiest way to cook pancakes. (If you don't have a griddle, a large skillet is fine.)

MAKES ABOUT 14 (4½- TO 5-INCH) PANCAKES; SERVES 4

- **2 cups all-purpose flour**
- **1½ tablespoons sugar**
- **1½ teaspoons coarse salt**
- **1 teaspoon baking powder**
- **½ teaspoon baking soda**
- **2½ cups buttermilk**
- **2 large eggs**
- **1½ tablespoons unsalted butter, melted**
- **1 cup pure maple syrup, for serving**
- **4 ripe bananas, sliced ¼ inch thick**
- **Unsalted butter, for serving**

1 Heat an electric griddle to 375°F. Lightly coat with butter.

2 In a large bowl, whisk together the flour, sugar, salt, baking powder, and baking soda.

3 In a medium bowl, whisk together the buttermilk and eggs. Add to the dry ingredients, and stir with a whisk just to combine and break up lumps. Stir in the melted butter. (It's fine if the batter is lumpy; it's important not to develop the gluten in the flour.)

4 In a small saucepan, heat the syrup over medium heat until warm, 3 to 5 minutes. Transfer to a serving pitcher.

5 Meanwhile, using a ¼-cup measure, spoon the pancake batter onto the hot griddle. Place 3 or 4 banana slices on top of each, and gently press the slices into the batter. Cook until the tops of the pancakes are bubbling, the edges begin to set, and the undersides are a nice golden brown, 2 to 3 minutes. Turn with a spatula and cook to brown the other sides, another 2 to 3 minutes. Serve immediately with butter and warm maple syrup.

Buttermilk

I use this acidic liquid often in my baking because it has a lot going for it. It's low in fat, it contributes a tangy flavor, and the acid hinders the development of gluten, creating an especially tender, moist crumb in pancakes, waffles, muffins, cakes, and quick breads. It's also convenient: It will keep for at least a month in the refrigerator.

Pumpkin-Spiced Pancakes with Cranberry Compote

The recipe for these fluffy, pumpkin-spiced pancakes was inspired by a breakfast at Campton Place Hotel in San Francisco, in the 1980s. I was there for a New Year's Eve Grateful Dead concert and I stayed at the hotel. The morning after the concert, I ordered these pancakes with cranberry compote, cinnamon whipped cream, and spiced pecans. It was a great weekend: good music, friends, nice weather, and delicious food. These pancakes were an excellent way to start the New Year.

MAKES ABOUT 16 (4½- TO 5-INCH) PANCAKES; SERVES 4 OR 5

Cranberry Compote

- **12 ounces fresh or frozen cranberries**
- **1 cup granulated sugar**
- **Zest of 1 orange, peeled off in strips**
- **½ cup freshly squeezed orange juice (from 1 to 2 oranges)**
- **1 cinnamon stick**
- **Pinch of coarse salt**

Pancakes

- **2 cups all-purpose flour**
- **2 tablespoons firmly packed light brown sugar**
- **1 tablespoon baking powder**
- **½ teaspoon ground cinnamon**
- **¼ teaspoon ground ginger**
- **¼ teaspoon grated nutmeg**
- **¼ teaspoon ground cloves**
- **2 teaspoons coarse salt**
- **1½ cups half-and-half**
- **¾ cup buttermilk**
- **½ cup pumpkin puree**
- **1 large egg**
- **6 tablespoons unsalted butter, melted, plus unsalted butter for serving**

1. To make the compote: In a medium saucepan, combine the cranberries, sugar, orange zest and juice, cinnamon stick, salt, and ½ cup water. Bring to a simmer and cook until the cranberries pop and the mixture thickens, about 5 minutes; set aside.

2. To make the pancakes: Heat an electric griddle to 375°F. Lightly coat with butter.

3. In a large bowl, whisk together the flour, brown sugar, baking powder, cinnamon, ginger, nutmeg, cloves, and salt; set aside.

4. In a medium bowl, whisk together the half-and-half, buttermilk, pumpkin puree, and egg. Add to the dry ingredients and stir with the whisk just to combine. Stir in the melted butter. (It's fine if the batter is lumpy; it's important not to develop the gluten in the flour.)

5. Using a ¼-cup measuring cup, spoon the batter onto the hot griddle. Cook the pancakes until the tops are bubbling, the edges are beginning to set, and the undersides of the pancake are a nice golden brown color, 2 to 3 minutes. Turn with a spatula and cook to brown the other sides, another 2 to 3 minutes.

6. Rewarm the compote over medium heat, 1 to 2 minutes. Serve the pancakes hot with the warm compote and extra butter.

Cousin John's Café Belgian Waffles

This is basically an éclair batter cooked in a waffle iron. The waffles cook up a beautiful golden brown on the outside and are so eggy and soft on the inside—I can't decide whether it's more like eating an omelet or a popover. Either way, they melt in your mouth. I used to make these at Cousin John's Café, a well-respected café in Park Slope, Brooklyn, that I owned with my cousin Louis. (He named the restaurant after me.) Cousin John's, which opened in 1986, is still around, and Louis is still serving these waffles. They are made with bread flour instead of all-purpose to give them the necessary structure to support the eggs and cream. At Cousin John's, we served them with whipped cream and berries. To turn them into a dessert, serve them with one of the ice creams or gelatos in Chapter 7 and top with hot Chocolate Sauce (page 218).

MAKES 8 (4-INCH) WAFFLES; SERVES 4

1 cup plus ¼ cup whole milk
¼ cup (½ stick) cold unsalted butter, cut into ½-inch pieces
½ teaspoon coarse salt
⅞ cup bread flour
4 large eggs
½ cup heavy cream, plus ¾ cup for whipping
2 tablespoons confectioners' sugar
1 cup pure maple syrup, for serving
3 cups mixed fresh berries

1 In a medium, heavy-bottomed saucepan, combine 1 cup of the milk, the butter, and salt and bring to a rolling boil over medium heat. Remove from the heat. Add the flour all at once and stir with a wooden spoon to incorporate. Return the pan to low heat and cook, stirring, until the dough comes together in a mass, pulls away from the sides, and leaves a film on the bottom of the pan, 2 to 3 minutes.

2 Transfer the dough to the bowl of a standing mixer fitted with the paddle attachment. Beat on low speed for 2 to 3 minutes to release excess steam. Increase the speed to medium. Add the eggs, one at a time, beating until fully incorporated after each addition and scraping down the sides and bottom of the bowl. Return the mixer to low speed. Beat in the remaining ¼ cup milk and the ½ cup of cream.

3 Combine the remaining ¾ cup of cream and the confectioners' sugar in a medium bowl. Whisk or beat with an electric mixer until medium peaks form; cover the whipped cream and refrigerate until ready to serve.

4 In a small saucepan, heat the syrup over medium heat until warm, 3 to 5 minutes. Transfer to a serving pitcher.

5 Heat an 8-inch round Belgian waffle iron. Scoop in half of the batter and spread over the grate. Cook until the steam dissipates

recipe continues

and you no longer see steam coming out the sides. Then open and check the waffle: It should be amber-brown with a soft interior. The total cooking time will be 5 to 8 minutes. Repeat with the remaining batter.

6 Serve immediately, with the berries, warm syrup, and whipped cream.

Perfect Whipped Cream

Crisps, cobblers, and brown bettys are delicious served with a dollop of whipped cream. Cream whips best if it is very cold. Before whipping, I recommend putting the bowl with the cream and sugar and the whisk in the freezer until ice begins to form on the top of the cream, about 10 minutes. Once whipped, the cream will hold for about 24 hours in the refrigerator. If it deflates, just whisk again. Whipped cream is an emulsion of air, water, and fat solids. Over time, the air escapes and the cream deflates. Whisking will re-create the emulsion. Confectioners' sugar also increases the stability of whipped cream.

Two cups of whipped cream would be sufficient for the crisps, cobblers, and brown betty in Chapter 6.

Whipped Cream

MAKES 2 CUPS

- **1 cup heavy cream**
- **½ teaspoon vanilla paste (see sidebar, page 212) or pure vanilla extract**
- **¼ cup confectioners' sugar**

Combine the heavy cream and vanilla in a medium bowl. Beat on medium speed until frothy. With the mixer running, gradually add the confectioners' sugar. Beat until thickened, 1 to 2 minutes, then increase the speed to medium-high and beat until firm peaks form. Cover and refrigerate until ready to serve.

Buttermilk-Pecan Waffles with Blueberry Maple Syrup

This recipe was inspired by the incredible waffles served at the Camellia Grill, an upscale diner in uptown New Orleans. I first tasted them while I was doing my internship there at the Louis XVI restaurant. I used to go to the Grill with co-workers on our day off. Every time I've returned to New Orleans since then, I try to go by the Camellia Grill for a plate of these waffles. This recipe is intended for a standard (not Belgian) waffle iron so that the waffles are very crisp. My kids find them irresistible drenched in vanilla-scented blueberry-maple syrup, and yours will too.

MAKES 12 (4-INCH) WAFFLES; SERVES 4

Blueberry-Maple Syrup

1 cup pure maple syrup
2 teaspoons vanilla paste (see sidebar, page 212)
2 cups fresh or frozen blueberries

Waffles

1¾ cups all-purpose flour
2 tablespoons sugar
1 teaspoon coarse salt
1½ teaspoons baking powder
¾ teaspoon baking soda
1½ cups buttermilk
3 large eggs
½ cup vegetable oil
1½ to 2 cups chopped pecans

TIP If you aren't eating the waffles right away, set them aside on a wire rack as they come off the waffle iron so they stay crisp. Reheat in a toaster oven, or on a baking sheet in a 300°F oven until crisp and heated through, 7 to 10 minutes.

1 To make the syrup: In a medium saucepan, heat the maple syrup with the vanilla paste over medium heat until warm, 3 to 5 minutes. Add the blueberries and continue cooking until the blueberries begin to break down and the syrup is infused with the taste of vanilla, about 5 more minutes. Set aside.

2 To make the waffles: Heat a waffle iron.

3 In a large bowl, whisk together the flour, sugar, salt, baking powder, and baking soda. In a 2-cup measure, stir the buttermilk and eggs with a fork to break up the eggs. Add the buttermilk mixture and the oil to the bowl with the dry ingredients and stir with the fork until just combined. (It's fine if the batter is lumpy; it's important not to develop the gluten in the flour.)

4 Cook the waffles according to the manufacturer's directions for the waffle iron (spray with nonstick spray, if needed), sprinkling each waffle with about ¼ cup of the pecans before closing the lid.

5 Rewarm the syrup over medium heat, 1 to 2 minutes. Serve the waffles hot, with the warm syrup.

Brioche French Toast with Vanilla Filling

This is a decadent weekend breakfast or brunch item. With brioche (or challah) from a bakery, a little vanilla pastry cream, and berries, it only takes a quick twenty minutes to put these warm, golden brown french-toast "sandwiches" on the table. Sliced bananas, chocolate chips, or Nutella are also crowd-pleasing options. You will only need about a half cup of pastry cream. The remainder will last about one week in the refrigerator. Eat it as a snack (since it's essentially vanilla pudding) or spread it on toast or a toasted slice of quick bread. An electric griddle works well for this recipe. If you don't have a griddle, a skillet is fine.

SERVES 4

Vanilla Filling

- **2 large egg yolks**
- **¼ cup sugar**
- **2 tablespoons cornstarch**
- **1 cup whole milk**
- **Pinch of coarse salt**
- **1 teaspoon vanilla paste (see sidebar, page 212) or pure vanilla extract**
- **1 tablespoon cold unsalted butter, cut into pieces**

French Toast

- **2 tablespoons unsalted butter, if using a skillet**
- **1 (8 by 4-inch) loaf of brioche or challah, ends trimmed, cut into eight ¾-inch-thick slices**
- **2 cups mixed fresh berries, at room temperature**
- **3 large eggs**
- **6 tablespoons whole milk**
- **1½ tablespoons sugar**
- **1½ teaspoons pure vanilla extract**
- **½ teaspoon ground cinnamon**
- **1 cup pure maple syrup, for serving**

1 To make the vanilla filling: In a medium, heat-proof bowl, whisk together the egg yolks, 2 tablespoons of the sugar, the cornstarch, and ½ cup of the milk.

2 In a medium saucepan, combine the remaining 2 tablespoons sugar, the remaining ½ cup milk, and the salt. Bring to a simmer. Whisking constantly, gradually pour the hot milk into the egg mixture to temper. Set a strainer over the saucepan. Strain the custard mixture back into the saucepan and bring to a boil over medium heat, whisking constantly. Boil for 10 seconds, whisking. (Make sure the custard boils for 10 seconds in the center of the pan, not just around the sides.) The mixture should thicken to a pudding-like consistency. Remove from the heat and transfer to a clean medium bowl. Whisk for a few minutes until cooled. Whisk in the vanilla and butter. Cover with plastic wrap, pressing it directly onto the surface to prevent a skin from forming. Refrigerate until chilled, 1 to 2 hours.

3 To make the french toast: Heat a griddle to 375°F and coat with butter, or heat 1 tablespoon butter in a large skillet over medium heat.

4 Spread 4 of the brioche slices with 2 generous tablespoons of pudding each. Arrange about ¼ cup of the berries on top of each, in a single layer. Top with another slice of bread and press gently to adhere.

5 In a large bowl, whisk together the eggs, milk, sugar, vanilla, and cinnamon to blend.

6 In a small saucepan, heat the syrup over medium heat until warm, 3 to 5 minutes. Transfer to a serving pitcher.

7 Dip both sides of each sandwich quickly into the milk mixture, allowing the bread to soak up a little of the mixture. Place directly on the heated grill or in the skillet and cook until golden brown on one side, 4 to 5 minutes. Flip and cook until the second side is golden brown and the filling is warmed through, 4 to 5 more minutes. (If using a skillet, cook 2 toasts at a time, adding the remaining tablespoon of butter for the second batch.)

8 Serve with the rest of the berries and the warm maple syrup.

Chelsea Buns with Currants

These shiny, currant-studded, brown sugar–cinnamon spirals are a British version of the French pastry called pain aux raisins. *Since these buns are somewhat time-consuming to make, I recommend immediately freezing what you don't eat. The buns thaw quickly and make a nice breakfast bread for weekends or weekdays.*

MAKES 12 BUNS

Dough

- **⅔ cup whole milk**
- **3½ tablespoons granulated sugar**
- **1 envelope (¼ ounce) active dry yeast**
- **3 cups all-purpose flour, plus extra for kneading**
- **5 tablespoons cold unsalted butter, cut into pieces**
- **1 teaspoon coarse salt**
- **2 large eggs**

Filling

- **⅔ cup firmly packed light brown sugar**
- **½ teaspoon ground cinnamon**
- **⅔ cup currants, plumped in boiling water (see page 22) and drained**
- **2 tablespoons melted unsalted butter**
- **½ cup granulated sugar, plus 1 teaspoon for sprinkling**

1 To make the dough: In a small saucepan, heat the milk with ½ tablespoon of the sugar to 110°F. (It should feel lukewarm, not hot.) Pour into a small heat-proof bowl or 2-cup measure. Sprinkle yeast over. Let stand until bubbling, about 5 minutes.

2 Combine the flour, butter, salt, and the remaining 3 tablespoons sugar in a bowl of a standing mixer fitted with the paddle attachment. Beat on low speed until the butter breaks down into tiny bits, 3 to 4 minutes.

3 Whisk the eggs into the yeast mixture one at a time. Add the yeast mixture to the flour-butter mixture and beat on low speed until the liquid is absorbed and the dough is smooth, about 2 minutes.

4 Turn the dough out onto a lightly floured work surface. Knead just until smooth and springy, 3 to 4 minutes. Stretching it gently, fold in the left and right sides of the dough to the center, then the top and bottom, to make a rough ball. Place smooth side down in a buttered bowl, and then turn so that the smooth side faces up and both sides are coated with butter. Cover with oiled plastic wrap. Let rise in a warm place (at least 70°F) until increased in bulk by 1½ times and very soft, 1 to 1½ hours.

5 Meanwhile, to make the filling: Stir together the brown sugar and cinnamon in a small bowl; set aside.

6 Pat the currants very dry with paper towels; set aside.

7 To deflate the dough, use a plastic pastry scraper to fold the sides in. Turn the dough out onto a lightly floured work surface so that the smooth side faces up. Using a rolling pin, roll the dough to a 12 by 12-inch square, about ¼ inch thick.

8 Leaving a ½-inch border at the top edge, use a pastry brush to brush the dough with the melted butter. Sprinkle the buttered dough evenly with the brown-sugar mixture and with the currants. Brush the unbuttered border with water. Starting from the bottom, use two hands to roll the dough tightly into a cylinder. Position the cylinder so that the seam is on the bottom, and press down gently with your hands to seal. Trim the ends.

9 Butter a 9 by 13-inch baking dish. Using a ruler, score the cylinder at 1-inch intervals; there should be 12. Use a sharp serrated knife to slice the cylinder into twelve 1-inch-thick rounds. Be careful not to compress the dough as you slice.

10 Arrange the buns in the prepared baking dish, allowing a little space between each. (Make sure that the spirals are well sealed; if not, tuck the loose "tail" underneath the bun.) Cover with an oiled sheet of plastic wrap and let rise in a warm place until increased in bulk by about 1½ times, about 30 minutes.

11 Set the oven rack in the lower third of the oven. Preheat the oven to 375°F. Place the baking dish on a baking sheet, and bake, rotating the sheet about two-thirds of the way through the baking, until the filling is bubbling and the buns are a pale golden brown (do not overbake), 20 to 25 minutes.

12 In a small saucepan, heat ½ cup water and the ½ cup of granulated sugar over medium-low heat until the sugar dissolves and the sugar syrup is clear.

13 Remove buns from the oven. With a pastry brush, immediately brush with sugar syrup. Sprinkle with the remaining 1 teaspoon granulated sugar. Let cool for 10 minutes. Serve warm.

TIP For ease of slicing the dough, fill a measuring cup or pitcher with hot water. Before each cut, dip the blade of the knife into the hot water and wipe with a towel.

Acadia Popovers with Strawberry Jam

I fell in love with the combination of strawberry jam and popovers one summer in Acadia National Park, which I think is one of the most beautiful spots in the country. There's a restaurant in the park where people go for tea, and they serve excellent popovers with strawberry jam. These popovers make a terrific weekend breakfast and they're no more difficult to make than waffles or pancakes. My kids slather them with the jam. Popovers are a little like Yorkshire pudding: crisp on the outside, and eggy and moist on the inside. Make sure not to pull them out of the oven too early. The outsides of the popovers will get fairly dark, but it's necessary that they cook through completely or they'll collapse when you take them out of the oven. You will need a six-cup popover mold (each cup holds one cup of batter).

MAKES 6 POPOVERS

1 cup bread flour or all-purpose flour
2 teaspoons coarse salt
1 cup whole milk
2 teaspoons sugar
3 large eggs
2 tablespoons melted unsalted butter
Strawberry jam

1 Set the oven rack in the lower third of the oven. Preheat the oven to 450°F. Lightly butter a 6-cup popover mold.

2 In a large bowl, whisk together the flour and salt; set aside.

3 In a medium bowl, whisk together the milk, sugar, eggs, and melted butter. Add to the bowl with the dry ingredients and stir with the whisk to combine. (This is a fairly liquid batter. It should be smooth, but try not to overwork it or the popovers will be tough.)

4 Divide the batter among the prepared popover cups and bake until the popovers are puffed and the outside is a nice dark brown color and crusty, 25 to 30 minutes. The color will be darker than a golden brown, and the popovers should be soft inside, but not doughy. You'll be able to pick up the popovers right out of the molds and they will feel light for their size.

5 Serve immediately with jam.

2

Just Fruit, Poached and Otherwise

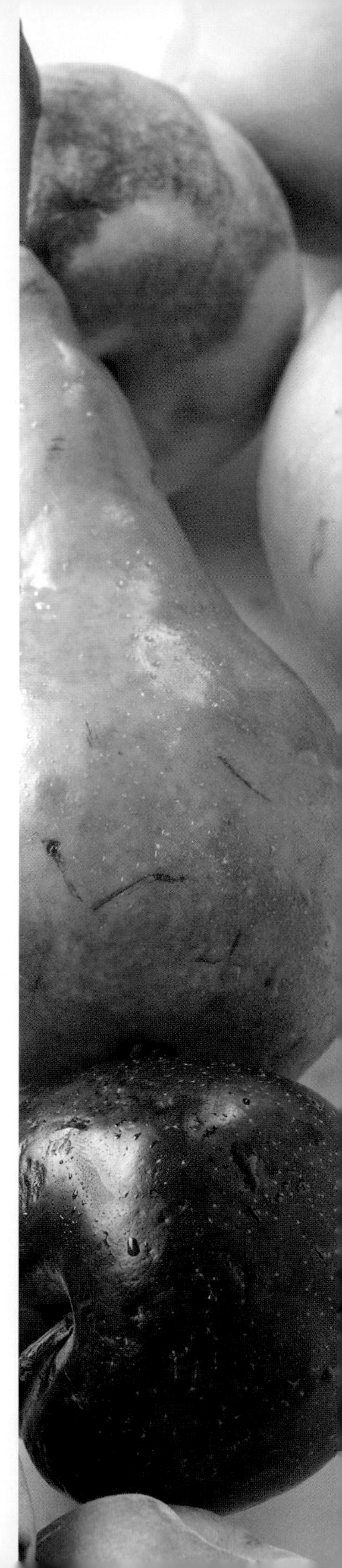

When you find great fruit, in season, sometimes the best way to treat it is hardly at all. This chapter is devoted to simple desserts to make at home: macerated fruit, poached and grilled fruit, and fruit soups. These recipes are particularly welcome for home cooks because they require minimal preparation. There are no doughs, batters, or egg custards to make. Many don't even demand cooking, so they're especially nice for summer meals.

Serving fresh fruit after dinner is typical Italian, whether it's cut up into a salad, macerated in lemon juice or wine, or just set out in a bowl to be eaten out of hand. I got into the habit of eating fresh fruit for dessert as a child, and to this day I enjoy doing the same with my family. Macerated Fruit with Prosecco (page 61) is an homage to my grandfather, who always macerated ripe peach slices in red wine during the summer. Watermelon Wedges with Ginger and Lime (page 73) is an easy, contemporary way to serve watermelon, and kids love watermelon "smiles."

Fresh fruit features nicely in summer soups such as a pureed Summer Melon Soup (page 64), and Gazpacho (tomato is also a fruit) on page 65. Served icy cold, both are refreshing antidotes to the heat of summer.

Some of the recipes, such as Pears "Belle Hélène" (poached pears with vanilla ice cream and warm chocolate sauce on page 68) and Strawberries Romanoff (page 62) are classics of French cuisine that were popular in New York restaurants where I worked in the early 1980s. Since then, these desserts are often, unfortunately, overlooked and I encourage you to try them. Despite their pedigree, they're not overly sophisticated and children will enjoy them as much as adults do.

Several recipes in this chapter feature poached fruit. Poaching simply means simmering very gently in a flavored liquid. The fruit may be poached whole or cut into pieces. It is very often poached in a sugar syrup, which is made by bringing water and sugar to a boil in a saucepan to dissolve the sugar. Spices in the syrup add exotic flavor to Chilled, Poached Pineapple with Vanilla and Spices (page 58). Fruit is also poached in sweetened red or white wine, and Poached Pears in Red Wine (page 66) has a beautiful, deep red color. If possible, the fruit should be juicy but not too ripe so that it doesn't fall apart during cooking. Poaching is also a practical way to treat less-than-perfect fruit because it boosts both flavor and sweetness.

Finally, I've included a recipe for warm, grilled figs wrapped in prosciutto and served on grilled toast (see page 74). As yet, Nik is the only one of my children who appreciates fresh figs as much as I do, but I'm hoping it's catching!

Chilled, Poached Pineapple with Vanilla and Spices

This is a simple summer dessert to make in a home kitchen. Chunks of fresh pineapple are poached in a sugar syrup steeped with vanilla, star anise, a cinnamon stick, and peppercorns. It only takes about fifteen minutes to put together, and it's very refreshing on a hot summer day, on its own or over ice cream.

SERVES 6

- **2 cups sugar**
- **1 tablespoon vanilla paste (see sidebar, page 212) or pure vanilla extract**
- **2 pieces of star anise**
- **1 cinnamon stick**
- **1 teaspoon whole white peppercorns**
- **1 ripe pineapple**
- **1 pint vanilla ice cream (optional)**

1 In a medium saucepan, combine the sugar and 2 cups water. Stir, then bring to a boil to dissolve the sugar. Remove from the heat. Add the vanilla paste, if using, the star anise, cinnamon, and peppercorns and let steep for 1 hour. Set a fine strainer over a large bowl and strain the syrup into the bowl, reserving the spices. Return the syrup to a clean saucepan.

2 Meanwhile, cut off the top and bottom of the pineapple with a large knife. Quarter the pineapple lengthwise, and cut out the core. Cut off all of the prickly skin. Cut the fruit into 1-inch chunks.

3 Add the pineapple pieces to the saucepan with the syrup. Bring to a simmer and cook until a skewer pierces the pineapple easily, 2 to 5 minutes depending on the ripeness of the pineapple. Remove the pan from the heat, transfer to a medium bowl, and let the pineapple cool completely in the liquid, about 1 hour. Add the reserved spices and the vanilla extract, if using, to the bowl and refrigerate the pineapple until very cold, 2 to 3 hours. Serve in small serving bowls or over ice cream.

Grilled Peaches with Mascarpone Mousse

This is a nice way to end a summer barbecue. Grilling enhances the flavor of many fruits and works well for peaches. The grill warms and softens the flesh while it caramelizes the sugars and adds a pleasant charred taste. The airy, sweetened mascarpone filling is flavored with orange and can be made several hours ahead and refrigerated.

SERVES 6

Mascarpone Mousse

- **¼ cup heavy cream**
- **¼ cup confectioners' sugar**
- **½ teaspoon vanilla paste (see sidebar, page 212) or pure vanilla extract**
- **½ teaspoon grated orange zest (from 1 orange)**
- **1 cup mascarpone cheese**

- **3 ripe but firm peaches, halved and pitted**
- **Honey, for drizzling**

1 Spray the clean grate of a gas or charcoal grill with nonstick cooking spray. Build a charcoal fire or preheat the grill.

2 To make the mousse: In a medium bowl, whisk the cream with the sugar to a soft peak. Whisk in the vanilla and orange zest.

3 In another medium bowl, stir a little of the whipped cream into the mascarpone cheese to lighten. Fold in the rest of the whipped cream.

4 Grill the cut sides of the peaches over medium heat until marked, about 2 minutes. Give the peaches a quarter turn and grill until marked with a crosshatch pattern, and until a knife inserted through the widest part enters without resistance, 2 to 5 more minutes.

5 Transfer the peaches to serving plates, cut sides up. Fill each peach half with a dollop of mousse. Serve warm, drizzled with honey.

Mascarpone Cheese

Mascarpone is a rich double-cream or triple-cream cheese. Made from cow's milk, this buttery cheese is traditionally produced in the Lombardy region of Italy. It has a pleasantly sour taste like that of crème fraîche. Mascarpone is also produced in America, but it's worth seeking out an Italian brand for this dessert because the flavor is richer. Mascarpone is available now at many grocery stores, in specialty stores and online (see Sources, page 281).

Macerated Fruit with Prosecco

In the summer, my grandfather used to macerate peach slices in red wine to serve—icy cold—at the end of Sunday dinner. This is my version of the family classic made with melon balls and Prosecco, Champagne's Italian cousin. The melon absorbs the flavors of the sweetened Prosecco while the Prosecco takes on the subtle taste of the melons. I love the pastel shades of these three melons, but feel free to use your favorite fruit.

SERVES 4

- **1 cup cantaloupe balls (from 1 cantaloupe) scooped with a 1-inch melon baller**
- **1 cup honeydew melon balls (from ½ honeydew melon) scooped with a 1-inch melon baller**
- **1 cup watermelon balls (from ½ seedless watermelon) scooped with a 1-inch melon baller**
- **1 tablespoon boiling water**
- **1 tablespoon sugar**
- **1 cup Prosecco**

1. Place the cantaloupe, honeydew, and watermelon balls in a medium bowl; set aside.
2. In a small measuring cup or heat-proof bowl, pour the boiling water over the sugar and stir to dissolve the sugar. Refrigerate until chilled, 10 to 15 minutes. Pour the sugar mixture over the melon balls. Add the Prosecco, stir gently, and chill until very cold, about 4 hours.
3. Spoon the melons into serving bowls with the sweetened Prosecco.

Strawberries Romanoff

This is one of the easiest desserts I know, which makes it perfect for a meal at my house when we're rushed for dinner. The mixture of fresh orange juice, orange zest, and orange liqueur brings out the sweetness of the strawberries. And despite its simplicity, this French dessert, named for the royal Russian family of Romanoff, is elegant enough to serve with pride at the finish of a dinner party.

SERVES 6

- **2 pints strawberries, hulled and quartered**
- **2 tablespoons sugar**
- **¼ cup orange liqueur or orange juice**
- **Finely grated zest of 1 orange**
- **2 tablespoons freshly squeezed orange juice (from 1 orange)**
- **⅛ teaspoon coarse salt**
- **1 recipe Whipped Cream (page 48)**

TIP Don't rinse the berries—they're too delicate. Just wipe them gently with a damp paper towel. To hull the berries, I use a strawberry huller instead of a knife. A huller looks something like tweezers. It removes the leaves and white center cores very precisely so that you don't lose much berry.

1 In a medium bowl, combine the strawberries, sugar, liqueur or orange juice, orange zest and juice, and salt. Cover and allow the strawberries to macerate in the refrigerator for at least 2 hours.

2 To serve, spoon the whipped cream into the bottoms of 6 martini glasses. Spoon the strawberries over. Serve immediately.

Rhubarb-Orange Compote

I love playing with sour flavors. As a professional baker, one of the things I like best when developing a recipe is to find just the right amount of sugar to blunt the mouth-puckering sourness of rhubarb and uncover its refreshingly tart flavor. In this case, I've sweetened the compote with both orange juice and sugar. Served over ice cream, this is a delicious, super easy spring dessert when rhubarb is in season.

SERVES 4

1 pound rhubarb (preferably 6 slender stalks), trimmed and cut into ½-inch sections

½ cup sugar

Zest of ½ orange, removed in strips with a zester

1 tablespoon freshly squeezed orange juice (from 1 orange)

½ cinnamon stick

1 teaspoon vanilla paste (see sidebar, page 212) or pure vanilla extract

Pinch of coarse salt

1 pint vanilla ice cream

TIP The key to cooking rhubarb is to not overcook it. It should retain some texture.

1 In a medium saucepan, combine the rhubarb, sugar, orange zest and juice, cinnamon, vanilla paste, if using, salt, and 2 tablespoons water. Bring to a boil over medium-high heat. Reduce the heat to low and simmer, stirring occasionally, until the rhubarb softens and just begins to fall apart, 3 to 5 minutes.

2 Transfer to a medium bowl and refrigerate for 3 hours. Stir in the vanilla extract, if using. Spoon into bowls over ice cream and serve.

Summer Melon Soup

In the heat of midsummer, my family can't get enough of chilled melons of all sizes, shapes, and colors. With its pretty yin-yang shape and contrasting pastel colors, this refreshing, no-cook soup is a lovely way to begin a summer meal. I serve it before the main course at an outdoor barbecue. It's light enough to leave plenty of room for the main event. The amount of sweetener will depend on the ripeness of the melons. Taste and add more sugar, as needed.

SERVES 8

- **1 large honeydew melon, halved and seeded**
- **2 small cantaloupes, halved and seeded**
- **2 tablespoons sugar, or as needed**
- **¼ teaspoon coarse salt**
- **Crème fraîche, for garnish**
- **8 sprigs of purple basil, for garnish**

1 Cut the honeydew halves into wedges and cut off the rind with a large knife. Cut the melon into 1-inch chunks and place in a medium bowl. Repeat to cut the cantaloupe into chunks and place those in a second medium bowl.

2 In a blender, puree the honeydew chunks with 1 tablespoon of the sugar and ⅛ teaspoon of the salt. Return the puree to the bowl it had been in. Rinse out the blender.

3 Puree the cantaloupe with the remaining 1 tablespoon sugar and ⅛ teaspoon salt. Return the puree to the second bowl. Cover and chill both soups until very cold, at least 4 hours.

4 To serve, pour each soup into a 2-cup liquid measure. With one cup in each hand, pour both soups at the same time into a serving bowl so that the soups wiggle around each other to create a yin-yang design. Use about ½ cup of each soup. Repeat to fill the remaining bowls. Set a basil sprig on top of each.

Gazpacho

Gazpacho is very satisfying on a hot summer evening when the kids and I don't have much of an appetite. Think of it as a cross between a soup and a salad. Use the shredding attachment on the food processor to ensure that the mixture retains a nice coarseness. I leave some peel on the cucumber for additional texture.

SERVES 8

- **8 very ripe plum tomatoes, stemmed and halved**
- **1 red bell pepper, stemmed, quartered, and seeded**
- **1 green bell pepper, stemmed, quartered, and seeded**
- **1 jalapeño pepper, halved, stemmed, and seeded (ribs removed)**
- **1 large seedless cucumber, peeled in strips (some peel left on) and cut in half**
- **½ small red onion, halved**
- **3 garlic cloves, halved**
- **2 cups tomato juice**
- **2 tablespoons sherry vinegar**
- **Coarse salt and freshly ground black pepper**
- **1 tablespoon sugar**
- **8 (¾-inch-thick) slices rustic bread**
- **1 cup extra-virgin olive oil, plus extra for grilling the bread**
- **¼ cup firmly packed fresh basil leaves, cut into very thin strips**

1 In the bowl of a food processor fitted with the shredding attachment, shred the tomatoes. Transfer to a large bowl. Repeat to shred the red and green bell peppers, jalapeño pepper, cucumber, onion, and 4 of the garlic halves. Add all to the bowl with the tomatoes.

2 Stir in the tomato juice, vinegar, 2 tablespoons salt, ¼ teaspoon black pepper, and the sugar. Cover and refrigerate until the soup is very cold, 3 to 4 hours.

3 To serve, heat a gas or charcoal grill. Spread the bread slices in a single layer on a rimmed baking sheet. Drizzle each side with oil and grill until lightly browned but still soft inside, 1 to 2 minutes on each side. Rub one side of each warm toast with the cut sides of the remaining 2 garlic halves.

4 Divide the gazpacho among the serving bowls. Sprinkle with the basil and drizzle each bowl with about 2 tablespoons olive oil. Serve each bowl with a slice of grilled toast.

TIP The heat of the jalapeño pepper is in the ribs and seeds. I remove both at my house. But if your family likes a little heat, leave in the ribs.

Poached Pears in Red Wine

I like whole Bosc pears in this gorgeous, classic fall dessert because their shape is so elegant. Chilling the pears overnight in the red-wine poaching liquid allows the beautiful burgundy color to penetrate the interior of the fruit. The combination of pears and cinnamon-scented red-wine sauce is delicious with a spoonful of crème fraîche, but serving the pears on their own makes for a light, fat-free dessert.

SERVES 4

4 Bosc pears
1 bottle (750 milliliters) red wine
¾ cup sugar
10 whole white peppercorns
1 cinnamon stick
2 whole cloves
⅛ teaspoon coarse salt
Zest of 1 orange, peeled in strips with a vegetable peeler
Zest of 1 lemon, peeled in strips with a vegetable peeler
1 cup crème fraîche, for serving

1 Peel the pears. Using a melon baller and working from the bottom end of the pears, scoop out the cores. Leave on the stems.

2 In a 3-quart saucepan, bring the wine to a simmer with the sugar, peppercorns, cinnamon stick, cloves, salt, and the orange and lemon zests. Stir to dissolve the sugar.

3 Add the pears to the pan. They should be completely submerged in the wine. (Add water to cover, if necessary.) Cover with a small plate to keep the pears submerged and simmer until a knife inserted through the widest part enters without resistance, 30 to 40 minutes.

4 Using a slotted spoon or a skimmer, lift the pears gently out of the saucepan and set them right side up on a large plate. Let cool to room temperature.

5 Set a fine strainer over a medium bowl and strain the poaching liquid into the bowl. Let cool to room temperature. Discard the spices and zests. Transfer the cooled pears to a medium bowl and pour over the cooled poaching liquid. Cover and refrigerate overnight.

6 The next day, gently transfer the pears to another medium bowl. Cover and return to the refrigerator. Pour the poaching liquid into a small saucepan and simmer until reduced by about two-thirds in volume, thickened, and syrupy, 20 to 30 minutes. Cool to room temperature, then refrigerate until cold.

7 To serve, place each chilled pear on a serving plate (or cut them in half lengthwise to show the interiors). Drizzle the sauce around the pears and garnish the plates with a dollop of crème fraîche.

Pears "Belle Hélène"

I prefer the buttery texture of Bartlett pears in this dish of poached pears and gelato or ice cream served under a blanket of warm chocolate sauce. (It's said to have been named after an operetta by the nineteenth-century French composer Jacques Offenbach.) The pears are traditionally served whole, but I cut them in half to speed up the cooking. This is a beautiful dessert for a dinner party. It's practical, too, because all components can be made the day ahead. For a decorative effect, peel the pears with a channel knife, a tool that removes long, narrow strips of peel, to leave slender stripes.

SERVES 4

Pears

- **4 Bartlett pears**
- **1 lemon, cut in half**
- **1 cup white wine**
- **1½ cups sugar**
- **2 teaspoons vanilla paste (see sidebar, page 212) or pure vanilla extract**
- **⅛ teaspoon coarse salt**

Chocolate Sauce

- **½ cup half-and-half**
- **⅔ cup bittersweet chocolate chips**
- **¼ cup unsweetened cocoa powder**
- **¼ cup sugar**
- **2 tablespoons corn syrup**
- **⅛ teaspoon coarse salt**

- **1 pint Vanilla Gelato (page 220), Nik's Raspberry Gelato (page 222), or vanilla ice cream**

1. To make the pears: Peel the pears and cut them in half lengthwise, leaving the stems attached to one half for presentation. Use a melon baller to scoop out the cores. Rub the pear halves all over with lemon as you work to prevent the pears from turning brown. Place the pears in a medium bowl; set aside.

2. In a 3-quart saucepan, combine 3 cups water, the wine, sugar, vanilla paste, if using, and salt. Stir, then bring to a simmer to dissolve the sugar.

3. Add the pears to the saucepan. Place a small plate on top of the pears to keep them submerged. Simmer until the pears are tender and a knife inserted into the thickest part enters without resistance, 12 to 15 minutes. Gently lift the pears out of the pan with a slotted spoon or skimmer and place them on a large plate or medium platter. Let cool to room temperature, about 1 hour.

4. Set a fine strainer over a medium bowl and strain the poaching liquid into the bowl. Let cool to room temperature, about 1 hour. Transfer the cooled pears to the bowl with the cooled poaching liquid. The liquid should completely cover the pears. Add the vanilla extract, if using. Cover and refrigerate overnight to allow the flavor of the white wine to penetrate the interior of the pears.

5. The next day, remove the pears from the poaching liquid and place them in another medium bowl. Cover and refrigerate while you make the chocolate sauce. Discard the poaching liquid (or see Tip, opposite).

6 To make the sauce: Combine the half-and-half, chocolate chips, cocoa powder, sugar, corn syrup, and salt in a small saucepan and bring to a boil. Stir until smooth. Set a fine strainer over a medium bowl and strain the sauce into the bowl.

7 To serve, place one scoop of gelato into the bottom of each of four small glass serving bowls or martini glasses. Add two pear halves to each. Pour the warm chocolate sauce over.

TIP The pears are also delicious served with just the reduced poaching liquid. Reduce the poaching liquid as for Poached Pears in Red Wine (page 66) and chill. Drizzle over the chilled pear halves on plates or in bowls.

Poaching Perfected

For perfect poached fruit, first, use a pan that will hold the fruit and liquid comfortably. Make sure the fruit is completely submerged in the poaching liquid; add water as needed. Set a plate, the diameter smaller than that of the saucepan, directly on top of the fruit. The plate will keep the fruit submerged during poaching. Simmer rather than boil; boiling will break the fruit down. When the fruit is cooked, remove it from the pan with a slotted spoon or skimmer so as not to mar the exterior. (Whole cored pears should stand on their ends; they will collapse if placed on their sides.) Once the fruit cools, store it in the cooled poaching liquid so it stays juicy. Serve warm or cold in some of the poaching liquid, or reduce the liquid until it thickens and serve it as a sauce.

River Café Poached Peaches with Raspberry Sauce

This dessert was popular at River Café, in Brooklyn, where it was one of the first desserts I ever made. We served the peaches in delicate almond cookie "bowls" called tuiles. At home, I simplify the dish with a crisp toasted-almond garnish in place of the tuiles. Almond crisps also taste great on fresh fruit salad, ice cream, mascarpone mousse (page 60)—anything that benefits from a little crunch.

SERVES 4

Peaches

4 peaches, skinned (see page 23)
2 cups granulated sugar
1 tablespoon vanilla paste (see sidebar, page 212) or pure vanilla extract
Pinch of coarse salt
4 whole cardamom pods

Raspberry Sauce

1 tablespoon cornstarch
2 pints fresh raspberries
1 cup granulated sugar
Pinch of coarse salt
1 tablespoon freshly squeezed lemon juice (from 1 lemon)

Almond Crisps

1 cup sliced blanched almonds
1 tablespoon (about ½ large) egg white
¼ cup confectioners' sugar

1 pint vanilla ice cream, for serving

1 Halve and pit the peaches; set aside.

2 In a 3-quart saucepan, combine 4 cups water, the granulated sugar, vanilla paste, if using, salt, and cardamom pods. Bring to a simmer. Add the peach halves; the poaching liquid should cover them completely. Cover with a small plate to keep the fruit submerged. Simmer until a knife inserted into the peaches meets no resistance, but the peaches are still firm, 7 to 10 minutes. Stir in the vanilla extract, if using, and let cool completely in the poaching liquid. Transfer the peaches and the poaching liquid to a large bowl and refrigerate until completely chilled, at least 4 hours or overnight.

3 To make the sauce: In a small bowl or measuring cup, stir together the cornstarch and 2 tablespoons water; set aside. Combine the raspberries, granulated sugar, salt, and lemon juice in a medium saucepan and mash with a fork. Bring to a simmer, stir, and cook just to dissolve the sugar, about 2 minutes. Add the cornstarch mixture as needed to thicken the sauce to the consistency of honey. Add the mixture a little at a time, simmering for about 30 seconds after each addition to allow the cornstarch to thicken. Set a fine strainer over a medium bowl and strain the sauce to remove the seeds. Cool; cover and refrigerate to chill completely, at least 1 hour.

4 To make the almond crisps: Preheat the oven to 350°F. Line a rimmed baking sheet with a nonstick silicone baking mat.

recipe continues

5 In a medium bowl, combine the almonds with the egg white and stir with a rubber spatula to moisten. Sift the confectioners' sugar over and fold into the almond mixture. Spread the mixture in an even layer over the prepared baking sheet and bake until the almonds are golden brown, 10 to 12 minutes. Let cool on the baking sheet, then break apart into pieces.

6 To serve, scoop a mound of ice cream into each serving bowl. Place two peach halves on top of each. Spoon the raspberry sauce on top and finish with crumbled almond crisp.

Cornstarch Slurries

Cornstarch is a convenient thickening agent for fruit mixtures and sauces such as the raspberry sauce on page 71, the cornstarch can't be added directly or it will clump, so it is mixed with a liquid to make what is called a slurry. Slurries are practical because they thicken quickly and add neither flavor nor fat.

Stir the cornstarch with twice its volume in *cold* liquid (water, in this case) until smooth. Drizzle some of the slurry into the raspberry sauce, bring to a boil, and boil for 30 seconds to 1 minute until you see the sauce thicken and the starchy taste cooks out. If the sauce is still too thin, repeat the process. Once the texture is to your liking, cook the sauce as little as possible. Overcooking will cause the cornstarch to lose its thickening power.

Watermelon Wedges with Ginger and Lime

At the finish of a summer barbecue there's nothing cooler—or more fun for the kids to eat—than these lime-and-ginger watermelon "smiles." I borrowed this recipe for my daughter Nola, my most appreciative watermelon-eater, from Lucinda Scala Quinn, my wonderful cohost of Everyday Food.

SERVES 6

- ½ **cup sugar**
- **Grated zest and juice of 1 lime**
- 1 **tablespoon grated peeled fresh ginger**
- ¼ **watermelon**

1 In a small saucepan, combine ½ cup water, the sugar, lime zest and juice, and ginger. Bring to a simmer and stir to dissolve the sugar. Transfer to a small bowl. Cover and refrigerate until chilled, at least 1 hour.

2 Cut the watermelon quarter crosswise into six ¾-inch-thick wedges. Transfer to a medium serving platter and chill for at least 1 hour.

3 To serve, shingle the watermelon "smiles" on the platter and spoon the syrup over the top.

Warm Figs and Prosciutto on Bruschetta

This simple, savory appetizer is my way of celebrating the arrival of figs in late spring and early summer. It's such a nice combination of flavors and textures. The figs are soft and sweet, the ham is salty, the toasts are crisp, and the glaze is sweet-and-sour. This recipe lends itself well to an outdoor barbecue party, but don't wait too long for an occasion.

MAKES 12 BRUSCHETTA; SERVES 6 TO 8

- **1 cup balsamic vinegar**
- **2 tablespoons honey**
- **24 slices (½-inch-thick) baguette, cut on the bias (from 1 baguette)**
- **2 to 3 tablespoons extra-virgin olive oil**
- **12 fresh figs, cut in half through the stem ends, stems left on**
- **4 ounces good-quality blue cheese such as Gorgonzola, Stilton, or Maytag, cut into ¾-inch chunks**
- **12 very thin slices prosciutto, each split lengthwise into two long strips**

1. In a small saucepan, simmer the vinegar with the honey over medium heat until reduced by about half and thickened to a glaze, about 15 minutes. Let cool to room temperature.
2. Preheat a gas or charcoal grill. Spread the baguette slices in a single layer on a rimmed baking sheet. Drizzle both sides of the baguette slices with oil. Grill until lightly browned but still soft inside, 1 to 2 minutes on each side.
3. Set the oven rack in the lower third of the oven. Preheat the oven to 350°F.
4. Press a chunk of cheese into the flesh of each fig half. Wrap each with a halved slice of prosciutto so the stems are exposed. Place on a rimmed baking sheet and bake until the cheese begins to melt, 3 to 5 minutes. Place each warm fig upright on a bruschetta. Arrange on a platter and drizzle with the sweetened vinegar glaze.

3

Cookies and Bars

ookies and bars are the backbone of most families' dessert collections, including my own. They're quick to make and sturdy enough to stash in lunch boxes. And they lend themselves well to different types of dried fruit, which adds flavor and keeps cookies moist. It's available year-round, and you can mix and match, depending on personal preferences.

I love cookies. I really don't have a favorite. But if I had to say, I'm more of a drop cookie kind of guy. I like a cookie that's basically lots of stuff held together with a little batter, like the cranberry-oatmeal cookies on page 81.

But I'm easy. This chapter pulls together my favorite fruit-flavored cookies and bars, plus a great recipe for carrot bars (page 98). You'll find different shapes, sizes, flavors, and textures to satisfy everyone in your family. For those who love drop cookies, there are fruit-packed chocolate chunk cookies as well as my oatmeal cookies and a trail mix cookie (page 82) that's loaded with dried fruit and white chocolate chips. Citrus-Glazed Sablés (page 89) are elegant, crisp, and buttery. Cranberry-Apple Tassies (page 94) are tiny, addictive fruit-filled tartlets.

I never go a day without eating a biscotti. When I was growing up, they were called *cantucci* in my house. They remind me of Sunday dinners with my grandparents. Dunking cantucci in a cup of espresso sweetened with a mountain of sugar was like heaven for a kid. Fellow fans of biscotti will find three of my favorite versions here, including a variation—with dried cherries and hazelnuts—on the cantucci I grew up on.

Once I knew my way around the stove, I got a kick out of improving on some of the store-bought cookies of my youth. Store-bought Fig Newtons will always have a place in my heart, but I think you'll enjoy the homemade version on page 91.

With the exception of Lemony Madeleines (page 86), which should be eaten within a few days, all of the cookies in this chapter will keep at least one week in an airtight container. Store biscotti with biscotti *only*. They will pick up moisture from other types of cookies and lose their crispness. (If they do get soft, pop them back into a 350°F oven for a few minutes to crisp them up.) Store the carrot bars in the refrigerator in an airtight container; bring them to room temperature before serving. And make sure to store mendiants in a cool place so that they do not melt, but do not refrigerate them.

All the drop cookies in this chapter are about 2½ inches in diameter—big enough to stay soft and chewy. A #40 ice cream scoop—about 2 tablespoons—is perfect and makes scooping the dough easy. For young children, you may want to reduce the size to 1 to 1½ inches. Just make sure to reduce the baking time by about half so as not to overbake the cookies.

Sour Cherry–Chocolate Chunk Cookies

These chunky cookies are probably my kids' all-time favorites. An amped-up version of chocolate chip cookies, my version benefits from a double dose—both dark and milk chocolates—and dried cherries. For my youngest, Peter, I bake them in miniature: 1 to 1½ inches in diameter. Let the cherries cool before adding them to the batter or the warmth from the fruit will melt the chocolate and streak the batter.

MAKES 32 (2½-INCH) COOKIES

- **1½ cups all-purpose flour**
- **½ teaspoon baking soda**
- **½ teaspoon coarse salt**
- **¾ cup dark chocolate chunks (about ½-inch chunks)**
- **½ cup milk chocolate chips**
- **½ cup (1 stick) unsalted butter, at room temperature**
- **½ cup firmly packed light brown sugar**
- **½ cup granulated sugar**
- **1 large egg**
- **2 teaspoons pure vanilla extract**
- **1 cup dried sour cherries, plumped in boiling water (see page 22), drained, and patted dry on paper towels**
- **½ cup (1¾ ounces) coarsely chopped pecans (optional)**

TIP It's very seldom that a cookie benefits from being completely cooked all the way through. (Biscotti, of course, are the exception.) The heat of the oven dries out the cookie, causing it to harden. For a chewier cookie, experiment with underbaking a bit.

1 Set the oven rack in the lower third of the oven. Preheat the oven to 350°F. Line two baking sheets with parchment paper or nonstick silicone baking mats; set aside.

2 In a medium bowl, whisk together the flour, baking soda, and salt; set aside. In another medium bowl, combine the dark chocolate chunks and milk chocolate chips; set aside.

3 In a large bowl, or in the bowl of a standing mixer fitted with the paddle attachment, beat the butter, brown sugar, and granulated sugar on medium-high speed until light and fluffy, 2 to 3 minutes, scraping down the bowl halfway through. Beat in the egg and then the vanilla.

4 Reduce the mixer speed to low, if using. Add the flour mixture and beat just until the flour is absorbed. Gently fold in the cherries, chocolate chunks, chocolate chips, and chopped pecans, if using, with a rubber spatula.

5 Scoop out the batter onto the prepared baking sheets, about 2 inches apart. Flatten gently with the palm of your hand.

6 Bake one sheet at a time, rotating the sheet about two-thirds of the way through the baking time, until the cookies are set and browned on the edges but still very soft in the center, 9 to 11 minutes.

7 Transfer the baking sheet to a wire rack and let cool for 10 minutes. Then remove the cookies to the rack with a spatula and cool completely.

Cranberry-Oatmeal Cookies with Coconut

Oatmeal cookies are one of my personal favorites. Coconut and dried cranberries make my version nice and chewy, and the tart, tangy cranberries counterbalance the sweetness of the coconut. Cranberry and coconut also keep the cookies moist, as long as you don't over-bake. They should look a little undercooked in the center when you remove them from the oven.

MAKES ABOUT 24 (2½-INCH) COOKIES

- **¾ cup all-purpose flour**
- **½ teaspoon baking soda**
- **½ teaspoon ground cinnamon**
- **¼ teaspoon coarse salt**
- **1½ cups old-fashioned oats**
- **½ cup dried cranberries, plumped in boiling water (see page 22), drained, and patted dry on paper towels**
- **½ cup sweetened flake coconut**
- **½ cup (1 stick) unsalted butter, at room temperature**
- **½ cup firmly packed light brown sugar**
- **¼ cup granulated sugar**
- **1 large egg**
- **½ teaspoon pure vanilla extract**

TIP I use old-fashioned oats for cookies because they hold their shape better than the quick-cooking variety.

1. Set the oven rack in the lower third of the oven. Preheat the oven to 350°F. Line two baking sheets with parchment paper or nonstick silicone baking mats; set aside.
2. In a medium bowl, whisk together the flour, baking soda, cinnamon, and salt; set aside. In a separate medium bowl, combine the oats, cranberries, and coconut; set aside.
3. In a large bowl, or in the bowl of a standing mixer fitted with a paddle attachment, beat the butter, brown sugar, and granulated sugar on medium-high speed until light and fluffy, 2 to 3 minutes, scraping down the bowl halfway through. Beat in the egg and then the vanilla. Scrape down the bowl.
4. Reduce the mixer speed to low, if using. Add the flour mixture and beat just to combine. Gently fold in the cranberry mixture with a rubber spatula.
5. Use a 2-tablespoon scoop to portion out the batter onto the prepared baking sheets, placing the batter about 2 inches apart. Flatten gently with the palm of your hand.
6. Bake one sheet at a time, rotating the sheet about two-thirds of the way through the baking time, until the edges and bottoms are set and golden brown but the cookies are still a little soft in the centers, 12 to 14 minutes.
7. Transfer the baking sheet to a wire rack and let cool for 10 minutes. Then remove the cookies to the rack with a spatula and cool completely.

Trail Mix Cookies

My son Peter, who has never met a cookie he doesn't like, particularly enjoys making these hearty drop cookies with his sister Nola, when their visits coincide. With repeated testing, the three of us have honed the perfect mix of oats, chocolate, dried fruits, nuts, and seeds. Depending on the tastes of your crew, you can swap out the dried cranberries for dried cherries, currants for raisins or sultanas, and the white chocolate for dark or milk chocolate chips. I prefer white chocolate here because its flavor is less assertive. It adds a rich, sweet, creamy hit of vanilla that allows the taste of the other ingredients to shine through.

MAKES 3 DOZEN COOKIES

- **1 cup all-purpose flour**
- **2 teaspoons baking powder**
- **¼ teaspoon coarse salt**
- **1 cup old-fashioned oats**
- **1 cup sweetened flake coconut**
- **¾ cup white chocolate chips**
- **½ cup dried cranberries, plumped in boiling water (see page 22), drained, and patted dry on paper towels**
- **½ cup currants, plumped in boiling water, drained, and patted dry on paper towels**
- **½ cup lightly salted or unsalted cashew pieces**
- **½ cup shelled sunflower seeds**
- **½ cup (1 stick) plus 3 tablespoons unsalted butter, at room temperature**
- **½ cup firmly packed light brown sugar**
- **⅓ cup granulated sugar**
- **2 large eggs**
- **1 teaspoon pure vanilla extract**

1. Set the oven rack in the lower third of the oven. Preheat the oven to 350°F. Line two baking sheets with parchment paper or nonstick silicone baking mats; set aside.
2. In a medium bowl, whisk together the flour, baking powder, and salt; set aside. In a separate medium bowl, combine the oats, coconut, chocolate chips, cranberries, currants, cashews, and sunflower seeds; set aside.
3. In a large bowl, or the bowl of a standing mixer fitted with a paddle attachment, beat the butter, brown sugar, and granulated sugar on medium-high speed until light and fluffy, 2 to 3 minutes, scraping down the bowl halfway through. Beat in the eggs, and then the vanilla. Scrape down the bowl.
4. Reduce the mixer speed to low, if using. Add the flour mixture and beat just to combine. Gently fold in the oats mixture with a rubber spatula.
5. Scoop out the batter onto the prepared baking sheets, placing the scoops about 2 inches apart.
6. Bake one sheet at a time, rotating the sheet about two-thirds of the way through the baking time, until the edges and bottoms of the cookies are set and golden brown but the cookies are still a little soft in the centers, 12 to 15 minutes.
7. Transfer the baking sheet to a wire rack and let cool for 10 minutes. Then remove the cookies to the rack with a spatula and cool completely.

Orange Sugar Cut-Out Cookies

Like most households, we have a variety of cookie cutters—Christmas tree shapes, Halloween pumpkins, and Easter bunnies—so these cookies appear at every holiday. Peter can't stop eating them, regardless of shape. The dough freezes well. If you like, roll half of the dough and freeze the rest for another occasion.

MAKES 36 COOKIES OF ASSORTED SHAPES (ABOUT 3½ INCHES EACH)

- **3¾ cups all-purpose flour**
- **1 teaspoon baking powder**
- **½ teaspoon coarse salt**
- **1 cup (2 sticks) unsalted butter, at room temperature**
- **2 cups sugar**
- **2 large eggs**
- **2 teaspoons vanilla paste (see sidebar, page 212) or pure vanilla extract**
- **Grated zest of 1 orange**

TIP It's a good idea to chill all rolled cookies after cutting and before baking. It keeps the dough from spreading during baking.

1. In a large bowl, whisk together the flour, baking powder, and salt; set aside.
2. In the bowl of a standing mixer fitted with a paddle attachment, beat the butter and sugar on medium-high speed until light and fluffy, 2 to 3 minutes, scraping down the bowl halfway through. Beat in the eggs one at a time.
3. Reduce the mixer speed to low. Add the flour mixture and beat just until the flour is absorbed. Beat in the vanilla and orange zest.
4. Turn the dough out onto a sheet of plastic wrap, shape into two disks, and refrigerate for 30 minutes.
5. Set the oven rack in the lower third of the oven. Preheat the oven to 350°F. Line two baking sheets with parchment paper or nonstick silicone baking mats; set aside.
6. Working with one dough disk at a time, on a lightly floured work surface, roll the dough until it is ⅛ inch thick. Cut out shapes for 18 cookies. Place on the prepared baking sheets and chill until firm, about 15 minutes.
7. Bake until the bottoms and edges of the cookies begin to turn a light golden brown, 9 to 11 minutes, depending on shape. (Don't let the edges go very brown; the cookies will harden as they cool.) Remove the baking sheet to a wire rack to cool completely.
8. Repeat to cut, chill, and bake the remaining disk of dough.

Hermits

Hermits are a type of American spice cookie that has been popular in New England for more than a century. Most recipes are made with raisins or currants, but you can add any dried fruit. (I like to use raisins, dried cranberries, dried dates, and walnuts.) The stiff batter is baked in logs, like biscotti, and sliced, then I finish them with a shiny coating of orange-flavored glaze. These moist, cakey cookies are a popular item in care packages for college students, summer campers, and military service personnel because they ship well and they stay fresh longer than most cookies. Hermits travel well in lunch boxes, too. They are even better a day later—and they'll last just fine for at least one week.

MAKES ABOUT 30 COOKIES

- **1 cup raisins, plumped in boiling water (see page 22), drained, and patted dry on paper towels**
- **½ cup dried cranberries, plumped in boiling water, drained, and patted dry on paper towels**
- **½ cup chopped dried dates, plumped in boiling water, drained, and patted dry on paper towels**
- **2½ cups all-purpose flour**
- **1 teaspoon coarse salt**
- **½ teaspoon baking soda**
- **½ teaspoon baking powder**
- **½ teaspoon ground cinnamon**
- **½ teaspoon ground mace**
- **½ teaspoon ground cloves**
- **½ teaspoon ground ginger**
- **½ cup (1 stick) unsalted butter, at room temperature**
- **½ cup granulated sugar**
- **2 large eggs**
- **½ cup molasses**
- **1 cup coarsely chopped walnuts**

1 In a medium bowl, combine the raisins, cranberries, and dates with ¼ cup of the flour and toss to coat; set aside.

2 Set the oven rack in the lower third of the oven. Preheat the oven to 350°F. Line a baking sheet with parchment paper or a nonstick silicone baking mat; set aside.

3 In a second medium bowl, whisk together the remaining 2¼ cups flour, the salt, baking soda, baking powder, cinnamon, mace, cloves, and ginger; set aside.

4 In the bowl of a standing mixer fitted with the paddle attachment, beat together the butter and sugar on medium speed until light and fluffy, 2 to 3 minutes. Beat in the eggs until blended. Add the molasses and beat until combined, scraping down the bowl halfway through. The batter will look curdled.

5 Add the flour mixture and beat until the flour is absorbed. Fold in the dried-fruit mixture and the walnuts.

6 Turn the dough out onto a lightly floured work surface. Divide the dough in half. Gently roll each half with lightly floured hands to a log about 17 inches long and 1½ to 2 inches wide. Using two spatulas, carefully transfer the logs to the prepared baking sheet. Press down on the logs with your palm to flatten.

7 Bake, rotating the baking sheet about two-thirds of the way through the baking time, until the tops of the logs are firm but the centers are soft and spring back when you press with a finger at the thickest point, about 20 minutes.

8 Transfer the baking sheet to a wire rack. Be sure to let the logs cool completely before glazing.

9 Meanwhile, to make the glaze: Sift the confectioners' sugar into a small bowl. Gradually whisk in the orange juice and then the zest until well combined.

10 Divide the glaze evenly between the two cooled logs, and spread with the back of a spoon or a spatula, allowing the excess to drip onto the sheet pan. Let dry completely.

11 Using two spatulas, very carefully transfer one log at a time to a cutting board. Using a serrated knife and a sawing motion, cut each log on the diagonal into 15 slices about ¾ inch thick.

Orange Glaze

½ cup confectioners' sugar

Grated zest of 1 orange plus 2 tablespoons freshly squeezed orange juice (from 1 orange)

TIP The fruit is tossed in flour to prevent it from sinking to the bottom of the batter.

Lemony Madeleines

Madeleines are soft, pale yellow, scallop-shaped cakes sold in pastry shops all over France. I was introduced to them on one of my early visits to Paris and have been making them ever since. Madeleines are traditionally made with butter and must be eaten the day they're baked or they lose their airy softness. That is impractical for home kitchens, so my recipe replaces half the butter with vegetable oil to extend their shelf life to a couple of days. You'll need a special pan with twelve scallop-shaped molds, available in metal and silicone. Both work well, but the metal pans give the cookies a light, crisp finish that I like. The batter will hold for a few hours. So let the pan cool completely before filling the molds for the second batch.

MAKES 20 MADELEINES

¾ cup plus 2 tablespoons sugar
⅔ cup cake flour
¾ teaspoon baking powder
3 tablespoons vegetable oil
3 tablespoons unsalted butter, melted, plus more for the pan
2 teaspoons lemon extract
Grated zest of 1 lemon
2 large eggs
1 large egg yolk
⅛ teaspoon coarse salt

1 In a medium bowl, whisk together the sugar, flour, and baking powder; set aside. In a small bowl, combine the oil, melted butter, lemon extract, and lemon zest; set aside.

2 In another medium bowl, whisk the 2 whole eggs plus the egg yolk with the salt until frothy. Whisk in the sugar-and-flour mixture until the dry ingredients are combined and the batter is smooth. Fold in the oil-and-butter mixture with the whisk. Cover and refrigerate for at least 2 hours, or overnight.

3 Set a rack in the lower third of the oven. Preheat the oven to 350°F. Brush a 12-mold madeleine pan well with melted butter, or spray with nonstick spray. Dust the molds with flour and tap out the excess.

4 Fill the molds about two-thirds full, about 1 tablespoon in a standard mold; do not overfill. Bake until golden brown and risen, 14 to 16 minutes, rotating the pan two-thirds of the way through the baking time.

5 Immediately invert the madeleines onto a wire rack and let cool completely. Let the mold cool completely. Then butter and flour 8 of the molds, fill with the remaining batter, bake, and cool.

Coconut-Blueberry Macaroons

This recipe is a variation on the sweet, chewy coconut macaroons that are popular at the bakery. I developed them with Peter in mind because he loves blueberries. Macaroons are great year-round, but these are perfect for the summer when the berries are in season. You'll need a candy or instant-read thermometer to measure the temperature of the egg-white mixture as it heats.

MAKES 26 COOKIES

1 cup (6 to 7 large) egg whites, at room temperature

½ cup sugar

¼ cup light corn syrup

3 tablespoons unsalted butter

2⅔ cups (8 ounces) unsweetened finely shredded dried coconut

½ teaspoon almond extract

½ teaspoon coarse salt

1¼ cups (½ pint) fresh blueberries

TIP For a professional look, melt white chocolate in a double boiler or microwave. Dip the bottoms of the cooled macaroons in the chocolate. Set the macaroons on a baking sheet lined with parchment paper or a nonstick silicone baking mat and let the chocolate dry completely.

1 Bring 1 inch of water to a simmer in the bottom of a double boiler. Combine the egg whites, sugar, corn syrup, and butter in the top of the double boiler. Set it over (not in) the simmering water and heat, whisking constantly, until the mixture reaches 140°F to 150°F on a candy or instant-read thermometer, about 15 minutes.

2 Transfer to the bowl of a standing mixer fitted with the paddle attachment. Add the coconut, almond extract, and salt. Beat on low speed until the mixture has cooled, 10 to 15 minutes. The mixture will have coalesced and will no longer be watery. Fold in the blueberries.

3 Set the oven rack in the lower third of the oven. Preheat the oven to 350°F. Line a baking sheet with parchment paper or a nonstick silicone baking mat.

4 Using a 1-inch (2-tablespoon) ice cream scoop, firmly pack the batter into the scoop, and press the flat side against the side of the bowl to flatten. Arrange the 26 scoops 1 to 2 inches apart on the prepared baking sheet.

5 Bake until the macaroons are a speckled light golden brown color and are still soft and moist in the centers, 20 to 25 minutes.

6 Cool on the baking sheet on a wire rack for 10 minutes. Then remove from the baking sheet with a metal spatula and let cool completely on the rack.

Citrus-Glazed Sablés

When I was in my early twenties, I used to vacation at the beaches of Key West whenever I got the chance. These buttery citrus rounds are reminiscent of cookies I tasted there. The tart-sweet icing adds a nice shine and an extra kick of citrus but can be omitted, if you like. This is the type of cookie we used to call "refrigerator," or "icebox" cookies. The dough is shaped into a log, rolled in sanding sugar for a nice edging, and chilled until firm enough to slice. The recipe makes two logs, so I bake one and put the unbaked log in the freezer or the fridge (it will last about two weeks in the fridge, even longer in the freezer). When the cookie cupboard is bare, these cookies are sliced and baked in less time than it takes to make a round trip to the supermarket.

MAKES 48 COOKIES

- **2½ cups plus 2 tablespoons sifted all-purpose flour**
- **1 teaspoon coarse salt**
- **1 cup (2 sticks) unsalted butter, at room temperature**
- **¾ cup granulated sugar**
- **1 large egg**
- **1 teaspoon lemon extract**
- **½ cup sanding sugar**

Citrus Icing

- **½ cup confectioners' sugar**
- **½ teaspoon grated orange zest plus 2 tablespoons freshly squeezed orange juice (from 1 orange), or more as needed**
- **½ teaspoon grated lemon zest**
- **½ teaspoon grated lime zest**

1 In a medium bowl, whisk together the flour and salt; set aside.

2 Combine the butter and granulated sugar in the bowl of a standing mixer fitted with the paddle attachment, and beat on medium speed until light and fluffy, 2 to 3 minutes, scraping down the bowl halfway through. Beat in the egg and lemon extract to combine. With the mixer on low, add the flour mixture and mix just until the flour is absorbed.

3 Turn the dough out onto an unfloured work surface. Divide the dough in half and roll with the palms of your hands into two logs, each 12 inches long and 1½ inches in diameter. Dust your hands with a little flour if the dough sticks. Wrap each in parchment paper, twist the ends to seal, and chill until firm, at least 1 hour or overnight. When ready to use, let stand at room temperature until soft enough to slice.

4 Set a rack in the lower third of the oven. Preheat the oven to 350°F. Line two baking sheets with parchment paper or nonstick silicone baking mats.

5 Working with one dough log at a time, open the parchment paper so that it lies flat on the work surface. Sprinkle each log with ¼ cup of the sanding sugar. Fold the parchment back over the log and roll, pressing the sugar into the dough to evenly and generously coat.

recipe continues

TIP When slicing the cookies, rotate the logs a quarter turn after each slice so that you don't get a flat side. If the cookies still aren't round, you can press them gently into shape on the baking sheet.

6 Slice each log into twenty-four ½-inch-thick rounds. Place the rounds on the prepared baking sheets, about 1 inch apart. Bake, rotating the sheet two-thirds of the way through the baking time, until the cookies are lightly colored and golden brown around the edges, 20 to 22 minutes.

7 Meanwhile, to make the icing: Sift the confectioners' sugar into a small bowl. Gradually whisk in the orange juice until smooth. Whisk in the grated orange, lemon, and lime zests. The icing should be fairly thin—a good spreading consistency. If it's too thick, add a little more orange juice.

8 Remove the sheets to a wire rack. Immediately swirl about ⅛ teaspoon of icing on top of each cookie, spreading with the back of a spoon. Let stand for 10 minutes to cool. Then remove the cookies to the wire racks with a metal spatula and let cool completely.

Better-Than-Store-Bought Fig Newtons

I grew up on Fig Newtons. They're one of America's favorite store-bought cookies but they're even better if you make them yourself. Orange juice and zest give the honey-fig filling a bright taste, and the buttery cream-cheese wrapping melts in your mouth. Stash a couple of these plump half-moons in your kids' lunch boxes and you're guaranteed to see some happy faces. You can use any kind of fig as long as they're dried. (You can substitute any dried fruit, in fact, or combination of fruits.) The flavor of the fig paste mellows as it ages, so these just keep getting better for up to two weeks.

MAKES 48 COOKIES

Cream Cheese Dough

- 2⅓ cups all-purpose flour
- ¼ teaspoon baking powder
- 1 cup (2 sticks) unsalted butter, at room temperature
- 8 ounces cream cheese, at room temperature
- ½ cup sugar
- ½ teaspoon coarse salt
- 3 large egg yolks
- 1 teaspoon pure vanilla extract

Filling

- 1⅓ cups (about 10 ounces) dried figs, woody stems removed
- 1 cup honey
- Grated zest of 1 orange
- 3 tablespoons freshly squeezed orange juice (from 1 orange)
- ¼ teaspoon coarse salt
- ½ teaspoon ground cinnamon

- 1 large egg
- 1 large egg yolk
- Pinch of coarse salt
- Sanding sugar (optional)

1 To make the dough: In a medium bowl, whisk together the flour and baking powder; set aside.

2 In the bowl of a standing mixer fitted with the paddle attachment, beat the butter and cream cheese on medium-high speed until lightened and blended, about 1 minute. Add the sugar and salt and beat until light and fluffy, 1 to 2 more minutes, scraping down the sides of the bowl halfway through. Add the egg yolks, and beat until blended. Beat in the vanilla.

3 Reduce the mixer speed to low. Add the flour mixture and beat just until the flour is absorbed.

4 Scoop about half of the dough onto a sheet of plastic wrap, shape into a flattened disk, and wrap in the plastic. Do the same with the other half. Refrigerate for at least 2 hours, or overnight.

5 To make the filling: Coarsely chop the figs and place them in a small saucepan. Add the honey, orange zest and juice, salt, cinnamon, and 1⅓ cups water. Bring to a simmer and cook until the figs have softened and the liquid evaporates, 30 to 40 minutes. Transfer to a food processor and process to a puree; set aside to cool. Refrigerate to chill.

6 Line two baking sheets with parchment paper or nonstick silicone baking mats; set aside.

recipe continues

7 On a lightly floured board, roll out one disk of dough about ⅛ inch thick. Cut into 2½-inch rounds and place about 1 inch apart on the prepared baking sheets. Press the scraps together and re-roll the dough to cut 24 rounds in total.

8 Set the oven rack in the lower third of the oven. Preheat the oven to 350°F.

9 In a small bowl, whisk the egg, egg yolk, and salt with a fork to blend, for the egg wash.

10 To fill the cookies, spoon 2 teaspoons of the fig filling onto the center of each dough round. Lightly brush the lower edge of the rounds with egg wash. Fold the top half of the dough over the filling to form a half-moon shape. Press to seal in the filling, and wipe off any excess, as needed.

11 Press along the folded edges of the half-moons with the tines of a fork to make a decorative edging. Brush the cookies all over with the egg wash. Sprinkle each with ⅛ teaspoon sanding sugar, if you'd like, and cut vents with the tips of kitchen scissors to allow steam to escape.

12 Bake one sheet of cookies at a time until the tops are golden brown, 20 to 22 minutes. Transfer the baking sheet to a cooling rack and let cool for 10 minutes. Remove the cookies from the baking sheet with a metal spatula and let cool completely.

13 Meanwhile, roll the second disk of dough. Cut, fill, and bake 24 more cookies.

TIP Brush egg wash on only one half of the dough round before filling. Egg-washed dough will stick best to dry dough.

Cranberry-Apple Tassies

Tassies are a classic Southern cookie that I grew to love when I was working in New Orleans. They're really miniature pies made with a cream cheese pastry, filled with a pecan pie–type filling, and baked in a mini muffin pan. When I introduced them to my family, I made them my own by substituting apples and dried cranberries for the pecans. The tart, caramelized cranberries are very nice against the sweet brown sugar filling and buttery crust. Traditionally, tassies are served at room temperature. But they're also excellent warm, as we found out when my wonderful pastry chef Val Denner tested these at the SoNo bakery and she couldn't fend off the hordes in time for the tassies to cool.

MAKES 24 COOKIES

Dough

- **½ cup (1 stick) unsalted butter, at room temperature**
- **3 ounces cream cheese, at room temperature**
- **½ teaspoon pure vanilla extract**
- **1 cup all-purpose flour**
- **¼ teaspoon coarse salt**

Fruit Filling

- **2 tablespoons unsalted butter**
- **1 cup peeled, cored, and diced (¼ inch) Granny Smith apple (about 1 apple)**
- **1 cup dried cranberries, plumped in boiling water (see page 22), drained, and patted dry on paper towels**
- **1 teaspoon granulated sugar**
- **½ teaspoon ground cinnamon**

Brown Sugar Filling

- **⅔ cup firmly packed light brown sugar**
- **1 large egg**
- **1 tablespoon unsalted butter, melted**
- **½ teaspoon pure vanilla extract**
- **¼ teaspoon coarse salt**

1. To make the dough: In the bowl of a standing mixer fitted with the paddle attachment, beat the butter and cream cheese on medium-high speed until light and fluffy, 1 to 2 minutes. Beat in the vanilla. Reduce the mixer speed to low. Add the flour and salt and beat until the flour is absorbed.

2. Turn the dough out onto a sheet of plastic wrap and shape into a disk. Wrap in the plastic wrap and refrigerate until chilled, at least 30 minutes.

3. To make the fruit filling: In a medium skillet, melt the butter over medium heat. Add the apples and cranberries. Sprinkle with the sugar and cinnamon and cook until tender, 10 to 15 minutes; set aside to cool.

4. To make the brown sugar filling: In a medium bowl, whisk together the brown sugar, egg, melted butter, vanilla, and salt to blend; set aside.

5. Set the oven rack in the lower third of the oven. Preheat the oven to 375°F. Lightly butter a mini muffin pan with 24 cups or two 12-cup pans.

6. To assemble the tassies, take half of the dough and pinch off twelve pieces, about 2 teaspoons each. Roll into balls and place one into each muffin cup. Using your thumbs, gently press the dough evenly over the bottoms and up the sides of the muffin cups. (If the dough gets too warm to handle while you're working, refrigerate for 5 to 10 minutes, then continue.)

Repeat with the remaining dough. Refrigerate the lined muffin cups for 10 minutes.

7 Fill each muffin cup with 1 teaspoon of the fruit filling. Pour in 1 teaspoon of the brown sugar filling. Place the muffin pan on a baking sheet and bake, rotating the baking sheet about two-thirds of the way through the baking time, until the crust is golden brown and the filling is cooked, 30 to 35 minutes. Transfer the muffin pan to a wire rack to cool for 10 minutes.

8 To unmold, gently run a knife around the edge of each tassie to loosen. Remove carefully with your fingers and let cool completely on the rack.

Mrs. Kostyra's Date Squares

This recipe came to me from Mrs. Kostyra, Martha Stewart's mother and adopted mother to all of us at Martha Stewart Living Omnimedia. She was truly a great lady and it was always a wonderful day when she was on Martha's show. I'm glad to have these bars to remember her by. I've replaced the lemon flavoring in Mrs. Kostyra's original bars with orange, which pairs nicely with dates. Oatmeal gives the bars a delicate, flaky crust.

MAKES 16 SQUARES

Date Paste

- **2 cups diced pitted dates**
- **1/8 teaspoon coarse salt**
- **Grated zest of 1 orange**
- **2 tablespoons freshly squeezed orange juice (from 1 orange)**

Crumb Mixture

- **1½ cups all-purpose flour**
- **1½ cups quick-cooking oats**
- **1 cup firmly packed light brown sugar**
- **½ teaspoon baking soda**
- **¼ teaspoon coarse salt**
- **¾ cup (1½ sticks) cold unsalted butter, cut into small cubes**

- **1 to 2 tablespoons confectioners' sugar, for dusting**

TIP Store-bought orange juice is a fine substitute for fresh in all of the recipes in this book.

1 Set the oven rack in the lower third of the oven. Preheat the oven to 350°F. Butter an 8 by 8-inch baking dish; set aside.

2 To make the date paste: Place the dates, salt, orange zest and juice, and 1 cup water in a medium saucepan. Simmer gently over medium heat until the dates are soft, 10 to 12 minutes. Let cool for at least 10 minutes.

3 To make the crumb mixture: In a large bowl, combine the flour, oats, brown sugar, baking soda, and salt. Add the cubed butter and blend with your fingertips until the mixture resembles coarse crumbs.

4 Transfer 3⅓ cups (about two-thirds) of the crumb mixture to the prepared baking dish. Press an even layer over the bottom and up the sides. Spread the date paste over the bottom with the back of a spoon or a spatula. Spread with the remaining 1⅔ cups of crumb mixture.

5 Bake, rotating the baking dish about two-thirds of the way through the baking time, until the crumb topping is golden brown, 40 to 45 minutes. Transfer to a wire rack and cool completely. Dust with confectioners' sugar. Cut the cooled bars into sixteen 2 by 2-inch squares.

Joan's Carrot Bars with Cream Cheese Frosting and Spiced Pecans

Over the years, I've bolstered my recipe collection with favorites borrowed from other families. This recipe came to me from my friend Amanda Graff's mother, Joan Graff. The crisp, ginger-spiced pecans really make these bars. The recipe for the pecans allows for plenty of extra nuts for snacking, or you can save them to decorate other desserts (Nik loves them on ice cream). For a little extra zip, add a sprinkle of cayenne pepper to the ginger-sugar mixture. The pecans will stay crisp for up to one month in an airtight container.

MAKES 16 BARS

Ginger-Spiced Pecans

- **1¼ cups (5 ounces) pecan halves, at least 16**
- **2 tablespoons granulated sugar**
- **½ teaspoon coarse salt**
- **¼ teaspoon ground ginger**
- **1½ teaspoons honey**
- **½ teaspoon canola oil**

Carrot Bars

- **1 cup plus 2 tablespoons all-purpose flour**
- **½ teaspoon baking soda**
- **¼ teaspoon coarse salt**
- **1 teaspoon ground cinnamon**
- **2 large eggs**
- **1 cup granulated sugar**
- **¾ cup vegetable oil**
- **1 cup grated carrots (about 3 carrots)**

1 To make the pecans: Set the oven rack in the lower third of the oven. Preheat the oven to 325°F. Spread the pecan halves (be sure there are at least 16) in a single layer on a rimmed baking sheet and toast until fragrant, 10 to 15 minutes; let cool.

2 Combine the sugar, salt, and ginger in a small bowl; set aside.

3 Combine the honey, oil, and 1½ teaspoons water in a medium (2½-quart) saucepan. Place over medium-high heat until the mixture boils, about 30 seconds. Add the toasted pecans and reduce the heat to medium. Cook, stirring once in a while, until all of the liquid has evaporated, 3 to 5 minutes. Immediately transfer to a large bowl, and sprinkle with the ginger-sugar mixture. Toss until well combined. Transfer to a sheet pan and spread to a single layer. Allow to cool completely, about 30 minutes.

4 To make the carrot bars: Preheat the oven to 350°F. Spray a 9 by 13-inch baking dish with nonstick cooking spray. Place the baking dish on a baking sheet; set aside.

5 Combine the flour, baking soda, salt, and cinnamon in a medium bowl; set aside. In the bowl of a standing mixer fitted with the paddle attachment, beat the eggs with the sugar on medium speed until blended. Add the oil and carrots and beat until blended. Turn the mixer to low speed. Add the flour mixture and beat until blended.

6 Pour the batter into the prepared baking dish and spread with a rubber spatula. Bake, rotating the baking sheet about two-thirds of the way through the baking time, until a toothpick inserted in the center comes out clean, 26 to 30 minutes. Transfer to a wire rack and let cool completely before frosting.

7 To make the frosting: In the bowl of a standing mixer fitted with the paddle attachment, beat the cream cheese with the butter on medium high speed until light and fluffy, scraping down the bowl often, 3 to 4 minutes. Add the confectioners' sugar, salt, and vanilla, and beat until smooth, light, and fluffy, 2 to 3 minutes.

8 Spread the cooled bars with the frosting. Refrigerate until chilled, at least 30 minutes. Cut into sixteen 3 by 2-inch bars. Set a pecan half on top of each bar.

Cream Cheese Frosting

3 ounces cream cheese, at room temperature

¼ cup (½ stick) unsalted butter, at room temperature

1 cup confectioners' sugar

Pinch of coarse salt

1 teaspoon vanilla paste (see sidebar, page 212) or pure vanilla extract

Apricot-Almond Biscotti

I made sure to taste a lot of biscotti while I was traveling in Italy. Almost every espresso bar I walked into had a jar of the cookies sitting on the counter. There's an enormous variety over there. Some are made with butter, others with olive oil, and the cantucci-style (see page 103) are made without fat. The flavorings are limitless: nuts, dried fruits, various alcohols, grains (such as cornmeal), and seeds, such as anise seed, to name a few. These biscotti are the cookies of choice in my household during the Christmas season. The dough is butter-based, and cornmeal adds texture. If you can't find blanched whole almonds, use almonds in the skin. There is no need to blanch the nuts yourself.

MAKES 30 COOKIES

1 cup blanched whole almonds
2½ cups all-purpose flour
2 tablespoons coarse yellow cornmeal
2 teaspoons baking powder
½ cup (1 stick) unsalted butter, at room temperature
¾ cup granulated sugar
1 teaspoon coarse salt
2 large eggs, at room temperature, lightly beaten, plus 1 large egg, lightly beaten with a pinch of coarse salt, for egg wash
2 teaspoons pure almond extract
½ cup chopped dried apricots, plumped in boiling water (see page 22), drained, and patted dry on paper towels
Sanding sugar (optional)

1 Set the oven rack in the lower third of the oven. Preheat the oven to 350°F. Line a baking sheet with parchment paper or a nonstick silicone baking mat; set aside.

2 Spread the almonds over a second, rimmed baking sheet and toast until lightly browned and fragrant, 7 to 10 minutes; set aside.

3 In a medium bowl, whisk together the flour, cornmeal, and baking powder; set aside.

4 In the bowl of a standing mixer fitted with the paddle attachment, beat the butter, granulated sugar, and salt on medium-high speed until light and fluffy, 2 to 3 minutes, scraping down the sides of the bowl halfway through. Add the 2 beaten eggs and beat until blended. Then beat in the almond extract.

5 With the mixer on low speed, add the flour mixture and beat until the flour is absorbed. Fold in the apricots and toasted almonds with your hands.

6 Divide the dough in half. On a lightly floured work surface, gently roll each half with lightly floured hands to a log about 17 inches long and 1½ to 2 inches wide. With both hands, carefully transfer the logs to the prepared baking sheet. Press down on the tops of the logs with your palm to flatten. Brush with the egg wash and sprinkle with sanding sugar, if using.

7 Bake, rotating the baking sheet about two-thirds of the way through the baking time, until the logs are a light golden brown and spring back when you press on them at the thickest point, about 20 minutes.

8 Remove the logs from the oven and let cool on the baking sheet on a wire rack for 10 minutes. Using two spatulas, very carefully transfer one log at a time to a cutting board. Using a serrated knife and a sawing motion, cut each log on the diagonal into fifteen slices about ¾ inch thick. Return the slices to the baking sheet, laying each one on its side, and bake until the biscotti are completely dried and browned on the edges, 16 to 20 minutes.

9 Cool the biscotti for 10 minutes on the baking sheet on a wire rack. Then transfer them to the wire rack with a metal spatula and let cool completely.

VARIATION: CRANBERRY-PECAN BISCOTTI

Follow the method for the Apricot-Almond Biscotti above, replacing the almond extract with 2 teaspoons pure vanilla extract; the apricots with ⅓ cup dried cranberries (plump cranberries in boiling water to cover for 5 to 10 minutes, then drain and pat dry); and the toasted almonds with ⅔ cup large untoasted pecan pieces. Omit the cornmeal.

Cherry-Nut Cantucci

My grandmother's basement was often the site of a cookie swap. My aunts made several Italian varieties, including cantucci, and everyone who visited brought a plateful, either homemade or from the local bakery. This is my version of traditional cantucci, which originated in the town of Prato, near Florence. The original cookies are made with almonds alone. (In Italy, they would be served with a sweet white wine. They're delicious dunked in coffee, too.) I love the flavor of hazelnuts alongside the almonds, and dried cherries add a little chew between the crunch of the nuts. The dough will look too dry to hold together, but don't worry. Once you begin working with it on the baking sheet, it will compress easily into nut-studded logs that look like big PayDay candy bars.

MAKES ABOUT 30 COOKIES

- **¾ cup whole blanched almonds**
- **2 cups all-purpose flour**
- **1 cup sugar**
- **½ teaspoon baking soda**
- **1 teaspoon coarse salt**
- **2 large eggs**
- **2 teaspoons almond extract**
- **¾ cup skinned hazelnuts (see page 112)**
- **¾ cup dried cherries, plumped in boiling water (see page 22), drained, and patted dry on paper towels**
- **1 large egg beaten with a pinch of coarse salt, for egg wash**
- **Sanding sugar (optional)**

1 Set the oven rack in the lower third of the oven. Preheat the oven to 350°F. Line a baking sheet with parchment paper or a nonstick silicone baking mat; set aside.

2 Spread the almonds over a second, rimmed baking sheet and toast until lightly browned and fragrant, 7 to 10 minutes; set aside.

3 In the bowl of a standing mixer fitted with the paddle attachment, beat the flour, sugar, baking soda, and salt on low speed to combine. In a bowl, whisk the eggs and almond extract with a fork; add to the flour mixture and beat on low speed until the flour is mostly incorporated.

4 Dump the mixture into a large bowl. Add the hazelnuts, almonds, and cherries and work the mixture together with your hands to form a rough dough. The dough will be dry and will not hold together easily.

5 Turn the dough out onto the prepared sheet pan. Divide the dough in half, and work each half into a 17-inch-long roll, about 2 inches wide. Press down on the tops of the logs with your palm to flatten. Brush with the egg wash and sprinkle with sanding sugar, if using.

recipe continues

TIP Make the egg wash a little ahead of time. The salt will break down the egg, making it easier to spread.

6 Bake, rotating the baking sheet about two-thirds of the way through the baking time, until the logs are a light golden brown and spring back when you press on them at the thickest point, 22 to 25 minutes.

7 Remove the logs from the oven and let cool on the baking sheet on a wire rack for 10 minutes. Using two spatulas, very carefully transfer one log at a time to a cutting board. Using a serrated knife and a sawing motion, cut each log on the diagonal into fifteen slices about ¾ inch thick. Return the slices to the baking sheet, laying each one on its side, and bake until the biscotti are completely dried and browned on the edges, 14 to 17 minutes.

8 Cool the biscotti for 10 minutes on the baking sheet on a wire rack. Then transfer them to the wire rack with a metal spatula and let cool completely.

Fruit-and-Nut Chocolate Mendiants

A mendiant is a French confection, something between a candy and a cookie. I make them at home during the holiday season because they're so festive looking and the kids have fun setting the dried fruit and nuts into the melted chocolate rounds. They also make great Christmas gifts. Mendiants were traditionally made with raisins, hazelnuts, dried figs, and almonds, but contemporary versions use a variety of nuts, dried fruits, seeds, and fruit peels. Over the years, my kids and I have settled on the combination below: almonds; pistachios; dried apricots, cherries, and cranberries; and candied orange peel. Other options to consider are hazelnuts, peanuts, walnuts, pecans, cashews, macadamia nuts, pine nuts, dark or golden raisins, dried figs, and candied lemon peel. Just make sure that your toppings are at room temperature so the chocolate doesn't harden too quickly.

MAKES 20 COOKIES

- **20 whole blanched almonds**
- **40 whole green pistachios**
- **5 dried apricot halves, each half cut like a pie into 8 wedges (40 pieces), plumped in boiling water (see page 22), and drained**
- **20 dried cherries, plumped in boiling water and drained**
- **40 dried cranberries, plumped in boiling water and drained**
- **20 pieces (diced, or 1-inch-long strips) candied orange peel**
- **8 ounces bittersweet 60% chocolate, finely chopped or shaved (about 1⅓ cups)**
- **1 teaspoon vegetable oil**
- **¼ teaspoon coarse salt**

1 Line a baking sheet with parchment paper or a nonstick silicone baking mat; set aside. On a work surface, set out the almonds, pistachios, apricots, dried cherries, dried cranberries, and orange peel, each in their own small bowl; set aside.

2 Place about one-third of the chopped chocolate (about ½ cup) in a small bowl; set aside. Place the rest of the chocolate in the top of a double boiler set over (not in) 1 inch of barely simmering water. Heat until melted. Remove the bowl from the heat and wipe the bottom. Add the remaining one-third of the chopped chocolate, a little at a time, stirring with a rubber spatula until most of the chunks have melted. Add the oil and salt and stir until smooth.

3 Counting about 2 teaspoons per mendiant, spoon the melted chocolate onto the prepared baking sheet. Use the back of the spoon to shape each into a disk 1½ to 2 inches in diameter. Make only 5 at a time so that the chocolate does not cool and set before you have a chance to add the nuts and fruit. Dot each chocolate round with 1 almond, 2 pistachios, 2 apricot wedges, 1 cherry, 2 cranberries, and 1 piece of orange peel.

recipe continues

4 Let the chocolate cool completely, at least 30 minutes. The mendiants are ready when they are completely set and can be removed easily from the parchment or silicone mat.

Tips for Tempering Chocolate

In order for mendiants to set correctly with a professional-looking sheen, the chocolate is put through a process called "tempering." When chocolate melts, the components—cocoa butter and solids—separate. Tempering is the process of re-emulsifying the components. Chocolate that looks dull, whitish, and cloudy is unemulsified cocoa butter.

There are three basic methods for tempering. The method I prefer here is called "seeding" the chocolate. About two-thirds of the chopped chocolate is melted over a double boiler. The remaining third, the "seed," is stirred, a little at a time, into the melted chocolate, off the heat. The "seed" chocolate will cool the warm, melted chocolate to the correct temperature.

When melting chocolate, it's very important not to allow any water or steam to get into the bowl. Water will cause chocolate to streak, or "seize," into a hard mass.

Chocolate should never be overheated; pull it off the heat before it melts completely (optimally, at about 100°F). If once the chocolate "seed" is added, the chocolate cools too quickly and thickens, put it back over the heat for a brief second. Then pull it off and stir. If it's still not smooth, return it to the heat briefly, and continue with this process until the chocolate is completely smooth.

4

Fruit Pies and Tarts

Pâte Brisée

Pâte Sucrée

Caramel-Apple Tart

Apricot-Plum "Pizza" with Pistachio Frangipane

Key Lime Pie

Bistro Blueberry Tart

Lemon Soufflé Tartlets

Banana Meringue Pie

Blackberry Pie with a Cornmeal Crust

Winter Blueberry Streusel Pie

Citrus Buttermilk Pie

Mixed Berry Turnovers

Banana–Macadamia Nut Tartlets

French Lemon Tart

Caramel Pear Tarts

Strawberry Frangipane Tartlets

Fig Tart

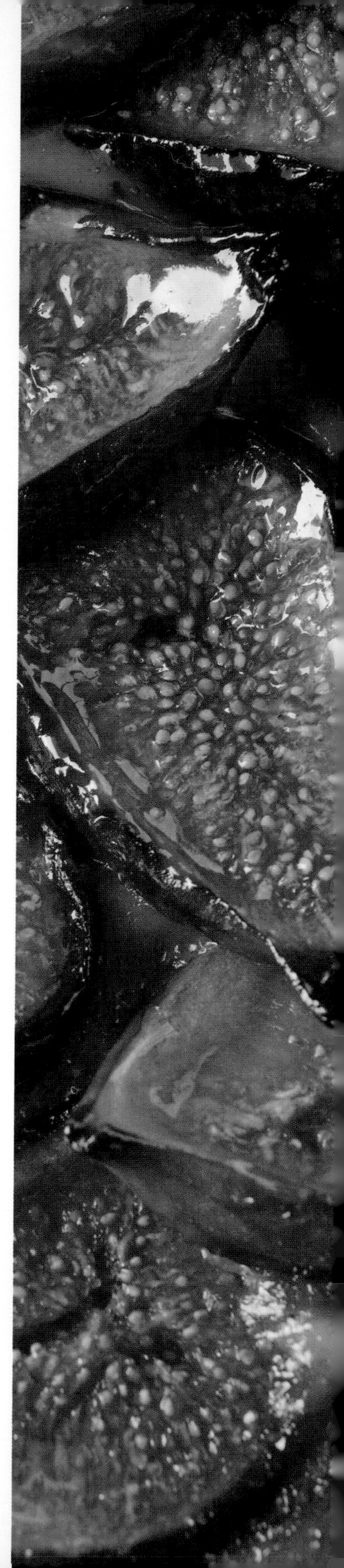

Summer is the peak time for many of the pies and tarts in this chapter. At the bakery, our selection is mostly determined by what we can access in the farmers' markets. We barter our baked goods for fresh fruit and vegetables from the farmers. Working this way allows us to use the fruits as they hit their season, so that our product remains local, seasonal, and fresh. We can see what's coming down the line because the farmers let us know that next week they'll have this or that, and in two weeks, they'll have something else for us.

We're fortunate to have fabulous relationships with our local farmers. We get fresh fruit from Rose's Berry Farm, out of Glastonbury, Connecticut, several times a week. They sell everything from plums, apples, peaches, nectarines, berries, and cherries to a range of vegetables. Their blueberries are fantastic. In July, at the beginning of plum season, we get their small, golf ball–size plums, both red and golden. The Italian prune plums come at the end of the season, in September. In the winter, we get cold-storage apples and pears.

I recommend that you bake seasonally from this chapter too. Nothing says summer like Blackberry Pie with a Cornmeal Crust (page 126). Caramel-Apple Tart (page 112) and Banana–Macadamia Nut Tartlets (page 134) are terrific fall and winter desserts. The airy Lemon Soufflé Tartlets (page 120) and French Lemon Tart (page 136) while very refreshing in warm weather, also make a nice ending to a hearty winter meal. Caramel Pear Tarts (page 139) are a fall spin on the French dessert Tarte Tatin, substituting pears for apples.

There are only three or four components in making fruit pies and tarts. First there is the fruit. Then there is a dough or press-in graham cracker crust. There is a filling, such as a pastry cream (see page 112) or almond cream (see page 142). Finally, there is a finishing element such as streusel (see page 128), apricot glaze, or confectioners' sugar. Once you get the hang of working with those components, you can mix and match, depending on what you've got in the house.

Pies and tarts are best eaten as soon as possible. If you are keeping them for a day or two, cover and refrigerate those that contain custards, such as Banana Meringue Pie (page 124), Citrus Buttermilk Pie (page 131), and French Lemon Tart.

I grew up on Table Talk pies, from Worcester, Massachusetts, sold in four-inch mini sizes. My brothers and I used to get Boston cream and cherry pie. I don't think there was a blessed thing that was real in them, but you got a quarter back if you returned the tin. The memory of those little handheld pies has often inspired me to make individual pies like Strawberry Frangipane Tartlets (page 142), Mixed Berry Turnovers (page 132), and Caramel Pear Tarts for my own children. I hope your family finds some favorites here, too.

Pâte Brisée

This flaky, buttery dough is very easily made in a food processor. It takes about five minutes to make and may be used for both sweet and savory pastries such as Banana Meringue Pie (page 124); Tomato, Smoked Mozzarella, and Pesto Pizette (page 244); and Spinach and Feta Turnovers (page 249). A small amount of sugar helps to brown the dough. Don't overwork the dough once you add the water. You should be able to see bits of butter.

MAKES ENOUGH FOR ONE DOUBLE-CRUST OR TWO SINGLE-CRUST 9-INCH PIES

- **2¼ cups all-purpose flour**
- **2 teaspoons sugar**
- **1 teaspoon coarse salt**
- **1 cup (2 sticks) cold unsalted butter, cut into small pieces**
- **¼ cup ice water**

TIP: To make ice water, combine ¼ cup water and 1 or 2 ice cubes in a bowl and let stand for 5 minutes to chill the water. Remove the ice.

1 In the bowl of a food processor, combine the flour, sugar, and salt. Add the butter and pulse until the mixture resembles coarse crumbs with visible, chickpea-size bits of butter, about 10 seconds. With the machine running, add the ice water through the feed tube, a little bit at a time, until everything is moistened and the dough begins to clump together, but has not yet formed a ball. You will see unincorporated bits of butter. If the dough is too dry and does not hold together, add a little more water.

2 Scoop about half of the dough onto a sheet of plastic wrap, shape into a flattened disk, and wrap in the plastic. Do the same for the other half. Chill for at least 1 hour before using.

Pâte Sucrée

This sweet, rich dough is delicious in dessert tarts and pies. It tastes just like a butter cookie, so any scraps can be rolled, cut into cookie shapes, and baked.

MAKES ENOUGH FOR ONE DOUBLE-CRUST OR TWO SINGLE-CRUST 9-INCH PIES

- **2 cups all-purpose flour**
- **1 cup (2 sticks) unsalted butter, at room temperature**
- **¼ cup sugar**
- **1 teaspoon coarse salt**
- **1 large egg**
- **1 large egg yolk**

1. In a bowl, whisk the flour to aerate it; set aside.
2. In the bowl of a standing mixer fitted with the paddle attachment, beat the butter, sugar, and salt on medium-high speed until light and fluffy, about 3 minutes, scraping down the sides of the bowl halfway through. Add the whole egg and the yolk, and mix to combine. Add the flour and beat until it has been absorbed. There will still be streaks of butter visible.
3. Scoop about half of the dough onto a sheet of plastic wrap, shape into a flattened disk, and wrap in the plastic. Do the same for the other half. Refrigerate until firm, at least 2 hours.

Caramel-Apple Tart

This rustic apple tart is something I like to make in the fall. The kids like it because it tastes like caramel apples. The sliced apples are cooked in a hazelnut linzer shell lined with a smear of caramel pastry cream. The cream keeps the apples moist and a dusting of confectioners' sugar encourages the apples to caramelize during baking.

MAKES ONE 9-INCH TART; SERVES 8

Linzer Dough

- **1½ cups (6 ounces) hazelnuts**
- **1 cup plus 2 tablespoons all-purpose flour**
- **½ teaspoon baking powder**
- **½ teaspoon ground cinnamon**
- **¼ teaspoon grated nutmeg**
- **1½ tablespoons plus ½ cup granulated sugar**
- **½ cup (1 stick) unsalted butter, at room temperature**
- **½ teaspoon coarse salt**
- **1 large egg, at room temperature**
- **¾ teaspoon vanilla paste (see sidebar, page 212) or pure vanilla extract**

Caramel Pastry Cream

- **2 large egg yolks**
- **1 tablespoon plus ¼ cup granulated sugar**
- **2 tablespoons cornstarch**
- **⅛ teaspoon coarse salt**
- **1 cup whole milk**
- **¼ teaspoon vinegar**
- **1 teaspoon pure vanilla extract**
- **1½ tablespoons cold unsalted butter, cut into pieces**

1 To make the dough: Preheat the oven to 350°F. Place the hazelnuts in a single layer on a rimmed baking sheet and bake until they are lightly colored and the skins are blistered and cracking, 10 to 15 minutes. Wrap in a kitchen towel and let steam for 1 minute. Rub the nuts in the towel to rub off as many of the skins as possible, but don't worry about the skins that stick; set aside to cool completely.

2 In a medium bowl, whisk together the flour, baking powder, cinnamon, and nutmeg; set aside.

3 In a food processor, pulse the toasted hazelnuts with 1½ tablespoons of the sugar until finely ground. (Be careful not to overprocess, as the nuts will turn into an oily paste.) Transfer to the bowl of a standing mixer fitted with the paddle attachment. Add the butter, the remaining ½ cup sugar, and the salt, and beat on medium-high speed until light and fluffy, about 2 minutes, scraping down the sides of the bowl halfway through. Beat in the egg and the vanilla.

4 Add the hazelnut mixture and beat on low speed until the flour is absorbed.

5 Scrape the dough onto a sheet of plastic wrap, shape into a flattened disk, and wrap in the plastic. Refrigerate until firm, at least 2 hours.

6 To make the pastry cream: In a medium, heat-proof bowl, whisk together the yolks, 1 tablespoon of the sugar, the cornstarch, salt, and ¼ cup of the milk; set aside.

7 In a medium saucepan, combine the remaining ¼ cup sugar, 3 tablespoons water, and the vinegar. Bring to a boil over medium-high heat, swirling the pan to dissolve the sugar. Boil until the mixture turns a deep amber color, 5 to 10 minutes. Remove from the heat and add the remaining ¾ cup milk. Stand back; the caramel will spit and the milk will boil up. Return the pan to medium heat and stir until the caramel melts and the mixture is smooth.

8 Whisking constantly, gradually pour the hot caramel-milk into the egg-yolk mixture to temper. Set a strainer over the saucepan; strain the mixture back into the pan. Bring to a boil over medium heat, whisking constantly. Let boil for 10 seconds (in the center of the pan, not just around the sides), still whisking. The mixture should thicken to a pudding-like consistency. Transfer to the bowl of a standing mixer fitted with the paddle attachment. Beat the cream for 2 to 3 minutes to cool slightly. Beat in the vanilla, then the butter. Beat until cooled, 5 to 10 more minutes. Press a piece of plastic wrap directly on the surface to prevent a skin from forming, and refrigerate.

9 On a lightly floured work surface, roll the chilled dough to a 12-inch round, about ⅛ inch thick. Fit the dough into a 9-inch fluted tart pan with a removable bottom and trim the dough so that it comes slightly above the rim of the tart pan. Then, with the heel of your hand, press the excess dough against the sharp edge of the rim of the pan to cut it level with the pan. Chill until firm, about 30 minutes.

10 Arrange the oven rack in the lower third of the oven. Preheat the oven to 375°F. Line a baking sheet with parchment paper or a nonstick silicone baking mat.

11 Spread the pastry cream over the bottom of the pie shell. Arrange the apple wedges on top in concentric circles. Brush the apples with the melted butter and sprinkle with the cinnamon. Sift confectioners' sugar generously over the top.

12 Bake, rotating the baking sheet about two-thirds of the way through the baking time, until the pastry is cooked through and the apples are tender and caramelized, about 40 minutes. Transfer to a wire rack to cool.

2 to 2½ Granny Smith apples, cored, peeled, and cut into ¼- to ⅓-inch wedges (cut each quarter into 4 slices)

2 tablespoons unsalted butter, melted

½ teaspoon ground cinnamon

Confectioners' sugar

TIP At the bakery, we beat pastry cream in a mixer to cool as quickly as possible. If you don't have a mixer, turn the cream out into a large bowl and refrigerate to cool as quickly as possible.

Apricot-Plum "Pizza" with Pistachio Frangipane

We sell a version of this dessert pizza in big sheet pans at the farmers' market when Italian prune plums arrive during the fall. The cooked apricots and plums present a gorgeous color, and the pistachios turn the cream a pale green. Italian prune plums are great for baking (in fact, better for baking than for eating). When they're cooked, the skin turns a beautiful, bright purple and the fruit tastes sweet and slightly sharp. Apricots are actually in season earlier than Italian prune plums. Canned apricots are a fine substitute. If substituting other, larger plum varieties for the Italian prune plums, quarter them.

SERVES 12

- **1 recipe Pâte Brisée (page 110), chilled**

Pistachio Cream

- **½ cup pistachios (or 10 tablespoons pistachio flour)**
- **6 tablespoons granulated sugar**
- **1 teaspoon coarse salt**
- **6 tablespoons (¾ stick) unsalted butter, at room temperature**
- **2 large eggs, at room temperature**
- **1½ teaspoons almond extract**
- **3 tablespoons all-purpose flour**

- **⅔ cup apricot jam, heated, strained, and cooled**
- **1½ pounds fresh plums (preferably Italian prune plums), halved and pitted (cut into ½-inch slices each, if not Italian)**
- **12 fresh or canned apricots, halved and pitted**
- **2 tablespoons sanding sugar, for sprinkling**

1. On a lightly floured surface, roll the dough to a 14 by 12-inch rectangle, ⅛ to ¼ inch thick. Roll the dough up around the rolling pin and transfer to an 8½ by 12-inch rimmed baking sheet. Trim the dough as necessary to about ½ inch above the rim of the pan. Crimp the edges. Chill until firm, about 30 minutes.

2. To make the pistachio cream: In a food processor, pulse the pistachios with the granulated sugar and salt until finely ground, 20 to 30 seconds. Add the butter and process to blend. Add the eggs, processing until blended and scraping the bowl after each addition. Add the almond extract and then the flour and process until combined.

3. Set the oven rack in the lower third of the oven. Preheat the oven to 425°F.

4. Use an offset spatula to spread the pizza shell with ⅓ cup of the apricot jam. Spread the pistachio cream on top of the jam. Arrange a line of apricot halves, cut side up, on top of the cream, along one short side of the shell. Press gently to settle the fruit. Arrange a line of plum halves, cut side up, next to and touching the plum halves. Continue with a row of apricots and then another row of plums until the shell is completely filled; there will be four rows of apricots and three rows of plums. Sprinkle all over with the sanding sugar.

recipe continues

5 Bake, rotating the pizza about two-thirds of the way through the baking time, until the crust is cooked through and golden brown and the pistachio cream is puffed and a rich golden brown color, 55 to 60 minutes. Wrap the edges of the crust in aluminum foil if it browns too much. Transfer to a wire rack.

6 While the pizza is still warm, in a small saucepan, warm the remaining ⅓ cup apricot jam over low heat until liquid. Brush the top of the pizza lightly with more jam to seal the fruit and give the tart a nice shine. Allow the pizza to cool completely.

7 Cut the pizza into twelve 3-inch squares to serve.

Key Lime Pie

I first tasted Key lime pie when I was in Key West in my early twenties, visiting my good friend Patricia. I remember thinking that the flavors seemed very fitting for the islands. It's like eating oysters in New Orleans. When you eat the real thing in the real place, you think, "Wow, this is why people talk about this all the time!" Key limes are a special variety of lime indigenous to the Florida Keys. Their peak season is from June through August, but they are available year-round from Mexico and Central America. They're smaller than the standard Persian limes sold in supermarkets, and you'll only get 2 to 3 teaspoons juice per lime. The yellowish juice has an exquisite flavor that's almost a fragrance. But Persian limes work fine too if that's all that is available. Traditionally Key lime filling isn't baked; the acid in the lime juice "cooks" the yolks, even without heat. I bake it very briefly, though, to accelerate the chemical reaction.

MAKES ONE 10-INCH PIE; SERVES 8 TO 10

Graham Cracker Crust

- 2 cups graham cracker crumbs
- ½ cup (1 stick) unsalted butter, melted slightly and cooled
- ⅓ cup sugar
- ¼ teaspoon coarse salt

Key Lime Filling

- 1 (14-ounce) can sweetened condensed milk
- 6 large egg yolks
- Pinch of coarse salt
- Grated zest of 1 Key lime
- 1 cup freshly squeezed Key lime juice (from 16 to 24 limes)

TIP When zesting the lime, make sure to get only the outer green of the peel; the underlying white pith is bitter.

1 Butter the bottom and sides of a 10-inch Pyrex or other oven-proof glass pie plate; set aside.

2 To make the crust: In a large bowl, combine the graham cracker crumbs, melted butter, sugar, and salt. Using your hands, mix thoroughly until the ingredients come together. Press the graham cracker mixture over the bottom and up the sides of the pie plate. Chill the crust for at least 20 minutes.

3 Set the oven rack in the lower third of the oven. Preheat the oven to 350°F.

4 Place the chilled piecrust on a baking sheet and bake until lightly browned on the edges, and firm, 18 to 20 minutes. Remove to a wire rack and let cool while you make the filling. Do not turn off the oven.

5 To make the filling: In the bowl of a standing mixer fitted with the whisk attachment, beat the sweetened condensed milk with the yolks, salt, and lime zest on medium speed until thick and pale, 2 to 3 minutes. Add the lime juice and beat until blended.

6 Pour the filling into the pie shell and bake, rotating the baking sheet about two-thirds of the way through the baking time, until the custard is set and just wiggles a bit in the center, 8 to 10 minutes. Remove to a wire rack and let cool for 15 minutes. Refrigerate until well chilled.

Bistro Blueberry Tart

This simple, rustic, blueberry-packed tart was inspired by fruit tarts I saw displayed on the counter of countless French bistros. Nola, a berry maven, is always delighted when I have it at home when she visits. It holds easily for two to three days (in fact, it's better the day after it's made), so it's convenient to have on hand. The filling is sweet and cakey with some vibrancy from lemon zest and juice. The dough, which may also be used in place of Pâte Brisée for quiches and other savory tarts, is very easy to work with. Make it the day ahead and serve plated with a little crème fraîche. Try this at your next dinner party.

MAKES ONE 10-INCH TART; SERVES 8 TO 10

Pâte à Foncer

- **1 large egg yolk**
- **¼ cup ice water**
- **2 cups all-purpose flour**
- **1 tablespoon granulated sugar**
- **2 teaspoons coarse salt**
- **½ cup (1 stick) cold unsalted butter, cut into small pieces**

Filling

- **2 large eggs**
- **1 large egg yolk**
- **6 tablespoons granulated sugar**
- **¼ teaspoon coarse salt**
- **⅛ teaspoon ground cinnamon**
- **1 teaspoon pure vanilla extract**
- **2 tablespoons all-purpose flour**
- **1 teaspoon baking powder**
- **Grated zest and juice of ½ lemon**
- **3 cups fresh blueberries**
- **1 tablespoon confectioners' sugar, for dusting**

1 To make the Pâte à Foncer: Stir together the egg yolk and the ice water in a small bowl; set aside.

2 In the bowl of a food processor, combine the flour, granulated sugar, and salt. Add the butter and pulse until the mixture resembles coarse crumbs with visible chickpea-size bits of butter, about 10 seconds. While pulsing, add the egg mixture and pulse about 10 more times until everything is moistened and the dough begins to clump together, but has not yet formed a ball.

3 Turn the dough out onto a lightly floured work surface. Press to form a ball. There will still be bits of unincorporated butter. Wrap in plastic and chill for at least 30 minutes.

4 Roll the dough to a 12-inch round, about ⅛ inch thick. Fit the dough into a 10-inch ceramic quiche pan and trim the dough with the heel of your hand. Chill while you make the filling.

5 Set the oven rack in the lower third of the oven. Preheat the oven to 375°F.

6 To make the filling: In a medium bowl, combine the eggs, egg yolk, granulated sugar, salt, cinnamon, and vanilla and whisk until frothy. Add all but 2 tablespoons of the flour and the baking powder and whisk until smooth. Whisk in the lemon zest and juice. Toss the blueberries in a medium bowl with the reserved 2 tablespoons flour; fold into the batter.

7 Place the chilled tart shell on a baking sheet. Pour in the blueberry mixture and bake, rotating the baking sheet about two-thirds of the way through the baking time, until the filling is set and the edges of the crust are golden brown, 45 to 50 minutes.

8 Transfer the tart to a wire rack and let cool completely. Let stand at room temperature for at least 3 hours before serving to allow the taste of the berries to permeate the filling. Dust with confectioners' sugar.

TIP Because it works well with any whole berry, or combination of berries, this recipe is a great way to use up leftover fruit. Substitute 3 cups fresh raspberries or blackberries, or any combination of raspberries, blackberries, and/or blueberries, for the blueberries in the recipe. You can also substitute 3 cups frozen berries; do not thaw before using and toss with flour as in step 6.

Lemon Soufflé Tartlets

Please don't be intimidated by individual tartlets like these. It's actually even easier to maneuver small rounds of dough for tartlets than it is large rounds for tarts. And tartlets are very impressive. For a change of pace, try serving these as an unusual finish to a Thanksgiving or Christmas meal. (Ask someone else to bring the pumpkin pie.) They come out of the oven looking just like a lemon soufflé—very high, light, and fluffy, with a subtle lemon flavor. The crisp, sweet crust is made from an Italian dough that my grandfather taught me to make. You'll need six 4-inch fluted tartlet molds. Serve the tartlets right out of the oven (after resting for ten minutes), or up to twenty-four hours later.

MAKES SIX 4-INCH TARTLETS

Pasta Frolla

- **2⅓ cups all-purpose flour**
- **1 teaspoon baking powder**
- **½ teaspoon coarse salt**
- **½ cup (1 stick) unsalted butter, at room temperature**
- **½ cup sugar**
- **Grated zest of 1 lemon**
- **1 large egg**
- **1 large egg yolk**

Lemon Soufflé Filling

- **5 large eggs, separated**
- **½ cup sugar**
- **Grated zest of 1½ lemons**
- **7 tablespoons freshly squeezed lemon juice (from 3 to 4 lemons)**
- **Coarse salt**
- **3 tablespoons cold, unsalted butter, cut into tablespoons**
- **2 teaspoons all-purpose flour**
- **1 tablespoon confectioners' sugar, for dusting**

1 To make the pastry: In a medium bowl, whisk the flour, baking powder, and salt; set aside.

2 In the bowl of a standing mixer fitted with the paddle attachment, or in a food processor, cream the butter with the sugar and lemon zest until lightened in color, and aerated, about 1 minute. Add the whole egg and yolk and beat or process to combine.

3 Add the flour mixture and beat or process just until the flour has been absorbed but the dough has not yet come together in a ball.

4 Turn the dough out onto a floured board. Fold it over on itself a few times just to incorporate; do not overwork. Flatten to a disk, wrap in plastic, and refrigerate for at least 30 minutes.

5 To make the filling: In a heavy-bottomed saucepan, combine the egg yolks, 5 tablespoons of the sugar, the lemon zest and juice, and a pinch of salt. Whisk to combine. Place over medium-low heat and cook, stirring constantly, until the mixture has thickened enough to coat the back of the spoon, about 5 minutes. Do not boil. Remove from the heat. Add the butter, 1 tablespoon at a time, and stir until smooth. Strain through a fine strainer into a bowl, pressing the curd through the strainer with a spoon. Refrigerate, uncovered, until chilled, about 1 hour.

recipe continues

TIP One of the major pitfalls when making meringue is adding the sugar all at once. The weight of the sugar inhibits the whites from incorporating air and leads to a heavy, runny meringue. Add the sugar gradually and slowly; in the industry, we call it "running sugar." Another way to make meringue is to melt the sugar with the whites in a double boiler over heat (see page 125).

6 On a lightly floured surface, roll the dough to about ⅛ inch thick. Cut as many 5-inch rounds as possible. Re-roll the scraps and cut more rounds; you should get 6 rounds. Fit the rounds into 4-inch fluted tart shells; the dough should extend slightly over the tops of the molds. Prick each round of dough all over with a fork. Chill for 15 minutes.

7 Set the oven rack in the lower third of the oven. Preheat the oven to 375°F. Line a baking sheet with parchment paper or a nonstick silicone baking mat; set aside.

8 Press the excess dough against the sharp edge of the rims of the molds with the heel of your hand to cut it level with the molds. Set the molds on the prepared baking sheet and bake, rotating the sheet about two-thirds of the way through the baking time, until the pastry is completely cooked through, lightly browned, and crisp, 15 to 18 minutes. Transfer the tart shells to a wire rack. Raise the oven heat to 400°F. Reserve the baking sheet.

9 In the bowl of a standing mixer fitted with the whisk attachment, combine the egg whites with a pinch of salt and beat on low speed until frothy and doubled in volume. Then, with the mixer going, gradually add the remaining 3 tablespoons sugar. Beat on medium-high speed until stiff peaks form and the meringue is glossy. Stir about one-quarter of the meringue into the chilled lemon curd to loosen it. Scrape the curd into the bowl with the meringue, sprinkle with the flour, and fold together with a rubber spatula to incorporate.

10 Remove the tartlet shells from the molds and return to the baking sheet. Divide the soufflé mixture among the baked shells, spreading over the bottoms. For a fluffy, rustic look, do not smooth the tops. Bake, rotating the baking sheet about two-thirds of the way through the baking time, until the filling has risen and is lightly browned on top, about 15 minutes. Transfer the tartlets to the wire rack and let cool for 10 minutes. Dust with confectioners' sugar.

Tips for Tarts and Pies

- **TEMPERATURE IS IMPORTANT:** Doughs are difficult to roll if they are warm. Chill the dough for 1 hour after you make it, and if it gets warm while you're working it, return it to the refrigerator for 5 minutes. Doughs are equally difficult to roll if they're too cold. If a dough has been refrigerated overnight, let it stand at room temperature for about 10 minutes (depending on the temperature of your kitchen), until it's malleable enough to roll without cracking.
- **RESTING:** As a general rule, doughs must rest in the refrigerator for at least 1 hour after you make them to allow the gluten in the dough to relax (see sidebar, page 174). If not, the dough will be elastic and difficult to roll. Flatten the dough first into a disk so that it chills evenly and rolls easily into a round.
- **ROLLING:** To ensure even thickness, roll the rolling pin back and forth from the center, pushing the rolling pin *out* to stretch the dough rather than pushing *down* to mash it. Do *not* roll sideways. Give the dough a quarter turn; roll again, back and forth. Continue until the dough has reached the correct thickness.
- **STICKY DOUGH:** Sprinkle the surface with a little more flour if the dough begins to stick, but try to use as little extra flour as possible because it will make the pastry tough. It's better to run a long metal spatula under the dough as you work to keep it from sticking.
- **LINING THE MOLD:** To transfer the dough round from the work surface to the mold, lightly flour the dough. Lift up the top edge of the dough round, place it over the rolling pin, and roll the pin toward you so that the dough rolls very loosely around the pin. Place the edge of dough that is hanging off the rolling pin at the bottom edge of the tart mold, allowing a 1/4-inch overhang. Roll the dough away from you, off the rolling pin and onto the mold. Press the dough into the mold. If the dough breaks, just patch it.
- **WORKING WITH SCRAPS:** Pastry scraps can be re-rolled effectively for the sweet, cookie-like dough called Pâte Sucrée (page 111). Flaky Pâte Brisée (page 110) does not re-roll as nicely. Save scraps for a bottom crust or cookies. The top crust should be new dough.

Banana Meringue Pie

This is a cross between two of my favorite pies, a lemon meringue and a banana cream. It's also a favorite of Peter's, a young man after my own heart. Meringue is a bit more delicate than whipped cream, so the bananas are very well highlighted. And the chocolate-painted crust makes it a slam-dunk success with other kids.

MAKES ONE 9-INCH PIE; SERVES 8

Vanilla Pastry Cream

4 large egg yolks
½ cup sugar
¼ cup cornstarch
2 cups whole milk
1 teaspoon vanilla paste (see sidebar, page 212) or pure vanilla extract
⅛ teaspoon coarse salt
2 tablespoons cold unsalted butter, cut into small pieces

½ recipe Pâte Brisée (page 110), chilled
2 ounces bittersweet chocolate, chopped into 2-inch pieces
2 to 3 ripe bananas, sliced about ¼ inch thick

Meringue

4 large egg whites
¾ cup sugar
Pinch of coarse salt

1 To make the pastry cream: In a medium, heat-proof bowl, whisk together the egg yolks, ¼ cup of the sugar, all of the cornstarch, and ½ cup of the milk; set aside.

2 In a medium saucepan, combine the remaining 1½ cups milk, the remaining ¼ cup sugar, the vanilla paste, if using, and the salt. Bring to a simmer. Whisking constantly, gradually pour the hot milk into the egg mixture to temper it. Set a strainer over the saucepan. Strain the custard mixture back into the saucepan and bring to a boil over medium heat, whisking constantly. Boil for 10 seconds, whisking. (Make sure the custard boils for 10 seconds in the center of the pan, not just around the sides.) The mixture should thicken to a pudding-like consistency.

3 Transfer the pastry cream to a bowl and whisk in the butter. Whisk in the vanilla extract, if using. Cover with plastic wrap, pressing it directly on the surface of the cream to prevent a skin from forming. Refrigerate until chilled, about 3 hours.

4 On a lightly floured work surface, roll out the dough to a 12-inch round, ⅛ inch thick. Fit the dough into a 9-inch Pyrex pie pan. Trim to a ½-inch overhang all around and use your fingertips to crimp the edges. Chill until firm, about 30 minutes.

5 Set the oven rack in the lower third of the oven. Preheat the oven to 375°F.

6 Line the chilled pie shell with parchment paper, leaving a 1-inch overhang. Fill with pie weights (see opposite). Place on a baking sheet and bake, rotating the sheet about two-thirds of the way through the baking time, until the edges of the crust are just

beginning to turn golden, 20 to 25 minutes. Remove the parchment paper and weights. Return the pie shell to the oven and continue to bake until the surface is golden all over, 20 to 25 minutes. Transfer to a wire rack and cool completely.

7 Place the chocolate in the top of a double boiler. Set it over (not in) 1 inch of simmering water and heat until melted. Stir until smooth.

8 Using a pastry brush, coat the bottom of the pie shell with the melted chocolate. Place in the refrigerator until the chocolate is set, about 15 minutes.

9 Using an offset spatula, spread the chilled custard evenly over the pie shell. Arrange the banana slices in a single layer over the custard to cover completely; refrigerate.

10 Preheat the oven to 400°F.

11 To make the meringue: Bring about 1 inch of water to a simmer in the bottom of a double boiler. Combine the egg whites, sugar, and a pinch of salt in the top of the double boiler, set it over (not in) the simmering water, and whisk to dissolve the sugar until it melts, 1 to 2 minutes. (The mixture should feel hot to the touch, and not gritty.) Remove from the heat and beat with an electric mixer on medium-high speed until the meringue is glossy and stiff peaks form when you lift the whisk.

12 Spread the meringue over the filling with a metal spatula so that the meringue has an attractive shape (it shouldn't be smooth). Place the pie on a baking sheet and bake without rotating until the meringue is nicely browned, 10 to 12 minutes. Cool on a wire rack for 10 minutes. Refrigerate until very cold, 2 to 3 hours.

TIP Pie weights are bean-size baking weights that help hold a crust in place during blind baking in order to maintain its shape and keep it from puffing up during baking. Ceramic or metal weights do a better job at this than dried beans or rice because they are heavier, conduct and retain heat better, and help to cook the pastry.

Blackberry Pie with a Cornmeal Crust

This double-crust pie is inspired by time spent in New Orleans over the years, where blackberry desserts such as crisps and cobblers are very popular. The cornmeal crust adds a delicate crunch that is wonderful against the soft texture of the fruit. The combination of the sweet berries and the cornmeal is fabulous, and it's even better with a scoop of vanilla ice cream.

MAKES ONE 9-INCH PIE; SERVES 8

Cornmeal Pastry Dough

- **2 cups all-purpose flour**
- **½ cup coarse yellow cornmeal**
- **1 tablespoon granulated sugar**
- **1 teaspoon coarse salt**
- **1 cup (2 sticks) cold unsalted butter, cut into small pieces**
- **5 to 6 tablespoons ice water**

Filling

- **5 (6-ounce) baskets fresh blackberries**
- **½ cup granulated sugar**
- **3 tablespoons cornstarch**
- **Grated zest of ½ orange**
- **2 tablespoons freshly squeezed orange juice (from 1 orange)**
- **1 teaspoon coarse salt**

- **1 large egg, beaten with a pinch of salt, for egg wash**
- **2 teaspoons sanding sugar**

1 To make the pastry: In the bowl of a food processor, combine the flour, cornmeal, sugar, and salt. Add the butter and pulse until the mixture resembles coarse crumbs, about 10 seconds. With the machine running, add the ice water through the feed tube in a slow and steady stream, a little bit at a time until the dough is moistened but does not form a ball. There will be unincorporated bits of butter. Pinch the mixture between two fingers. The dough should not be wet or sticky. If it is too dry and does not hold together, add a little more water. Turn the dough onto a clean work surface. Divide in half and shape each into a disk. Wrap in plastic wrap and chill for at least 1 hour.

2 To make the filling: In a large bowl, toss the blackberries with the sugar, cornstarch, orange zest and juice, and salt; set aside.

3 Set an oven rack in the lower third of the oven. Preheat the oven to 425°F. Line a baking sheet with parchment paper or a nonstick silicone baking mat.

4 On a lightly floured work surface, roll out one dough disk to a 12-inch round, ⅛ inch thick. Fit the dough into a 9½-inch fluted Pyrex pie plate. Mound the filling mixture into the crust. Brush the rim of the pie shell with egg wash.

5 Roll the second dough disk to an 11-inch round, about ⅛ inch thick. Place it on top of the blackberries, and press the top and bottom edges together to seal. Trim the dough to a 1-inch overhang and crimp the edges. Brush the top crust all over with egg wash and sprinkle with the sanding sugar. Cut an X in the center of the top crust, each cut about 2 inches long, and gently

fold back the corners to make a "chimney" to allow the steam to escape.

6 Set the pie plate on the prepared baking sheet. Place the sheet in the oven and immediately reduce the oven temperature to 400°F. Bake for 20 minutes. Rotate the baking sheet, reduce the heat to 350°F, and bake until the crust is golden brown and the juices are bubbling through the "chimney," 40 to 50 more minutes.

7 Transfer the pie to a wire rack to cool for at least 30 minutes to allow the juices to be absorbed.

Winter Blueberry Streusel Pie

Blueberries freeze very well in a home freezer, and this streusel-topped dessert is a terrific way to take advantage of your frozen berries during the winter months. I picked up the filling recipe for this pie at the Culinary Institute of America. It has a rich cinnamon-berry flavor, brightened with lemon. It will only work with frozen berries, which give off juice when they thaw. The juices are thickened with a cornstarch slurry (see sidebar, page 72) In the middle of a Connecticut winter, when we're stuck at home and buried in snow, this pie is a whiff of summer to come.

MAKES ONE 9-INCH PIE; SERVES 8

Filling

- **3 cups (1⅔ pounds) frozen, unsweetened blueberries (see page 21)**
- **¼ cup plus ⅔ cup granulated sugar**
- **¼ cup cornstarch**
- **¾ teaspoon coarse salt**
- **¾ teaspoon ground cinnamon**
- **1 teaspoon grated lemon zest (from 1 lemon)**
- **1 tablespoon freshly squeezed lemon juice (from 1 lemon)**

Streusel Topping

- **2½ cups all-purpose flour**
- **1 cup firmly packed light brown sugar**
- **2 teaspoons ground cinnamon**
- **½ teaspoon coarse salt**
- **1 cup (2 sticks) unsalted butter**

- **½ recipe Pâte Brisée (page 110), chilled**

1 To make the filling: Thaw the berries at room temperature in a strainer or colander set over a bowl. Transfer the berries to a medium bowl. Measure the juice from the drained berries, and add water, if needed, to measure ½ cup of juice. Transfer to a saucepan and stir in ¼ cup of the granulated sugar. In a small bowl, whisk ¼ cup cold water with the cornstarch.

2 Bring the juice mixture to a boil over medium heat. Add the cornstarch mixture, return to a boil, and cook, stirring, until thickened, 1 to 2 minutes. Add the remaining ⅔ cup granulated sugar, the salt, cinnamon, and lemon zest and juice. Cook, stirring, until the sugar dissolves. Pour over the thawed blueberries and mix gently. Let cool completely.

3 To make the streusel topping: In a large bowl, sift the flour with the brown sugar, cinnamon, and salt. Melt the butter in a small saucepan. Let cool for 2 minutes. Pour the melted butter over the flour mixture. Work the mixture with your fingertips to press into nice large crumbs.

4 On a lightly floured surface, roll out the pastry dough to a 12-inch round and fit it into a 9-inch Pyrex pie plate, pressing into the edges. Trim to a ½-inch overhang all around and use your fingertips to crimp the edges. Chill until firm, at least 1 hour.

5 Set the oven rack in the lower third of the oven. Preheat the oven to 450°F. Line a baking sheet with parchment paper or a nonstick silicone baking mat.

6 Transfer the cooled berry filling to the prepared pie shell. Sprinkle the streusel topping over the top, covering the filling completely.

7 Place the pie on the prepared baking sheet, and transfer to the oven. Immediately reduce the oven temperature to 425°F. Bake for 20 minutes. Rotate the baking sheet. Reduce the heat to 350°F. and continue baking until the streusel turns golden brown and the juices are bubbling, 40 to 50 more minutes. Transfer to a wire rack and let cool completely, at least 1 hour, to allow the juices to be absorbed. Serve at room temperature.

SAFE

Citrus Buttermilk Pie

Buttermilk pie is a Southern specialty. It combines a tangy, buttermilk custard with a crust. I love the combination of citrus and buttermilk—the more sour the better. So I've upped the tang of the traditional recipe by adding lemon and orange extracts and zest. Because the recipe doesn't call for citrus juice, it's easy to make the custard with zest that you've previously frozen (page 22). Then, if you have eggs, butter, and buttermilk in the refrigerator, the pie comes together at a moment's notice, year-round. It's perfect for a spring or summer meal, but I've also served it at Thanksgiving, sometimes switching out the Pâte Brisée for a graham cracker crust (see page 117). If you've never tasted this classic, you're in for a treat.

MAKES ONE 9-INCH PIE; SERVES 8

½ recipe Pâte Brisée (page 110), chilled
1 cup sugar
3 tablespoons cornstarch
½ teaspoon coarse salt
1½ cups buttermilk
2 large eggs
2 large egg yolks
6 tablespoons unsalted butter, melted
1 teaspoon lemon extract
1 teaspoon orange extract
½ teaspoon grated lemon zest (from 1 lemon)
½ teaspoon grated orange zest (from 1 orange)

1 On a lightly floured work surface, roll out the dough to a 12-inch round, ⅛ inch thick. Fit the dough into a 9-inch Pyrex pie plate. Trim to a ½-inch overhang all around and use your fingertips to crimp the edges. Chill until firm, about 30 minutes.

2 Set the oven rack in the lower third of the oven. Preheat the oven to 375°F.

3 Line the chilled pie shell with parchment paper, leaving a 1-inch overhang. Fill with pie weights (see page 125). Bake until the edges of the shell are just beginning to turn golden, 15 to 20 minutes. Remove the parchment paper and weights. Return the pie shell to the oven and continue to bake until the surface is golden all over, 25 to 30 minutes. Transfer to a wire rack and cool completely.

4 Increase the oven temperature to 400°F. Place the pie shell on a baking sheet.

5 In a medium bowl, whisk together the sugar, cornstarch, and salt; set aside. In a large bowl, whisk together the buttermilk, whole eggs, yolks, melted butter, and lemon and orange extracts and zests. Pour into the cooked pie shell. Bake, rotating the baking sheet about two-thirds of the way through the baking time, until the filling is slightly browned and set at the edges when you touch it, 40 to 45 minutes. Transfer to a wire rack to cool to room temperature.

Mixed Berry Turnovers

Turnovers are also called hand pies because you can just pick them up and eat them out of hand. Since they're so portable, they make good treats for kids' lunch boxes, and for picnics. These are made with a Pâte Brisée, but you can substitute a store-bought puff pastry or Pâte à Foncer (page 118). At the bakery, I usually make them with an apple filling because it's ever-popular. But my kids love this version, so this is what I make for them at home. Some of the juices will bubble out of the turnovers during cooking, so it's crucial to bake them on a rimmed baking sheet lined with parchment or a nonstick silicone baking mat.

MAKES FOUR 5-INCH TURNOVERS

- **¼ cup fresh blueberries**
- **¼ cup fresh, quartered strawberries**
- **¼ cup fresh raspberries**
- **¼ cup fresh blackberries**
- **¼ cup granulated sugar**
- **½ teaspoon coarse salt**
- **Grated zest of ½ lemon**
- **1 teaspoon freshly squeezed lemon juice (from 1 lemon)**
- **2 teaspoons cornstarch**
- **½ recipe Pâte Brisée (page 110), chilled**
- **1 large egg whisked with a pinch of coarse salt, for egg wash**
- **½ teaspoon sanding sugar**

1. In a medium bowl, toss the blueberries, strawberries, raspberries, and blackberries with the granulated sugar, salt, and lemon zest and juice. Transfer to a colander set over a plate or bowl; set aside to drain for 2 to 3 hours.

2. Use a rubber spatula to scrape the drained juice into a small saucepan. Add about half of the berries and mash with a fork. Place over medium heat and bring to a simmer. Meanwhile, stir the cornstarch with 1 tablespoon water in a cup. Add the cornstarch mixture to the pan with the simmering fruit syrup and simmer, stirring, until the mixture thickens, 2 to 3 minutes. Transfer to a medium bowl and stir in the remaining berries. Refrigerate until chilled, about 30 minutes.

3. Line a rimmed baking sheet with parchment paper or a nonstick silicone baking mat; set aside.

4. On a lightly floured surface, roll the dough about ⅛ inch thick and about 11 inches square. Use a pizza cutter and a ruler to trim the edges to a 10-inch square and cut four 5-inch squares. Brush two adjacent edges of each square with egg wash. Divide the berry mixture among the four squares, spooning it into the center. Starting with the half that has not been egg-washed, fold the dough diagonally over the filling to form a triangle, and press to seal. Crimp the edges using the floured tines of a fork.

5. Set the oven rack in the lower third of the oven. Preheat the oven to 425°F.

6 Place the turnovers on the baking sheet and freeze for 20 minutes. Brush with more egg wash and sprinkle each turnover with about ⅛ teaspoon sanding sugar. Cut vents in the center of each with the tips of kitchen scissors to allow steam to escape. Bake the turnovers, rotating the baking sheet about two-thirds of the way through the baking time, until the pastries are golden brown, about 15 minutes. Transfer to a wire rack and let cool completely.

TIP For apple turnovers, follow the directions for making apple compote on page 204, using 1 tablespoon butter, 2 large Granny Smith apples, a pinch of coarse salt, ½ teaspoon lemon juice, 2 tablespoons sugar, a pinch of cinnamon, 2 tablespoons wine or apple juice, and 2 tablespoons golden raisins. In step 1, cook the apples 7 to 8 minutes. In step 2, cook about 2 minutes to evaporate the liquid. Let the compote cool completely before filling the turnovers.

Banana–Macadamia Nut Tartlets

These individual filo tartlets are inspired by a similar dessert that we used to make at the Elms Restaurant and Tavern in Ridgefield, Connecticut. The filo crust is crisp and delicate and the maple–brown sugar filling, reminiscent of a pecan pie filling, brings out the flavor of the bananas. These warm tartlets make an elegant plated dessert with Banana Sorbet (page 228) and Chocolate Sauce (page 218) if you're throwing a party. But at my house we usually keep things simple and eat them as is because they're so delicious! It's very important that the bananas be ripe so that their texture is soft against the crisp filo. You'll need four 4-inch straight-sided tartlet molds. Serve these immediately before the filo crust has a chance to soften.

MAKES FOUR 4-INCH TARTLETS

Filling

- **1 tablespoon unsalted butter, melted**
- **¼ cup light brown sugar**
- **2 tablespoons light corn syrup**
- **2 tablespoons pure maple syrup**
- **1 large egg**
- **Pinch of coarse salt**
- **¼ teaspoon pure vanilla extract**

- **3 (17 by 12-inch) sheets frozen filo, thawed in the refrigerator**
- **2 tablespoons unsalted butter, melted, for brushing the filo**
- **2 to 3 ripe bananas, sliced about ¼ inch thick**
- **6 tablespoons chopped macadamia nuts (from one 2¼-ounce package nuts)**

1 To make the filling: In a medium bowl, whisk together the melted butter, brown sugar, corn syrup, maple syrup, egg, salt, and vanilla; set aside.

2 Set the oven rack in the lower third of the oven. Preheat the oven to 400°F. Place four unbuttered straight-sided 4-inch tartlet pans (without removable bottoms) on a parchment-lined baking sheet; set aside.

3 Stack the 3 filo sheets on a cutting board. Trim to a 10 by 15-inch rectangle. Score six 5 by 5-inch squares with a ruler and knife, then cut out the eighteen squares. Divide into four stacks of four, with two spares in case the filo rips.

4 Place one filo square on the work surface and brush the square very lightly with melted butter, leaving a ½-inch border unbuttered. Overlap with a second filo square, at a slight angle, so that the corners make a star design. Brush with butter, leaving the border unbuttered. Overlap with a third square, on an angle, and brush with butter. Overlap with a fourth square, on an angle, and brush with butter. You will have created a stack that is roughly round in shape, with a multipoint, star-shaped edge. Press the stack into one of the tartlet molds on the prepared baking sheet. The filo dough will stick up above the rim of the mold like tissue paper by about 1 inch. Repeat to line the remaining 3 tartlet molds.

5 Arrange 6 to 7 banana slices in a single layer over the bottom of each tartlet shell. Divide the nuts among the shells (1½ tablespoons per tartlet). Pour 2 tablespoons of the filling into each shell. Bake, rotating the baking sheet about two-thirds of the way through the baking time, until the filling puffs and sets, 18 to 20 minutes. Transfer to a wire rack and let cool for 2 minutes. Then carefully lift thc tartlets out of the pans by the edges. The filo will break a little; don't worry about it. But if the tartlets stick, run a small offset spatula between the filo and the pan to loosen. Set on the rack to cool for 5 minutes. Serve warm.

French Lemon Tart

I recommend this French lemon tart to anyone who loves lemon curd. The soft, silky, ultra-lemony custard filling tastes similar, but it's even easier to make and the almond extract is a delicious match with the lemon. I decorate the tart with a ring of lemon slices, candied in sugar syrup. They give the tart a professional touch but they're not mandatory at home. The tart tastes fabulous without them. Although I usually grate zest on a Microplane, I use the 1/8-inch holes on a box grater for this filling. It makes for a coarser zest, which gives the filling more texture.

MAKES ONE 9-INCH TART; SERVES 8

½ recipe Pâte Sucrée (page 111), chilled

Filling

- **3 large eggs**
- **1 cup sugar**
- **6 tablespoons (¾ stick) unsalted butter, melted**
- **3 tablespoons crème fraîche or sour cream**
- **Zest of 3 lemons, grated on a box grater**
- **½ cup freshly squeezed lemon juice (from 3 to 4 lemons)**
- **¾ teaspoon coarse salt**
- **½ teaspoon almond extract**

Candied Lemon Slices

- **2 cups sugar**
- **2 lemons, sliced uniformly but no less than 1/8 inch thick with a sharp knife**

- **1/3 cup apricot jam**
- **1 tablespoon freshly squeezed lemon juice (from 1 lemon)**
- **Crème fraîche, for serving**

1 On a lightly floured work surface, roll the dough about 1/8 inch thick. Fit the dough into a 9-inch fluted tart pan with a removable bottom and trim the edges so the dough comes slightly above the rim of the tart pan. Then press the excess dough against the sharp edge of the rim with your fingers to cut it level with the pan. Chill until firm, about 30 minutes.

2 Set the oven rack in the lower third of the oven. Preheat the oven to 375°F.

3 Line a baking sheet with parchment paper or a nonstick silicone baking mat. Line the chilled pie shell with parchment paper, leaving a 1-inch overhang, and fill with pie weights (see page 125). Bake until the edges of the tart are just beginning to turn golden, 15 to 20 minutes. Remove the parchment paper and weights. Return the tart shell to the oven and continue to bake until the surface is golden all over, about 10 minutes. Transfer to a wire rack and cool completely.

4 To make the filling: In a medium bowl, whisk together the eggs, sugar, melted butter, crème fraîche, lemon zest and juice, salt, and almond extract. Let stand for 5 minutes.

5 Place the tart shell on the prepared baking sheet. Place the baking sheet in the oven. Carefully pour the filling mixture into the tart shell. Bake until the filling is completely set and no

recipe continues

TIP When working with a very fluid filling mixture like this one, it's best to put the tart shell in the oven first, then pour in the filling. The filling is likely to slosh out of the shell if you try to transfer it from a work surface to the oven.

longer jiggles in the center, 30 to 35 minutes. (The filling will remain bright yellow.)

6 Transfer to a wire rack and let cool. Chill completely in the refrigerator.

7 To make the candied lemon slices: In a medium saucepan, bring the sugar and 1 cup water to a boil. Reduce to a simmer. Add the lemon slices and poach at a very low simmer until the rinds are translucent, about 40 minutes. (Simmer gently so the membranes do not break.) Let cool completely in the syrup, 40 to 45 minutes. Drain the slices and pat dry with paper towels.

8 Set the cooled tart on top of a large (such as 28-ounce) can and allow the sides of the pan to fall. Place the tart on a serving plate. Ring the edge of the tart with single lemon slices without overlapping. Cut one slice almost in half, twist, and place in the center of the tart. In a small saucepan, stir together the jam, lemon juice, and 1 tablespoon water. Bring to boil. Set a fine strainer over a small bowl. Strain the glaze into the bowl. With a pastry brush, brush the glaze over the lemon slices and the crust. Serve with crème fraîche.

Caramel Pear Tarts

These individual warm pear-shaped tarts are a takeoff on the famous French Tarte Tatin. They make a great fall dessert when pears are in season that is popular with our catering clients. But they're not difficult to make at home. You will need a pear-shaped cookie cutter with a long stem and a body wide enough to cover the fanned pear halves (about 4½ to 5 inches long and at least 3½ inches wide at the widest point). The pear halves are cupped by the pastry and the stems peek out from underneath. These are delicious as is, or served with caramel or vanilla ice cream. I like to serve them at Christmas dinner because they're elegant, easy, and can be made a day ahead. Cover the tarts, still in their pans, and leave them overnight at room temperature. Rewarm the next day on a baking sheet at 300°F until the pears are warmed through and the juices are liquid, ten to fifteen minutes.

MAKES 4 INDIVIDUAL PEAR-SHAPED TARTS

½ recipe Pâte Brisée (page 110), chilled

2 pears, peeled, halved with the stem left on one side, and cored with melon baller

Caramel

¾ cup sugar

¾ teaspoon white vinegar

8 teaspoons unsalted butter

1 Set the oven rack in the lower third of the oven. Preheat the oven to 400°F. Have ready four 6-inch slope-sided pie pans. Line a baking sheet with a sheet of parchment paper or a nonstick silicone baking mat; set aside.

2 On a lightly floured work surface, roll the dough ⅛ to ¼ inch thick. Using a pear-shaped cookie cutter, cut out four pear-shaped pieces of dough (otherwise, cut the dough into quarters and roll each to a round the size of one of the pie pans). Place on the prepared baking sheet; chill.

3 Thickly slice each pear half lengthwise (six or seven ½-inch-thick slices), up to ½ inch from the stem ends; leave the stem ends intact so that the slices do not separate. Press gently with the palm of your hand to fan the slices; set aside.

4 To make the caramel: In a small saucepan, combine the sugar, ¼ cup water, and the vinegar. Bring to a boil over medium-high heat, swirling the pan to dissolve the sugar. Boil until the mixture turns a deep amber color, 5 to 10 minutes.

5 Remove from the heat and add 2 tablespoons water; stand back—the caramel will spit. Swirl to combine. Return to the heat if necessary to re-melt the caramel.

recipe continues

TIP Their firm texture and buttery flavor make Anjou pears a perfect choice for these tarts. If you can't find them, substitute Bosc, Bartlett, or Cornice varieties.

6 Divide the caramel evenly among the four pie pans. Dot each surface with 2 teaspoons of the butter.

7 Arrange a pear half, rounded side down, on top of the caramel in each pie pan. Top each pear with a pastry "pear," stretching the dough and tucking it around the pear halves to cover them entirely. Place the pie pans on the lined baking sheet.

8 Bake, rotating the baking sheet about two-thirds of the way through the baking time, until the crust is cooked through, you see caramel bubbling from the bottom, and the pears are tender when you peek under the dough and pierce with a tester, 33 to 37 minutes. Remove from the oven and let stand for 5 minutes. Using tongs, carefully invert the pans onto a wire rack set over a sheet pan to catch the drippings; remove the pans with the tongs. Immediately place the tarts on serving plates and top with the remaining pan drippings.

Strawberry Frangipane Tartlets

These tartlets remind me of the individual Table Talk fruit pies my brothers and I loved as kids. (Except they're a lot better!) The filling is soft, and the strawberry jam echoes the flavor of the fresh strawberries on top. They're easy to make because the filling cooks along with the pastry, and the kids love having their own tartlet. You will need six 3½-inch fluted molds (no removable bottoms) and a round cutter, 4½ inches in diameter (the lid of a standard quart-size deli container works perfectly). It's a very pretty presentation and you can vary the tart with whatever berries are available. The important part is not to overbake the filling.

MAKES SIX 3½-INCH TARTLETS

1 recipe Pâte Sucrée (page 111), chilled

Almond Cream

- **¼ cup whole blanched almonds (or 6 tablespoons almond flour)**
- **3 tablespoons granulated sugar**
- **½ teaspoon coarse salt**
- **3 tablespoons unsalted butter**
- **1 large egg, at room temperature**
- **¾ teaspoon almond extract**
- **1½ tablespoons all-purpose flour**
- **¼ cup strawberry jam**
- **24 medium strawberries, hulled**
- **1 tablespoon confectioners' sugar, for dusting**

1. On a lightly floured surface, roll the dough about ⅛ inch thick. Use a standard quart-size deli container to cut as many 4½-inch rounds as possible. Press the scraps together in a ball; chill. Re-roll the scraps as necessary to make six rounds. Fit the dough rounds into six 3½-inch fluted tartlet pans and trim the dough so that it comes slightly above the rim of the pan. Then press the excess dough against the sharp edge of the rim of the pan with the heel of your hand to cut it level with the pan. Chill until firm, about 30 minutes.
2. To make the almond cream: In a food processor, pulse the almonds with the sugar and salt for about 10 seconds, until finely ground. Add the butter and process to blend. Add the egg, processing until blended and scraping the bowl. Add the almond extract. Add the all-purpose flour and process until combined.
3. Set the oven rack in the lower third of the oven. Preheat the oven to 375°F.
4. Use the back of a spoon to spread each tartlet shell with 1 teaspoon of the strawberry jam. Spread 2 tablespoons of the almond cream on top of the jam in each shell. Place the tartlet shells on a baking sheet and chill for 5 minutes.
5. Bake, rotating the baking sheet about two-thirds of the way through the baking time, until the pastry is cooked through and golden brown and the almond cream is puffed and golden, 22 to 26 minutes. Transfer the tartlets to a wire rack. Let cool

completely. Remove the tartlets from the molds. Spread the top of each with a thin layer of the remaining strawberry jam.

6 Stand a strawberry, pointed side up, in the center of each tartlet. Cut the remaining strawberries in half. Arrange 4 to 6 strawberry halves, depending on size, over the top of each tartlet, standing them on the wide end and leaning them against the center berry. Dust with confectioners' sugar.

Fig Tart

My grandparents usually had fresh figs on the table at their home from late spring into fall, when figs are in season. As a child, I wasn't a big fan of their soft, moist texture. But as an adult I can't stop eating them. When figs bake, they soften and release their juices, so the flavor of the fruit concentrates. A butter-sugar glaze gives the fruit a beautiful sheen and boosts the flavor of less than perfect fruit. If you have beautiful, ripe figs, you can simplify this recipe by leaving the figs raw and brushing them with a glaze of melted, strained, cooled apricot jam. This is a tasty alternative to traditional pumpkin pie for Thanksgiving if figs are still available where you live.

MAKES ONE 9-INCH TART; SERVES 8 TO 10

½ recipe Vanilla Pastry Cream (page 124)
Grated zest of ½ orange

½ recipe Pâte Sucrée (page 111), chilled
18 to 20 fresh figs, halved through the stem ends, leave 1 fig whole
2 tablespoons unsalted butter, melted
2 tablespoons sanding sugar

1 Make the pastry cream, adding the orange zest to the saucepan with the milk along with the vanilla. Refrigerate.

2 On a lightly floured work surface, roll the dough to a 12-inch round, about 1/8 inch thick. Fit the dough into a 9-inch fluted tart pan with a removable bottom and trim the dough so that it comes slightly above the rim of the tart pan. Press the excess dough against the sharp edge of the rim of the pan with the heel of your hand to cut it level with the pan. Chill until firm, about 30 minutes.

3 Arrange the oven rack in the lower third of the oven. Preheat the oven to 425°F. Line a baking sheet with parchment paper or a nonstick silicone baking mat.

4 Spread the pastry cream over the bottom of the pie shell. Arrange the fig halves on top, rounded edges down, shingled tightly and in concentric circles. Quarter the remaining whole fig, leaving the quarters connected at the base. Place in the center of the tart so that the quarters open like the petals of a flower. Brush the figs with the butter and sanding sugar evenly over the top.

5 Bake, rotating the baking sheet about two-thirds of the way through the baking time, until the pastry is cooked through and the figs are tender and caramelized, about 40 minutes. Transfer to a wire rack to cool.

5

Cupcakes and Cakes

Chocolate-Cherry Cupcakes

Banana–Chocolate Chip Cupcakes

Strawberry-Pecan Cupcakes

Cran-Raspberry Buckle

Banana–Chocolate Chip Kugelhopf

Chestnut Layer Cake with Raspberries

Lemon Daisy Cake

Italian Wedding Cake

Lemon-Almond Cake with Macerated Strawberries

Persimmon Pudding Cake with Ginger-Walnut Frosting

Gingerbread-Pineapple Upside-Down Cake

Elenore's Plum Cake

Blueberry Crumb Cake

Polenta Pound Cake

Citrus Angel Food Cake

Blueberry Cheesecake in Glass Jars

Banana Pudding Icebox Cake

Warm Hazelnut Shortcakes with Sautéed Plums

Pavlovas with Sautéed Plums, Peaches, and Nectarines

Pumpkin Roulade

Babette's Banana Éclairs

Pumpkin Whoopie Pies with Cinnamon Cream

In Valley Stream, Long Island, we lived down the block from a bakery called Everbest, owned by the Calabrese family. (I can still remember their motto: "Where butter makes the difference.") The bakery has been in business since 1949 and it's still going strong. Everbest was famous for their crumb cakes—a layer of vanilla cake topped with a streusel crumb topping. My brothers and I hung around with the Calabrese sons, and our whole gang used to play stickball behind the bakery. The bakery was a second home for me and my brothers. I was fascinated by the amount of baked goods that came out of that small kitchen! A few years after I opened the SoNo Baking Company in South Norwalk, Mr. Calabrese, now retired, came up from Florida to bake with me. It was one of those "Lion King," full-circle-of-life moments.

This chapter includes a variety of cakes, including a Blueberry Crumb Cake (page 172) in honor of Everbest. Some of the cakes, such as the Citrus Angel Food Cake (page 177) are classics. Others come from family members: Elenore's Plum Cake (page 171) was given to me by my mother-in-law and the Banana Pudding Icebox Cake (page 182) is a version of the cake my own mother used to make. Chocolate-Cherry Cupcakes (page 148), Banana–Chocolate Chip Cupcakes (page 150), and Strawberry-Pecan Cupcakes (page 151) are favorites of children and adults in my family. Making two or three kinds for a birthday party ensures that all the guests get their favorite flavor, and you can mix and match the frostings to suit preferences.

Cake making requires concentration and a little skill. You may find some to be challenging. The layer cakes—Lemon Daisy Cake (page 158), Italian Wedding Cake (page 163), and Chestnut Layer Cake with Raspberries (page 156)—are for when you want something really impressive and have plenty of time. I recommend devoting parts of two or even three days so that you're not rushed. But other cakes in this collection are no more difficult than making muffins or cookies. Elenore's Plum Cake is just a simple batter plus plums, and it's fantastic. Polenta Pound Cake (page 175) has only eight ingredients and comes together in about ten minutes.

All the recipes are do-able if you follow the instructions carefully. I always tell people: If you can fold an origami shape, you can easily put together a cake. It's not hard, you just have to start at the beginning and carefully follow the directions all the way through. If you try to take a shortcut with origami, you end up having to start over, right? There are no shortcuts with baking either, as far as I know.

With the exception of those made with whipped cream or frosted with a buttercream, store the cakes in this chapter at room temperature under a cake dome. A cake dome will prevent whipped cream–filled cakes from picking up refrigerator odors, too.

Chocolate-Cherry Cupcakes

Cupcakes are a must for children's birthday parties and these days they're just as popular with adults. The current trend is to fill the cupcakes with a little something delicious to match the cake and frosting, like the Hostess cupcakes I grew up on! These moist, super-chocolatey cakes are filled with cherries that have been softened and sweetened in a sugar syrup.

MAKES 18 CUPCAKES

Chocolate Ganache

- **½ pound semisweet chocolate, finely chopped (about 1⅓ cup)**
- **½ pound bittersweet chocolate, finely chopped (about 1⅓ cup)**
- **2 cups heavy cream**
- **2 tablespoons honey**
- **1½ teaspoons vanilla paste (see sidebar, page 212) or pure vanilla extract**
- **¼ teaspoon coarse salt**

Cherries in Syrup

- **1 cup sugar**
- **54 fresh or frozen pitted cherries**

Cupcakes

- **⅔ cup good-quality unsweetened cocoa powder, plus extra for dusting**
- **1 cup all-purpose flour**
- **1⅓ cups sugar**
- **¾ teaspoon baking powder**
- **1¼ teaspoons baking soda**
- **¼ teaspoon coarse salt**
- **2 large eggs, at room temperature**
- **1 teaspoon pure vanilla extract**
- **5½ tablespoons unsalted butter, melted**
- **⅔ cup buttermilk**
- **⅔ cup brewed coffee (not espresso)**

1 To make the ganache: Place the semisweet and bittersweet chocolate in a heat-proof bowl; set aside. In a medium saucepan, combine the cream, honey, vanilla paste, if using, and salt. Bring the cream mixture to a boil, pour over the chocolate, and let stand for 5 minutes to melt the chocolate. Whisk until smooth. Strain through a fine strainer into a bowl. Stir in the vanilla extract, if using. Cover with plastic wrap and let stand at room temperature until the ganache stiffens, at least 6 hours or overnight. (Or place in the refrigerator and chill, stirring every 20 to 30 minutes, until the ganache stiffens.)

2 To make the cherries in syrup: In a small saucepan, combine the sugar and 1 cup water and bring to a boil over medium-high heat, swirling to dissolve the sugar. Remove from the heat. Transfer to a bowl; refrigerate until chilled. Add the cherries. Refrigerate for at least 2 hours or overnight.

3 Preheat the oven to 350°F. Butter a standard 12-cup muffin pan with softened butter. Coat the muffin cups with cocoa and tap out the excess. (Or line with cupcake liners.) Place the muffin pan on a baking sheet; set aside.

4 To make the cupcakes: In the bowl of an electric mixer fitted with the paddle attachment, sift in the flour, cocoa, sugar, baking powder, baking soda, and salt. Mix on low speed to combine.

5 Add the eggs, vanilla, melted butter, buttermilk, and coffee. Mix on low speed until fully combined. Pour the batter into the prepared muffin cups so that the batter comes to about ⅜ inch from the tops; do not overfill. Set the remaining batter aside.

Bake, rotating the baking sheet about two-thirds of the way through the baking, until a cake tester inserted in the middle comes out clean and the tops are lightly browned, 24 to 26 minutes. Cool in the muffin cups on a wire rack for 10 minutes, then unmold and cool completely on the rack.

6 Fill, bake, and cool the remaining 6 cupcakes.

7 Strain the cherries. Pat dry on a paper towel. Using your thumb or the back of a teaspoon, scoop out the center of each cooled cupcake with a melon baller, creating an indentation deep enough to hold three cherries. Press the cherries into the indentation. Frost the filled cupcakes with the ganache.

TIP For the professional touch, frost the cupcakes with a pastry bag and tip. For Chocolate-Cherry Cupcakes (opposite), I use a fluted tip such as Ateco #828 (see Sources, page 281); for Banana–Chocolate Chip Cupcakes (page 150), I use a round tip such as Ateco #806; the Strawberry-Pecan Cupcakes (page 151) are frosted with the same round tip, and the frosting is flattened with a small offset spatula.

Banana–Chocolate Chip Cupcakes

My son Peter loves my Banana-Chocolate Kugelhopf, so when it was time to come up with a cupcake for his third birthday party, SoNo Baking Company pastry chef Val Denner devised these sensational cupcakes. The chocolate chips in the cake echo the rich, dark chocolate ganache filling, and the creamy hazelnut frosting complements both bananas and chocolate. Peter was delighted and had a generously frosted face to prove it.

MAKES 18 CUPCAKES

1 recipe Banana–Chocolate Chip Kugelhopf (page 154)

Nutella Frosting

1¼ cups (2½ sticks) unsalted butter, at room temperature
2½ cups confectioners' sugar
Pinch of coarse salt
2 tablespoons heavy cream
2 teaspoons pure vanilla extract
2 tablespoons Nutella

¼ recipe Chocolate Ganache (page 148)
18 skinned hazelnuts (page 112), for garnish

1 Set the oven rack in the lower third of the oven. Preheat the oven to 350°F. Spray a standard 12-cup muffin pan with nonstick cooking spray or line with cupcake liners. Place the muffin pan on a baking sheet.

2 Fill the cupcake molds with the cake batter so that it comes to within about ¼ inch from the top of the cups. Reserve the remaining batter. Bake, rotating the sheet about two-thirds of the way through the baking time, until a cake tester inserted into the center of a cupcake comes out clean and the tops are lightly browned, 24 to 26 minutes. Cool in the muffin pan on a wire rack for 10 minutes. Unmold and cool completely on a wire rack.

3 Fill, bake, and cook the remaining 6 cupcakes.

4 To make the frosting: In the bowl of a standing mixer fitted with a whisk attachment, beat the butter at medium-high speed until smooth and creamy. Add the confectioners' sugar and salt and beat at medium speed until blended. Scrape down the bowl, add the cream and vanilla, and beat on medium speed until blended. Increase the speed to medium-high and beat, scraping down the bowl about halfway through, until light and fluffy, about 4 minutes. Beat in the Nutella until incorporated.

5 Using a melon baller, scoop out the center of each cooled cupcake, creating an indentation deep enough to hold the filling. Fill a pastry bag fitted with a large plain tip, or a resealable plastic bag, with the ganache (snip the corner, if using plastic) and pipe in about 2 teaspoons of ganache. Spread with the frosting and center a hazelnut on top of each cupcake.

Strawberry-Pecan Cupcakes

These cupcakes, favorites of my daughter Nola, are a triple strawberry threat: A strawberry cake with a strawberry jam center, and a smooth strawberry frosting. Swap out the frosting for Chocolate Ganache (page 148) or Orange Cream Cheese Frosting (page 188) if you like. These are perfect for all the strawberry lovers in your family.

MAKES 18 CUPCAKES

1 recipe Strawberry-Pecan Coffee Cake (page 43)

Strawberry Frosting

1¼ cups (2½ sticks) unsalted butter, at room temperature

2½ cups confectioners' sugar

Pinch of coarse salt

2 tablespoons heavy cream

2 teaspoons pure vanilla extract

3 tablespoons strawberry jam, plus 3 to 4 tablespoons more for filling

18 perfect hulled fresh strawberries, for garnish

1 to 2 tablespoons confectioners' sugar, for dusting

1 Set the oven rack in the lower third of the oven. Preheat the oven to 350°F. Spray a standard 12-cup muffin pan with nonstick cooking spray or line with cupcake liners. Place the muffin pan on a baking sheet.

2 Make the coffee cake as on page 43, but drain the mashed strawberries in step 2 before folding into the batter. Fill the cupcake molds with the cake batter so that the batter comes to within about ¼ inch from the top of the cups. Reserve the remaining batter. Bake until a cake tester inserted into the center of a cupcake comes out clean and the tops are lightly browned, 24 to 26 minutes. Cool in the muffin pan on a wire rack for 10 minutes. Unmold and cool completely on a wire rack.

3 Fill, bake, and cool the remaining 6 cupcakes.

4 To make the frosting: In the bowl of a standing mixer fitted with a whisk attachment, beat butter at medium-high speed until smooth and creamy. Add confectioners' sugar and salt and beat at medium speed until blended. Scrape down the bowl, add cream and vanilla, and beat on medium speed until blended. Increase speed to medium-high and beat, scraping down the bowl about halfway through, until light and fluffy, about 4 minutes. Beat in 3 tablespoons of the strawberry jam until incorporated.

5 Using a melon baller, scoop out the center of each cooled cupcake, creating an indentation deep enough to hold ½ teaspoon jam. Fill a pastry bag fitted with a large plain tip, or a resealable plastic bag, with the strawberry jam (snip the corner, if using plastic) and pipe in about ½ teaspoon of jam. Spread with the frosting. Set a strawberry on top of each cupcake and dust with confectioners' sugar.

Cran-Raspberry Buckle

A buckle is an old-fashioned fruit dessert and it tastes fantastic. A buttery, egg-rich batter is mingled with fresh fruit and topped with a pecan streusel mixture. As the cake rises during baking, the weight of the streusel topping causes the cake to collapse in places, or buckle. The brown sugar–cinnamon streusel gets jumbled up with the fruit and cake. This is a great end-of-summer treat when raspberries are on their way out and cranberries are just starting to come in. But since both fruits are available year-round now, we eat this at my house all year long. My kids love warm, fruity cakes like this in the morning. But it's also a good choice for dessert, topped with a scoop of Vanilla Gelato (page 220) or ice cream, or Nik's Raspberry Gelato (page 222).

SERVES 8

Streusel Topping

- **1 cup all-purpose flour**
- **1 cup firmly packed light brown sugar**
- **1 teaspoon coarse salt**
- **½ teaspoon ground cinnamon**
- **½ cup coarsely chopped pecans**
- **½ cup (1 stick) cold unsalted butter, cut into ¼-inch cubes**

Batter

- **1¼ cups all-purpose flour**
- **2 teaspoons baking powder**
- **1 cup (2 sticks) unsalted butter, at room temperature**
- **1 cup granulated sugar**
- **½ teaspoon coarse salt**
- **4 large eggs**
- **2 teaspoons pure vanilla extract**
- **2 cups fresh or frozen cranberries (frozen cranberries needn't be thawed)**
- **2 cups fresh or frozen raspberries**

- **1 tablespoon confectioners' sugar, for dusting**

1. To make the streusel topping: In a medium bowl, use a fork to stir together the flour, brown sugar, salt, cinnamon, and pecans. Add the butter, and using your fingertips, quickly work into the dry ingredients until pea-size crumbs form; set aside in the refrigerator.

2. Set the oven rack in the lower third of the oven. Preheat the oven to 350°F. Butter a 9 by 13-inch baking dish with softened butter; set aside.

3. To make the batter: In a medium bowl, whisk together the flour and baking powder; set aside. In the bowl of a standing mixer fitted with the paddle attachment, beat the butter, granulated sugar, and salt on medium-high speed until light and fluffy, 2 to 3 minutes. Beat in the eggs one at a time, and then the vanilla. On low speed, beat in the flour mixture just until absorbed. Fold in the cranberries and raspberries. Transfer to the prepared baking dish. Sprinkle the streusel over the top.

4. Set the baking dish on a baking sheet. Bake, rotating the sheet about two-thirds of the way through the baking time, until a cake tester inserted in the thickest part of the buckle comes out clean and the topping is nicely browned and crisp, 55 to 60 minutes. Transfer to a wire rack to cool for 10 minutes. Dust with confectioners' sugar and cut into 8 squares.

Banana–Chocolate Chip Kugelhopf

This moist, chocolate chip–studded banana cake is Peter's favorite whether it's baked in a kugelhopf mold, as it is in this recipe, or as a cupcake (see page 150). I like the mold because it turns a straightforward banana bread batter into a very pretty and unusual-looking cake. It tastes so good warm, when the chocolate chips melt in your mouth with each bite. A true kugelhopf, however, is a yeasted cake of Eastern European origin; there are German, Austrian, Swiss, and Hungarian versions, to name a few.

MAKES ONE 8-INCH CAKE; SERVES 12 TO 16

- **2 cups all-purpose flour**
- **1 teaspoon baking powder**
- **1 teaspoon baking soda**
- **½ cup (1 stick) unsalted butter, at room temperature**
- **1 cup granulated sugar**
- **1½ teaspoons coarse salt**
- **2 large eggs, at room temperature**
- **2 teaspoons pure vanilla extract**
- **3 very ripe bananas, mashed**
- **½ cup buttermilk**
- **⅔ cup mini semisweet chocolate chips**
- **1 tablespoon confectioners' sugar, for dusting**

TIP Nonstick cooking spray works better than butter for the ring mold because it gets into those tricky ridges.

1 Set the oven rack in the lower third of the oven. Preheat the oven to 350°F. Spray a 6½-cup kugelhopf mold (8 inches in diameter and 3½ inches tall) with nonstick cooking spray; set aside.

2 In a medium bowl, whisk together the flour, baking powder, and baking soda; set aside.

3 In the bowl of a standing mixer fitted with the paddle attachment, beat the butter, granulated sugar, and salt on medium speed until light and fluffy, 4 to 5 minutes, scraping down the sides of the bowl halfway through. On low speed, add the eggs, one at a time, beating after each addition. Scrape down the bowl. Beat in the vanilla and the bananas. The mixture will look curdled, as it should.

4 With the mixer on low speed, add the flour mixture in three batches, alternating with the buttermilk, beginning and ending with the flour mixture. Scrape down the bowl and paddle twice during mixing. Beat until the flour is absorbed. Remove the bowl from the mixer stand and fold in the chocolate chips.

5 Scrape the batter into the prepared mold. Place the mold on a baking sheet and bake, rotating the sheet about two-thirds of the way through the baking time, until a cake tester inserted in the center of the cake comes out clean, 50 to 55 minutes.

6 Transfer to a cooling rack and cool in the pan for 10 minutes. Invert the pan on the rack and turn the cake out. Let the cake—still inverted—cool completely on the rack.

7 Sift confectioners' sugar over the cooled cake.

Chestnut Layer Cake with Raspberries

MAKES ONE 9-INCH THREE-LAYER CAKE; SERVES 12

*Chestnuts—*castagne, *in Italian—are a traditional Italian treat and I've always loved them. (In savory dishes, too: Mashed chestnuts with heavy cream and brown sugar is one of my favorite Thanksgiving side dishes.) I have particularly fond memories of my grandparents sitting around the table after dinner at Christmastime, cracking walnuts and pecans and teaching us how to peel freshly roasted chestnuts. We peeled back the skin, which had been cut with an* X *at the bottom before roasting, and popped the warm nuts into our mouths. What a treat! This is one of my favorite layer cakes and it's fantastic for celebrations. Fresh raspberries brighten the flavor of the tender sponge cake and sweet chestnut buttercream and a bittersweet chocolate sauce complements all three. There are a lot of components, but the sponge cake and chocolate sauce can be made in advance. The buttercream frosting should be made the day you plan to serve.*

Chestnut Sponge Cake

- ½ cup cake flour
- 6 tablespoons cornstarch
- 3 tablespoons chestnut flour
- 3 large eggs, at room temperature
- 3 large egg yolks, at room temperature
- ½ cup sugar
- ¾ teaspoon coarse salt
- 1 tablespoon pure vanilla extract
- ¾ cup vegetable oil
- 3 (6-ounce) baskets fresh raspberries

Sugar Syrup

- ¼ cup sugar

1. Set the oven rack in the lower third of the oven. Preheat the oven to 375°F. Butter a 9 by 2-inch round cake pan with softened butter; coat with flour and tap out the excess.

2. To make the cake: In a medium bowl, sift together the flour, cornstarch, and chestnut flour; set aside.

3. In the bowl of a standing mixer fitted with the whisk attachment, beat the whole eggs, the egg yolks, the sugar, salt, and vanilla on medium-high speed until thick and pale yellow, about 5 minutes. The mixture should hold a thick ribbon when the whisk is lifted from the bowl. Remove the bowl from the stand. Add the flour mixture gradually by ½ cup measure, folding in each portion completely with a rubber spatula before adding the next. Gradually add the oil, drizzling it toward the edge of the bowl while folding.

4. Pour the batter into the prepared cake pan, set it on a baking sheet, and bake until a tester comes out clean when inserted into the center of the cake, 24 to 27 minutes. Remove from the oven and turn the cake out immediately onto a wire rack. Let cool for at least 1 hour. Wrap and refrigerate for at least 2 hours or up to 2 days.

5. To make the sugar syrup: In a small saucepan, combine the sugar and ¼ cup water. Stir, and bring to a boil over medium-

high heat, swirling to dissolve the sugar. Remove from the heat. Transfer to a bowl; refrigerate until chilled.

6 To make the buttercream: Bring about 1 inch of water to a boil in the bottom of a double boiler. In the top of a double boiler, whisk the egg whites with the sugar and salt over (not in) the simmering water until hot to the touch, 1 to 2 minutes (make sure the bottom of the top of the double boiler doesn't touch the water). Transfer to the bowl of a standing mixer fitted with the whisk attachment and beat until stiff peaks form. With the machine running, gradually beat in the butter, piece by piece. When all the butter is added, the mixture will break, but it will become smooth again as you continue to beat. Beat in the vanilla, then ¾ cup of the chestnut puree. Reserve the puree remaining in the can to fill the layers.

7 To assemble the cake: Trim the cake and split into even thirds (see page 166). Place one layer on a 9-inch cake round. Generously brush with about half the sugar syrup to evenly moisten the cake and spread with half of the remaining chestnut puree (about 5 tablespoons). Spread with ¾ cup of the buttercream. Set the second layer on top. Brush with sugar syrup and spread with the remaining chestnut puree. Spread with ¾ cup of the buttercream. Add the final cake layer and spread a thin "crumb" layer of buttercream over the top and sides of the cake (see page 166). Refrigerate the cake for 30 minutes, or until the crumb layer is set. Then spread the cake with the rest of the buttercream. Cover the top of the cake with a single layer of raspberries.

8 To make the sauce: Combine the cocoa powder, sugar, half-and-half, corn syrup, chocolate chips, and salt in a medium saucepan and bring to a boil. Strain through a fine strainer into a medium bowl.

9 To serve, cut the cake into slices. Spoon a pool of warm chocolate sauce onto each plate and set a slice of cake on top.

Chestnut Buttercream

- **5 large egg whites, at room temperature**
- **1⅓ cups sugar**
- **Pinch of coarse salt**
- **1 pound (4 sticks) unsalted butter, firm but not chilled, cut into cubes**
- **½ teaspoon vanilla paste (see sidebar, page 212) or pure vanilla extract**
- **1 (17½-ounce) can sweetened chestnut puree, such as Clément Faugier brand**

Bittersweet Chocolate Sauce

- **¼ cup unsweetened cocoa powder**
- **¼ cup sugar**
- **½ cup half-and-half**
- **2 tablespoons corn syrup**
- **4 ounces bittersweet chocolate chips**
- **⅛ teaspoon coarse salt**

TIP For all buttercreams, the butter should be firm but not straight out of the refrigerator. Set it out for 30 to 60 minutes (depending on the temperature of your kitchen) before using.

Lemon Daisy Cake

MAKES ONE 9-INCH 4-LAYER CAKE; SERVES 12

This absolutely gorgeous layer cake is one that your guests will remember. Layers of light-yellow sponge cake are filled with tart lemon curd and frosted with lemon buttercream. It's decorated with a scattering of 1960s-style, flower-power meringue daisies, each finished with a bright-yellow lemon-curd center. The fresh spring look practically jumps off the plate. The sponge cake, the lemon curd, and the daisies can be made up to two days ahead. Wrap and refrigerate the cake and curd; store the meringues in an airtight container at room temperature. Make the buttercream and ice the cake the day of the event (see Tips, page 166). It can be refrigerated for up to six hours (without the meringue flowers), but bring it to room temperature for four hours before serving.

Lemon Curd

- **1½ teaspoons powdered unflavored gelatin**
- **9 large egg yolks**
- **Grated zest of 6 lemons**
- **¾ cup freshly squeezed lemon juice (from 5 to 6 lemons)**
- **1 cup plus 2 tablespoons sugar**
- **¼ teaspoon coarse salt**
- **¾ cup (1½ sticks) cold unsalted butter, cut into ½-inch pieces**

1 To make the curd: In a small bowl, sprinkle 3 tablespoons cold water over the gelatin; set aside. In a small saucepan, combine the egg yolks, lemon zest and juice, sugar, and salt, and whisk well. Set over medium heat and cook, stirring constantly, until the mixture has thickened enough to coat the back of a wooden spoon, about 5 minutes. Do not boil. Whisk in the gelatin mixture.

2 Transfer to the bowl of a standing mixer fitted with the paddle attachment. Beat on medium speed for 5 minutes. Turn the mixer speed to low and beat in the butter a little at a time, until smooth. Strain through a fine sieve into a medium bowl to remove any bits of overcooked egg. Cover with plastic wrap, pressing it directly onto the surface of the curd to prevent a skin from forming. Refrigerate until chilled, at least 1 hour.

3 Set the oven rack in the lower third of the oven. Preheat the oven to 375°F. Butter two 9 by 2-inch round cake pans and dust the bottom and sides with flour; tap out the excess.

4 To make the sponge cake: In a medium bowl, sift together the flour and cornstarch; set aside.

5 In the bowl of a standing mixer fitted with the whisk attachment, beat the whole eggs, the yolks, the sugar, salt, and lemon extract on high speed until the mixture is thick and pale yellow and holds a thick ribbon when the whisk is lifted from the bowl,

about 5 minutes. Remove the bowl from the stand. Add the flour mixture gradually by ½-cup measure, folding in each portion completely with a rubber spatula before adding the next. Gradually and gently add the oil, drizzling it toward the edge of the bowl, and folding it in until it is blended completely. You want to be sure not to deflate the whipped eggs.

6 Divide the batter between the prepared cake pans. (There will be bubbles in the batter.) Bake, rotating the pans about two-thirds of the way through the baking time, until a cake tester comes out clean when inserted into the center of the cakes, about 25 minutes. Remove from the oven and invert the pans on wire racks. Immediately remove the pans and turn the cakes rounded sides up. Let cool for at least 1 hour.

7 To make the syrup: In a small saucepan, combine the sugar and ½ cup water and bring to a boil over medium-high heat, swirling to dissolve the sugar. Remove from the heat. Transfer to a bowl; refrigerate until chilled.

8 To make the buttercream: Set a strainer over the bowl of a standing mixer; set aside. Bring about 1 inch of water to a boil in the bottom of a double boiler. In the top of a double boiler, whisk the egg whites with the sugar and salt over (not in) the simmering water until hot to the touch, 1 to 2 minutes (make sure the bottom of the top of the double boiler doesn't touch the water). Strain into the mixer bowl. Set the bowl on the mixer stand and fit the mixer with the whisk attachment. Beat the egg whites until stiff peaks form. With the machine running, gradually beat in the butter, piece by piece. When all the butter is added, the mixture will break, but it will become smooth again as you continue to beat. Beat in the lemon extract. Transfer to a large bowl; set aside at room temperature.

9 Wash and dry the mixer bowl. Put the curd in the bowl and beat with the paddle attachment on low speed until the curd is fluffy but still bright yellow in color, about 1 minute. Scoop 3 to

Lemon Sponge Cake

1 cup plus 2 tablespoons cake flour

¾ cup cornstarch

6 large whole eggs, at room temperature

6 large egg yolks, at room temperature

1 cup sugar

1½ teaspoons coarse salt

4 teaspoons lemon extract

1½ cups vegetable oil

Lemon Syrup

⅓ cup sugar

1½ tablespoons freshly squeezed lemon juice (from 1 lemon)

Lemon Buttercream

10 large egg whites, at room temperature

2⅔ cups sugar

⅛ teaspoon coarse salt

2 pounds (8 sticks) unsalted butter, firm but not chilled, cut into cubes (see Tip, page 157)

1 teaspoon lemon extract

recipe continues

4 tablespoons of the curd into a small bowl for the meringue daisies (see sidebar, page 162). Place plastic wrap directly onto the surface; refrigerate.

10 To assemble the cake, stir the lemon juice into the chilled sugar syrup; set aside. Trim the cakes and split each into two rounds (see Tips, page 166). Scoop some of the buttercream into a pastry bag fitted with a plain tip about 5⁄16 inch in diameter (such as Ateco #12). Set one cake layer on a 9-inch cardboard cake round, secured with a dab of buttercream. Use a pastry brush to brush the cake with about one-third of the lemon syrup. Pipe a line of buttercream around the edge of the cake layer to create a dam. Spread about one-third of the lemon curd (a generous 2⁄3 cup) over the cake, inside the buttercream dam. Set the second cake layer on top, brush with the remaining syrup, make a buttercream dam, and spread with another third of the lemon curd. Set the third layer on top and repeat to brush with another one third of the syrup, make a buttercream dam, and spread with the rest of the lemon curd. Set the fourth cake layer on top and spread the top and sides of the cake with a crumb layer of buttercream. Refrigerate the cake for 30 minutes, or until the buttercream is set. Spread the cake with the remaining buttercream.

11 Just before serving, whisk the reserved lemon curd to loosen and use it to fill the meringue daisies. Decorate the tops and sides of the cake with the daisies.

recipe continues

Meringue Daisies

2 large egg whites, at room temperature
½ cup superfine sugar
⅛ teaspoon coarse salt
3 to 4 tablespoons lemon curd (see page 158)

1 Preheat the oven to 200°F. Bring 1 inch of water to a simmer in the bottom of a double boiler. Combine the egg whites, sugar, and salt in the top of the double boiler, stir the mixture over (not in) the simmering water, and whisk until the mixture is hot and the sugar is dissolved, 2 to 3 minutes. Transfer the mixture to the bowl of a standing mixer fitted with the whisk attachment. Beat on medium-high speed until stiff peaks form when you lift the whisk, about 6 minutes. The egg whites will start off glossy and damp, like the inside of a marshmallow, and eventually get drier and stiffer.

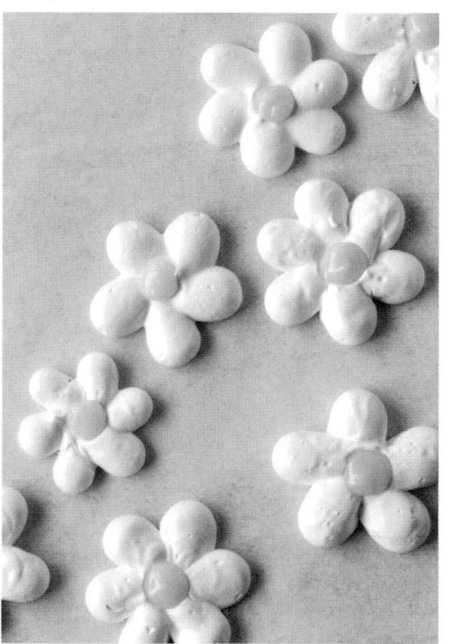

2 Line a baking sheet with parchment paper. Dab a little meringue under each corner of the paper to secure it. Scoop the meringue into a pastry bag fitted with a plain tip, about 5⁄16 inch wide (such as Ateco #12). Pipe several daisies about 2 inches in diameter: From the center point, pipe six teardrop-shaped petals. Leave an indentation in the centers of the daisies to fill with lemon curd. (If necessary, use the end of a wooden spoon dipped in water to indent the centers.) Bake until the exterior of the daisies is very dry but the color is still white, about 45 minutes. Remove to a wire rack and let cool completely.

3 Spoon the lemon curd into a pastry bag fitted with a small plain tip; or spoon into a resealable plastic bag, and snip the corner. Fill the center of each meringue daisy with a dot of lemon curd.

Italian Wedding Cake

In 2002, Martha Stewart took me to Fairfield, Connecticut, to a newly opened restaurant called Liana's Trattoria to taste their chiffon-style cake layered with whipped cream. But the chef and owner, Liana DiMeglio, has consistently refused to give up the recipe. She went on Martha's show one day with Joe Bruno, another local restaurateur (he owns Pasta Nostra in Norwalk, Connecticut); even then, she wouldn't make the cake. This has been a running joke between Liana and me for years. So I developed my own recipe. The cake is a light Italian sponge called pan di Spagna, *meaning "Spanish bread." I fill the layers with whipped cream and assorted berries. It's a great choice for any summer occasion, for a birthday party, and, of course, for a wedding (the 8-inch will give you the taller, more impressive cake). Once frosted, the cakes will hold for thirty-six to forty-eight hours in the refrigerator. Thank you, Liana, for your inspiration.*

MAKES ONE 8- OR 9-INCH 4-LAYER CAKE; SERVES 10

Italian Sponge Cake

- **½ teaspoon vanilla paste (see sidebar, page 212) or pure vanilla extract**
- **¾ cup cake flour**
- **4 large eggs, separated, at room temperature**
- **¾ cup granulated sugar**
- **¼ teaspoon cream of tartar**
- **¼ teaspoon coarse salt**

Filling

- **1 quart heavy cream**
- **1 tablespoon vanilla paste or pure vanilla extract**
- **⅔ cup confectioners' sugar**
- **1 (6-ounce) container (about 2 cups) fresh raspberries**
- **1 (6-ounce) container (about 2 cups) fresh blackberries**
- **1 pint fresh strawberries, hulled and quartered**

1 Set the oven rack in the lower third of the oven. Preheat the oven to 350°F. Coat the bottoms of two 8- or 9 by 2-inch round cake pans with nonstick spray. Line each with a parchment round, then spray the parchment (do not spray the sides of the pans). Set aside.

2 To make the cake: In a small cup, combine the vanilla and 2 tablespoons cold water; set aside. Sift the cake flour into a small bowl; set aside.

3 In the bowl of a standing mixer fitted with the whisk attachment, beat the egg yolks with ½ cup of the granulated sugar on medium-high speed until thick and pale yellow, about 5 minutes. The mixture should hold a thick ribbon when the whisk is lifted from the bowl. On low speed, beat in the cake flour in three batches, alternating with the vanilla-water mixture, beginning and ending with the flour. Scrape the bowl halfway through. Transfer the batter to a large bowl; set aside.

4 Wash and dry the mixer bowl and whisk. Add the egg whites to the bowl with the cream of tartar and salt. Beat on low speed until frothy, about 1 minute. With the mixer running, gradually sprinkle in the remaining ¼ cup of sugar. Raise the speed to

recipe continues

TIP If the whipped cream is not kept very cold, it will soften and become difficult to work with on the cake. Follow the tips on page 48.

medium-high and beat the meringue until stiff peaks form (just short of dry), 4 to 5 minutes.

5 Remove the bowl from the mixer stand. Fold 2 spoonfuls of the meringue into the batter with a rubber spatula to lighten. Then fold in the rest of the meringue until incorporated. Do not overmix; it's fine to leave a few streaks of white in the batter. Divide the batter between the prepared pans. Tap the pans a few times on the counter to remove air bubbles. Bake, rotating the pans two-thirds of the way through the baking time, until a cake tester inserted in the center comes out clean, 15 to 18 minutes.

6 Invert the cakes onto a wire rack. Immediately remove the pans and the parchment paper. Let the cakes cool completely, about 1 hour. Refrigerate until chilled, about 2 hours.

7 To make the filling: Combine the heavy cream and vanilla in the bowl of a standing mixer fitted with the whisk attachment. Turn the mixer to medium speed. With the mixer running, gradually add the confectioners' sugar. Beat until thickened, 1 to 2 minutes, then increase the speed to medium-high and beat until firm peaks form. Cover and refrigerate.

8 In a medium bowl, combine the raspberries, blackberries, and strawberry quarters; set aside.

9 To assemble the cake: Use your fingers to gently rub off the skin on the tops and bottoms of the cakes. Using a long serrated knife, split each cake into two even rounds. Set one cake layer on a 9-inch cake round and spread with about ¼ inch whipped cream (about 1¼ cups). Cover with a single layer of mixed berries (about 1½ cups berries), and spread thinly with whipped cream to cover the berries. Set the second cake layer on top and spread with ¼ inch of whipped cream. Cover with a single layer (about 1½ cups) of mixed berries and spread thinly with whipped cream. Add the third cake layer and spread with ¼ inch whipped cream. Cover with a single layer of mixed berries

(about 1½ cups) and spread thinly with whipped cream. Top with the final layer of cake. Reserve the remaining berries.

10 Frost the cake with a "crumb" layer by spreading a thin layer of whipped cream over the top and sides of the cake (see page 166). Refrigerate for 15 minutes, or until the crumb layer is set. Then spread the cake with the rest of the whipped cream. Serve the reserved berries in a bowl on the side.

Tips for Perfect Layer Cakes Every Time

- **TEMPERATURE:** Eggs and dry ingredients should be at room temperature, meaning that unless your kitchen is very hot, they should sit out on the counter for at least four hours before you start to bake. Otherwise, two hours will suffice.
- **PREPARING THE CAKE PANS:** For recipes that call for coating pans with butter, put softened (rather than melted) butter in a bowl. Use a 1-inch pastry brush to brush the sides and bottom of the pans. (Make sure to get in the crease where the sides meet the bottom.) For recipes that call for flouring the pan after buttering, add a little all-purpose flour, and tap the sides while tilting the pan to coat the bottom and sides entirely. Some cakes benefit from lining the pans with parchment paper, for easy turn-out: With a pencil, trace around the bottom of the cake pan on a sheet of parchment paper. Cut out the round with scissors.
- **THE RIGHT EQUIPMENT:** If you like to bake and decorate cakes, there are three pieces of equipment that will change your life. A 12-inch serrated knife, a standing mixer with whisk and paddle attachment, and a revolving cake decorating stand. (I also encourage you to buy an extra bowl for the mixer. It will make your life much easier for cakes that call for beating egg yolks and whites separately.) If you are decorating on a cake platter instead, you can keep things neat by cutting strips of parchment paper, about 12 inches long and 3 inches wide. Slip the strips between the cake and the serving platter. When you're finished decorating, just pull out the parchment strips and your platter will be clean.
- **SPLITTING THE CAKE INTO LAYERS:** A chilled cake is easier to split into layers. Cool the cake completely, wrap it in plastic, and refrigerate it before decorating—ideally one to two days. With a serrated knife, trim the bottom of the cake if it is dark (it will taste bitter). Place the cake right side up on a cake stand or platter. Score all around the top edge of the cake where the top begins to dome (notice the mark from the ridge of the cake pan). With the knife held parallel to the cake stand, use a sawing motion to cut all the way through the cake, turning the cake stand as you work. Score around the middle of the cake if splitting the cake into two layers; score in thirds, if splitting into three layers. Using a sawing motion, split the cake into two or three layers.
- **DECORATING THE CAKE:** When you're ready to frost the cake, dab a little of the frosting on a cardboard cake round to secure the cake. Set the cake on top. Fill the layers, then use a metal spatula or a paint scraper from a hardware store to apply a crumb layer—a very thin layer of frosting used to capture any loose crumbs and prevent them from getting into the outer frosting. Clean the spatula of excess buttercream on the edge of a bowl as you work. Discard that buttercream. It may seem wasteful, but once it has crumbs in it, it's no good to you.
- **SERVING:** Cakes taste best at room temperature. If refrigerated, let stand at room temperature for about four hours before serving to make sure the interior has come to temperature.

Lemon-Almond Cake with Macerated Strawberries

I came across a version of this rustic, lemon-almond cake on one of my trips to Italy. It's light and moist, with the tender crumb of a pound cake, and I love its elegant almond flavor. It's also practical at home: olive oil's low moisture content gives the cake a longer-than-usual shelf life, so it will hold very nicely for four to five days. Serve warm with cold, macerated strawberries as a tea cake or afternoon snack.

MAKES ONE 9-INCH CAKE; SERVES 10

Cake

1½ cups all-purpose flour
½ cup almond flour
1 teaspoon coarse salt
¾ teaspoon baking soda
1¼ cups granulated sugar
3 large eggs, at room temperature
1 cup buttermilk
6 tablespoons extra-virgin olive oil
2 teaspoons pure almond extract
Grated zest of 1 lemon
2 tablespoons freshly squeezed lemon juice (from 1 lemon)
1 tablespoon confectioners' sugar, for dusting

Macerated Strawberries

1 pint fresh strawberries, hulled and thinly sliced
1 tablespoon granulated sugar, or more as needed
1 teaspoon freshly squeezed lemon juice (from 1 lemon)

1 Place the oven rack in the lower third of the oven. Preheat the oven to 350°F. Coat the bottom and sides of a 9 by 2-inch cake pan with softened butter. Line the bottom with a parchment round. Coat the parchment and the sides of the pan again with softened butter; set aside.

2 To make the cake: In a large bowl, whisk together the all-purpose flour, almond flour, salt, and baking soda; set aside.

3 In a medium bowl, whisk together the sugar and eggs. Whisk in the buttermilk, olive oil, almond extract, and lemon zest and juice. Add the buttermilk mixture to the flour mixture and whisk until the flours have been absorbed.

4 Scrape the batter into the prepared pan. Place on a baking sheet and bake, rotating the sheet about two-thirds of the way through the baking time, until a tester inserted into the center of the cake comes out clean, 40 to 45 minutes. Transfer to a wire rack and let cool for 10 minutes. Turn the cake out of the pan, then invert so that the rounded side is up. Let cool completely.

5 To macerate the strawberries: In a small bowl, combine the sliced strawberries with the sugar and lemon juice. Chill for 2 hours, stirring every now and then. After about 1 hour, taste the berries, and if they are not sweet enough, add another teaspoon of sugar.

6 Sift the confectioners' sugar over the top of the cooled cake. Cut into wedges and serve with a spoonful of the strawberries.

Persimmon Pudding Cake with Ginger-Walnut Frosting

I urge people to take advantage of persimmons during late fall and early winter when they're in season. Once ripened (see page 25), they make a delicious cake that's almost as moist as a traditional steamed persimmon pudding. This is a perfect cake for a winter holiday meal.

MAKES ONE 9 BY 13-INCH CAKE; SERVES 12

Cake

- **3 cups all-purpose flour**
- **2 tablespoons baking soda**
- **1 teaspoon coarse salt**
- **2 teaspoons ground cinnamon**
- **1 teaspoon ground ginger**
- **½ teaspoon grated nutmeg**
- **5 to 6 persimmons (enough to yield 2 cups pureed fruit)**
- **1½ cups whole milk**
- **¾ cup (1½ sticks) unsalted butter, at room temperature, plus extra for the baking dish**
- **1½ cups granulated sugar**
- **3 large eggs, at room temperature**

Ginger-Walnut Frosting

- **3 ounces cream cheese, at room temperature**
- **¼ cup (½ stick) unsalted butter, at room temperature**
- **1 cup confectioners' sugar**
- **Pinch of coarse salt**
- **1½ teaspoons molasses**
- **½ teaspoon vanilla paste (see sidebar, page 212) or pure vanilla extract**
- **¼ teaspoon finely grated peeled fresh ginger**
- **⅛ teaspoon ground cinnamon**
- **¼ cup chopped walnuts**

1 Set the oven rack in the lower third of the oven. Preheat the oven to 350°F. Coat a 9 by 13-inch baking dish with softened butter or nonstick cooking spray.

2 To make the cake: In a medium bowl, whisk together the flour, baking soda, salt, cinnamon, ginger, and nutmeg; set aside. Cut the tops off the persimmons and squeeze the pulp into the bowl of a food processor. Process to a puree. Measure 2 cups, and transfer to a medium bowl. (You'll be left with about ¼ cup puree; it makes a nice snack.) Stir in the milk; set aside.

3 In the bowl of a standing mixer fitted with the paddle attachment, beat butter and sugar on medium-high speed until fluffy, 2 to 3 minutes. Beat in the eggs, one at a time, beating well after each addition. On low speed, beat in the flour mixture, alternating with the persimmon mixture, beginning and ending with the flour mixture. Scrape down the bowl and paddle as needed. Beat just until the flour is absorbed; do not overmix.

4 Scrape the batter into the prepared baking dish. Bake, rotating the pan two-thirds of the way through the baking time, until a cake tester inserted in the center of the cake comes out clean, 55 to 60 minutes. Transfer to a wire rack and let cool completely.

5 To make the frosting: In the bowl of a standing mixer fitted with the paddle attachment, beat the cream cheese with the butter on medium-high speed until light and fluffy, scraping down the bowl often, 3 to 4 minutes. Add the confectioners' sugar and salt and beat until light and fluffy, 2 to 3 minutes. Beat in the molasses, vanilla, ginger, and cinnamon. Fold in the walnuts.

6 Spread the cooled cake with the frosting. Cut into 12 squares.

Gingerbread-Pineapple Upside-Down Cake

In this American classic, pineapple rounds are arranged in a mixture of brown sugar and butter, then the batter goes on. Once the cake is turned out, the sweet glazed pineapple winds up on top. While other fruits are often substituted, I kept the pineapple and changed the cake to my favorite gingerbread.

MAKES ONE 9-INCH CAKE, SERVES 10

- **¾ cup (1½ sticks) unsalted butter, at room temperature, plus extra for the cake pan**
- **½ cup firmly packed light brown sugar**
- **1 ripe pineapple, leaves and prickly skin removed (see page 25)**
- **1½ cups all-purpose flour**
- **1 teaspoon baking soda**
- **¾ teaspoon coarse salt**
- **1 teaspoon ground cinnamon**
- **1 teaspoon ground ginger**
- **1 teaspoon ground allspice**
- **½ cup molasses**
- **½ cup buttermilk**
- **½ cup granulated sugar**
- **2 large eggs, at room temperature**

1 Set oven rack in lower third of the oven. Preheat oven to 350°F. Coat the bottom and sides of a 9 by 2-inch cake pan with softened butter. Fit a parchment round over the bottom of the pan. Add ¼ cup (½ stick) of the butter and place the pan in the oven until the butter melts completely, 2 to 4 minutes.

2 Remove the pan from the oven. Sprinkle the brown sugar evenly over the bottom and level with a fork.

3 Cut four ¼-inch-thick slices of pineapple (reserve the remainder for another use). Cut out the woody centers with a melon baller. Arrange the pineapple slices in the pan on top of the butter-sugar mixture. Then cut more slices, remove the woody cores, and cut to fill the open spaces in the pan; set aside.

4 In a medium bowl, sift together the flour, baking soda, salt, cinnamon, ginger, and allspice; set aside. In a small bowl, stir together the molasses and buttermilk; set aside.

5 In the bowl of a standing mixer fitted with the paddle attachment, beat remaining ½ cup of butter and all the granulated sugar on medium speed until light and fluffy, 2 to 3 minutes. Add eggs, one at a time, beating well after each addition. Turn mixer to low speed. Add flour mixture in 3 batches, alternating with buttermilk mixture, beginning and ending with flour mixture.

6 Using an offset spatula, carefully spread the batter over the pineapple. Bake, rotating the pan two-thirds of the way through the baking time, until a cake tester inserted in the center comes out clean, 40 to 45 minutes. Remove pan from the oven. Invert the pan onto a heat-proof serving plate. Let stand for 5 minutes. Remove the pan and the parchment round. Allow the cake to cool for 30 minutes. Serve warm or at room temperature.

Elenore's Plum Cake

This soft, light, buttery German-style plum cake is a great, easy recipe from my German-born mother-in-law. While it bakes, the batter billows up around the tart fruit. The plums melt into the sweet batter and color it a beautiful shade of pink-purple. The cake is particularly good warm, although my family has no problem polishing it off at room temperature either. It's very nice for a weekend breakfast, an afternoon snack, or as dessert. It's incredibly simple to make, and tastes fantastic. What else is there to say?

MAKES ONE 8 BY 8-INCH CAKE; SERVES 9

- **1 cup all-purpose flour**
- **1 teaspoon baking powder**
- **1 teaspoon coarse salt**
- **½ cup (1 stick) unsalted butter, at room temperature**
- **1 cup plus 2 tablespoons sugar**
- **2 large eggs, at room temperature**
- **1¾ pounds (5 to 6 large) black plums, halved and pitted, each half cut into ¼-inch-thick wedges**
- **¼ teaspoon ground cinnamon**

TIP One of the great things about baking with Pyrex is that you can peek through the glass to see when the cake is well browned on the sides and bottom, as well as on the top.

1 Set the oven rack in the lower third of the oven. Preheat the oven to 350°F. Butter an 8 by 8-inch Pyrex baking dish.

2 In a medium bowl, sift the flour with the baking powder and salt; set aside.

3 In the bowl of a standing mixer fitted with the paddle attachment, beat the butter with 1 cup of the sugar on medium speed until light and fluffy, 2 to 3 minutes. Add the eggs, one at a time, beating well after each addition. Turn the mixer to low speed. Add the flour mixture and beat until the flour is absorbed.

4 Scrape the batter into the prepared baking dish and smooth the top with an offset spatula. Arrange a line of plum wedges along one side, skin sides down, and press gently to settle them. Arrange another line of plum wedges right next to and touching the first. Continue to use up the plums and cover the batter.

5 In a small bowl, stir together the remaining 2 tablespoons sugar and the cinnamon. Sprinkle the mixture over the plums. Place the cake on a baking sheet and bake, rotating the sheet about two-thirds of the way through the baking time, until the top is golden brown, the plums are tender and bubbling, and a cake tester inserted in the center comes out clean, 70 to 75 minutes. Transfer to a wire rack to cool for at least 10 minutes. Cut into nine squares to serve warm, or let cool completely.

Blueberry Crumb Cake

This cake was inspired by a crumb cake developed by Sara Foster, a wonderful chef and award-winning cookbook author. My blueberry version combines a layer of vanilla cake—not too sweet—with fresh blueberries and a chunky cinnamon–brown sugar crumb topping. It makes a nice snack cake, but everyone in my family likes it for breakfast, too. You can vary the batter with chocolate chips, or add chopped nuts to the topping. My kids, who love this kind of breakfast pastry, eat the cake warm, right out of the oven. But it's also a great favorite at the farmers' market, where folks enjoy it at room temperature.

MAKES TWELVE 3-INCH SQUARES

Crumb Topping

- **2½ cups all-purpose flour**
- **1 cup firmly packed light brown sugar**
- **2 teaspoons ground cinnamon**
- **½ teaspoon coarse salt**
- **1 cup (2 sticks) unsalted butter**

Cake

- **1½ cups plus 1 tablespoon all-purpose flour**
- **2½ teaspoons baking powder**
- **1 teaspoon coarse salt**
- **½ cup whole milk**
- **½ cup granulated sugar**
- **2 tablespoons vegetable oil**
- **1 large egg, at room temperature**
- **1 tablespoon pure vanilla extract**
- **1 pint (2 cups) fresh blueberries**
- **1 to 2 tablespoons confectioners' sugar**

TIP The pan I use for this cake is sold in specialty cookware stores. You can find aluminum pans of exactly the same size (and much more easily) at most supermarkets and retail stores.

1 Set the oven rack in the lower third of the oven. Preheat the oven to 350°F. Spray a 12¼ by 8¼ by 1¼-inch baking sheet with nonstick cooking spray. Coat with flour and tap out the excess.

2 To make the crumb topping: In a large bowl, sift the flour with the brown sugar, cinnamon, and salt. Melt the butter in a small saucepan; let cool for 2 minutes. Pour the melted butter over the flour mixture. Work the mixture with your fingertips to press into nice large crumbs; set aside.

3 To make the cake: In a large bowl, stir together 1½ cups of the flour, the baking powder, and salt; set aside.

4 In a medium bowl, whisk together the milk, granulated sugar, oil, egg, and vanilla and add to the flour mixture. Stir until the flour is absorbed. Using a small offset spatula, spread the batter over the prepared pan.

5 In a medium bowl, toss the blueberries with the remaining 1 tablespoon of flour. Sprinkle evenly over the cake. Scatter the crumb topping over the top; it will completely cover the berries. Bake, rotating the pan about two-thirds of the way through the baking time, until the topping is golden brown, the blueberries are bubbling, and a cake tester inserted in the center of the cake comes out clean, 45 to 50 minutes. Remove to a cooling rack and allow to cool for 10 minutes, or completely.

6 Sift confectioners' sugar over the top. Cut into twelve 3-inch squares to serve.

Gluten Guide

Gluten is an elastic substance that is produced when flour is mixed with water or another liquid. The more you mix, the stronger and more elastic the web-like strands of gluten become. Gluten is critical for making breads and other yeasted items such, as the Chelsea Buns on page 65, because it enables the dough to trap the air and gases necessary to make the bread rise. Yeast doughs are therefore kneaded vigorously to encourage gluten production.

This elasticity, however, isn't desirable in most pastry batters because it will make the pastries tough. You can avoid the production of gluten by being careful not to overmix these batters. So, with the exception of Cousin John's Café Belgian Waffles on page 46, for all the muffins, quick breads, pancakes, and waffles recipes in Chapter 1, mix just until the flour is absorbed.

You can also encourage the gluten web to relax by allowing the dough or batter to stand for a while and by chilling. This is why almost all recipes for pie doughs call for allowing the dough to "rest" in the refrigerator for at least one hour before rolling.

Flour in the United States is categorized by protein content. It's the protein in the flour that forms gluten, so the higher the percentage of protein, the more gluten will be created. A high-protein flour such as bread flour is excellent for yeast-risen doughs and some pastries, such as Babette's Banana Éclairs (page 191) and my Acadia Popovers (page 55). Low-protein flours, such as cake and pastry flours, create the most tender cakes and pastries. With its mid-range protein content, all-purpose flour is appropriate for most of the recipes in this book.

Polenta Pound Cake

A favorite dessert in my household when I was growing up was store-bought pound cake topped with ice cream and chocolate sauce. This less traditional pound cake–and–ice cream combo is inspired by a dessert we served at the Elms Restaurant and Tavern in Ridgefield, Connecticut. The crisp, toasted cake contrasts nicely with the subtle, silky corn ice cream. Outside of summer when corn is in season, the cake is delicious on its own or with vanilla ice cream.

MAKES ONE 7-INCH TUBE CAKE; SERVES 10

- **1½ cups all-purpose flour**
- **¼ cup coarse cornmeal**
- **1 tablespoon coarse salt**
- **1 teaspoon baking powder**
- **1 cup (2 sticks) unsalted butter, at room temperature**
- **1½ cups sugar**
- **4 large eggs, at room temperature**
- **1 tablespoon vanilla paste (see sidebar, page 212) or pure vanilla extract**

- **1 recipe Sweet Corn Ice Cream (see page 223)**

1. Set the oven rack in the lower third of the oven. Preheat the oven to 350°F. Generously butter a 7-inch tube pan with a removable bottom; set aside.

2. Combine the flour with the cornmeal, salt, and baking powder in a medium bowl; set aside.

3. In the bowl of a standing mixer fitted with the paddle attachment, beat the butter with the sugar until light and fluffy, 1 to 2 minutes. Add the eggs, one at a time, beating well after each addition. Beat in the vanilla. On low speed, beat in the flour mixture just until the flour is absorbed. Do not overmix.

4. Pour the batter into the prepared pan and spread with an offset spatula to even the top. Place on a baking sheet and bake, rotating about two-thirds of the way through the baking time, until a cake tester inserted in the center of the cake comes out clean, 55 to 60 minutes. Let cool for 10 minutes in the pan on a wire rack. Run a knife around the sides of the pan, and lift the cake out by the center tube. Let cool completely.

5. To serve, heat a griddle. Cut the cake into 10 slices and cook on the griddle until lightly browned, 2 to 3 minutes each side. (Or toast the slices in a toaster oven.) Serve each slice with a scoop of ice cream.

Citrus Angel Food Cake

As a birthday ritual, my mother allowed each of us brothers to choose a special dinner and dessert. We all had different dinner favorites; mine were chicken and lasagna. But we all opted for my mother's chocolate layer cake filled with whipped cream. It was simple and delicious and back then seemed about a mile high. At my house, my children often ask for this fluffy angel food cake. A tart citrus glaze brings out its delicate flavor and the orange, green, and yellow ribbons of zest make a beautiful, confetti-like topping. A lemon zester, a small tool with sharp round holes in the head that strips off long, thin ribbons of zest, is useful for making the glaze. Be sure to zest the citrus before cutting and juicing it.

MAKES ONE 10-INCH TUBE CAKE

Cake

- **12 large egg whites (1½ to 1¾ cups), at room temperature**
- **1½ cups granulated sugar**
- **1 teaspoon freshly squeezed lemon juice (from 1 lemon)**
- **½ teaspoon cream of tartar**
- **½ teaspoon coarse salt**
- **1 tablespoon orange extract**
- **1 cup cake flour, sifted**

Citrus Glaze

- **1 cup confectioners' sugar**
- **¼ cup lemon juice, or as needed (from 2 lemons)**
- **Zest of 1 orange, in long strands**
- **Zest of 1 lemon, in long strands**
- **Zest of 1 lime, in long strands**

1. Set the oven rack in the lower third of the oven. Preheat the oven to 350°F.

2. To make the cake: Bring about 1 inch of water to a simmer in the bottom of a double boiler. Combine the eggs whites, ¾ cup of the sugar, the lemon juice, cream of tartar, salt, and orange extract in the bowl of a standing mixer. Whisk over the simmering water until the whites are hot to the touch and the sugar dissolves, 3 to 5 minutes. Return the bowl to the mixer stand and beat with the whisk attachment until the meringue is glossy and stiff peaks form. Be careful not to overbeat the whites; they should be stiff, but not dry. With a large rubber spatula, fold in the flour and the remaining ¾ cup sugar.

3. Scrape the batter into an unbuttered 10-inch tube pan with a removable bottom, preferably nonstick. Tap the filled pan a couple of times on the countertop to remove air bubbles. Bake on a baking sheet until the cake springs back when touched and is lightly browned, 35 to 40 minutes. Do not rotate while baking.

4. Invert the pan on its legs and let cool for 1 hour. Set the pan back on the bottom and use your fingers to gently pull the cake away from the sides of the pan to release it. Invert the pan on a wire rack and remove the rim. Gently pull the cake away from the bottom and from around the center tube, and carefully remove the tube. Let the cake cool entirely on the rack.

recipe continues

5 To make the glaze: Sift the confectioners' sugar into a medium bowl. Gradually whisk in the lemon juice until smooth. Whisk in the orange, lemon, and lime zests. (The icing should be fairly thin. If it's too thick, add a little more lemon juice.)

6 Place a baking sheet under the cooling rack. Spoon the glaze over the cooled cake, allowing the excess to drip onto the baking sheet. Let the glaze dry completely, about 30 minutes. Cut the cake into wedges with a serrated knife or angel food cake cutter, and serve.

Tips for Making Angel Food Cakes

- **PREPARING THE PAN:** Never butter the pan; the pan must be dry so that the batter will cling and rise. It's best to use a nonstick pan.
- **BEATING THE WHITES:** When you heat the egg whites, be sure that the bottom of the bowl doesn't touch the simmering water; if it does, the whites will cook and the texture will be grainy when you beat it. You'll need at least a 4-quart bowl on your standing mixer to handle the volume of whites. Beat the whites until stiff but not dry; overbeaten whites will not produce the fluffy cake that you want. A little lemon juice helps to lighten the egg whites, and it keeps them nice and white when baked.
- **UNMOLDING THE CAKE:** So as not to tear the delicate cake, use your fingers rather than a knife to loosen the cooled cake from the pan.

Blueberry Cheesecake in Glass Jars

This is an example of a tried-and-true recipe updated with a clever presentation. I borrowed the idea from Frederic Kieffer, one of our chefs at SoNo Baking Company, and simplified the recipe for home cooks. With a layer of cooked blueberries on the bottom of a glass jar, these individual cheesecakes sell very well at the bakery. They don't last long at home either. Eight-ounce Ball jars come in two different shapes—tall and slender or more rounded—and you can use either one. Wrap a pretty ribbon around the necks of the jars and place them on decorative plates, and your table will look as if it had been catered by a professional.

SERVES 6

- **1½ pints fresh blueberries**
- **¼ cup plus ⅔ cup granulated sugar**
- **¼ teaspoon finely grated lemon zest**
- **1 teaspoon freshly squeezed lemon juice**
- **2 tablespoons cornstarch**
- **1 pound cream cheese, at room temperature**
- **½ teaspoon coarse salt**
- **1 teaspoon vanilla paste (see sidebar, page 212) or pure vanilla extract**
- **3 large eggs, at room temperature**
- **⅓ cup sour cream**

1 In a medium saucepan, combine 1 pint of the blueberries, ¼ cup of the sugar, and the lemon zest and juice and cook over medium heat until the blueberries pop, 5 to 7 minutes. In a 1-cup Pyrex measure, stir together the cornstarch and 2 tablespoons cold water until smooth. Add to the saucepan with the blueberry mixture and simmer until thick and bubbly, 1 to 2 minutes. Transfer to a bowl and refrigerate while you make the filling.

2 In the bowl of a standing mixer fitted with the paddle attachment, beat the cream cheese, the remaining ⅔ cup of sugar, the salt, and vanilla on medium-high speed, scraping down the bowl and paddle several times, until the mixture is completely smooth, about 5 minutes.

3 Preheat the oven to 300°F. Bring a medium saucepan of water to a boil for a water bath.

4 Turn the mixer to low and beat in the eggs one at a time, until blended, scraping down the sides of the bowl after each addition. Beat in the sour cream until blended.

5 Divide the chilled blueberry mixture among six 8-ounce Ball jars (about 3 tablespoons per jar). Divide the cream cheese filling among the jars (a little more than ½ cup per jar) and smooth the tops. Place the filled jars in a roasting pan and put

recipe continues

the pan in the oven. Pour in the boiling water to come about ½ inch up the sides of the jars. Bake until the cheesecakes are set but still jiggle slightly in the center, 35 to 40 minutes for the taller jars, 40 to 45 minutes for the rounder jars. (The filling will not brown and the centers will dimple.)

6 Remove the jars from the water bath with tongs and let cool to room temperature. Chill overnight.

7 To serve, top each cheesecake with some of the remaining blueberries if you like.

Egg Tips

Ideally, for all recipes in this book that use eggs, the eggs should be at room temperature. This means removing the eggs from the refrigerator two to four hours before you plan to bake, depending on how hot your kitchen is. Why? The addition of cold eggs to a creamed butter-sugar mixture will cause the mixture to "break" and look curdled, like a broken mayonnaise. This happens because the cold makes the butter congeal into small, cold lumps. Because the congealed butter will not emulsify properly into the batter, once baked, the texture of the pastry will not be perfectly uniform.

I want busy bakers to be able to make these recipes on the fly, however. And since proper emulsification is somewhat less noticeable in cookies, muffins, quick breads, pancakes and waffles, I don't call for room temperature eggs in those recipes. (Where it's important, however, as in this chapter, recipes do call for "eggs, at room temperature.") If your batter does curdle, add a pinch of flour and keep beating until it smoothes out again.

Banana Pudding Icebox Cake

This is a banana variation on the icebox cake my mom used to make. It's the classic family dessert because it's very quick to put together and everyone enjoys it, regardless of age. Even after all my sophisticated training, this homey dessert hasn't lost one ounce of appeal. I prepare five individual 6-ounce Pyrex cups because my children covet their own individual dessert, but you can also use an 8 by 8-inch Pyrex baking dish (that's how my mother made it). This cake is best if you let it sit overnight in the refrigerator to allow the flavors to develop. In a pinch, four to six hours is the minimum.

SERVES 5

16 to 20 vanilla wafers (for ⅔ cup crumbs)

Banana Custard

- **3 large egg yolks**
- **¼ cup sugar**
- **2 tablespoons cornstarch**
- **1 cup whole milk**
- **¼ teaspoon coarse salt**
- **¼ cup mashed banana (about 1 banana)**
- **2 tablespoons cold unsalted butter, cut into ½-inch cubes**
- **1 tablespoon banana liqueur (optional)**

- **2 ripe bananas, sliced about ¼ inch thick**
- **½ cup heavy cream**
- **¼ teaspoon vanilla paste (see sidebar, page 212) or pure vanilla extract**
- **2 tablespoons confectioners' sugar**

1 Put the vanilla wafers in a resealable plastic bag and crush with a rolling pin to make ⅔ cup chunky crumbs. Do not crush too fine; you want the texture. Set aside.

2 To make the custard: In a medium, heat-proof bowl, whisk together the egg yolks, 2 tablespoons of the sugar, all the cornstarch, and ¼ cup of the milk; set aside.

3 In a medium saucepan, combine the remaining ¾ cup milk, the remaining 2 tablespoons sugar, and the salt. Bring to a simmer. Whisking constantly, gradually pour the hot milk mixture into the egg mixture to temper it. Set a strainer over the saucepan. Strain the custard mixture back into the saucepan and bring to a boil over medium heat, whisking constantly. Boil for 10 seconds, whisking. (Make sure the custard boils for 10 seconds in the center of the pan, not just around the sides.) The mixture should thicken to a pudding-like consistency.

4 Transfer the pastry cream to a bowl and whisk in the mashed banana, butter, and liqueur, if using.

5 In each of five 6-ounce glass custard cups, layer 1 tablespoon crushed wafers over the bottom. Arrange 4 banana slices in a single layer on top. Spoon over 2 tablespoons of the custard and smooth with the back of the spoon. Top with a second layer of 1 tablespoon crumbs. Add a second layer of 4 banana slices, and spoon over 2 more tablespoons of the custard. Smooth with the back of the spoon.

6 Beat the cream with the vanilla until frothy. With the mixer running, gradually beat in the confectioners' sugar. Beat until medium firm peaks form. Spread over the custard in the bowls. Cover the cups with plastic wrap and chill for at least 6 hours, or overnight.

Warm Hazelnut Shortcakes with Sautéed Plums

This recipe tastes so good that it got me fired. I'm not kidding. I had been working as Martha Stewart's commissary chef and there wasn't anything I loved more than baking, so I used to bake for the staff in my free time. There were croissants in the morning and fresh bread for lunch sandwiches. I'd make these warm hazelnut shortcakes with sautéed plums as an afternoon snack when plums were in season. One day, I was called to Martha's office and reprimanded for these shortcakes. I believe the exact words were: "You're making the staff fat." I was "retired" from the commissary and moved to the magazine staff. I think the story speaks for itself. The shortcakes with plum filling are warm, and the whipped cream is nice and cold. It's a great combination.

SERVES 4

Hazelnut Shortcakes

- **1½ cups all-purpose flour**
- **3 tablespoons hazelnut flour (such as Bob's Red Mill brand)**
- **3 tablespoons granulated sugar**
- **2 teaspoons baking powder**
- **½ teaspoon coarse salt**
- **1 teaspoon finely grated orange zest**
- **¼ cup (½ stick) cold unsalted butter, cut into small pieces**
- **⅔ cup heavy cream**
- **1 teaspoon sanding sugar**

Plum Filling

- **¼ cup (½ stick) unsalted butter**
- **4 ripe plums, halved, pitted, and cut into wedges**
- **2 tablespoons granulated sugar**
- **Pinch of coarse salt**

- **½ recipe Whipped Cream (page 48)**

1. Set the oven rack in the lower third of the oven. Preheat the oven to 375°F. Line a baking sheet with parchment paper or a nonstick silicone baking mat.
2. To make the shortcakes: In a large bowl, whisk together the all-purpose and hazelnut flours, the granulated sugar, baking powder, salt, and orange zest.
3. Work the butter into the dry ingredients with your fingers until the mixture resembles coarse crumbs. Add ½ cup of the cream and fold with a rubber spatula or your hands until the cream has been completely absorbed. Then continue adding cream by the tablespoon just until the dough comes together and there are no dry patches. You will not use all the cream; reserve the remainder for brushing the shortcakes.
4. Turn out the dough onto a lightly floured work surface. With lightly floured hands, pat the dough 1 inch thick. Using a 2¼-inch round floured cookie or biscuit cutter, cut out four shortcakes and place them on the prepared baking sheet. Brush the tops with the remaining cream, and sprinkle each with ¼ teaspoon sanding sugar.
5. Bake, rotating the sheet about two-thirds of the way through the baking time, until the tops and bottoms of the shortcakes are nicely browned, 22 to 24 minutes.
6. Cool on the baking sheet on a wire rack for 10 minutes. Transfer to a wire rack to cool for at least 15 minutes.

7 To make the filling: Melt the butter in a large skillet over medium heat. Add the sliced plums, sugar, and salt. Cook until the plums let go of their juices and the skins are slightly softened, 10 to 12 minutes.

8 To serve, split the shortcakes. Place a shortcake bottom on each of four serving plates. Divide the plum mixture among the cakes. Add a dollop of whipped cream to each, and top with the shortcake tops. Transfer the remaining whipped cream to a serving bowl and serve on the side.

TIP When sautéing fruit such as these plums, the amount of sugar will depend on the ripeness of the fruit. Fruit that is under-ripe will benefit from the addition of a few teaspoons more sugar.

Pavlovas with Sautéed Plums, Peaches, and Nectarines

A pavlova is a classic meringue dessert named after the Russian ballet dancer Anna Pavlova. The meringue is shaped into a round with a concave center and is baked until crisp on the outside but still marshmallowy soft on the inside. The center is filled with fruit and whipped cream. This is a great celebratory dessert, stunningly attractive and dead simple to make. Although individual-size pavlovas are not traditional, I prefer them for home bakers. Their smaller size makes them easier to handle. At the bakery, we pipe the meringue with a round or fluted tip, but at home, a spoon works nicely and gives this dessert an attractive, rustic look. You can make the meringues the day before you plan to serve them and store them wrapped in plastic. Do not refrigerate or the meringue will soften.

SERVES 6

Meringue

- **2 large egg whites, at room temperature**
- **½ cup superfine sugar**
- **2¼ teaspoons cornstarch**
- **¼ teaspoon coarse salt**
- **⅛ teaspoon cream of tartar**
- **1 teaspoon freshly squeezed lemon juice (from 1 lemon)**
- **Confectioners' sugar, for dusting**

- **3 tablespoons unsalted butter**
- **1 medium plum, halved, pitted, and cut into ½-inch wedges**
- **1 medium nectarine, halved, pitted, and cut into ½-inch wedges**
- **1 medium peach, halved, pitted, and cut into ½-inch wedges**
- **2 tablespoons granulated sugar**
- **⅛ teaspoon coarse salt**
- **½ recipe Whipped Cream (page 48)**

1 Set the oven rack in the lower third of the oven. Preheat the oven to 200°F. Line a baking sheet with parchment paper; set aside.

2 To make the meringue: Bring about 1 inch of water to a simmer in the bottom of a double boiler. Combine the egg whites, superfine sugar, cornstarch, salt, cream of tartar, and lemon juice in the bowl of a standing mixer. Whisk over the simmering water until the whites are warm to the touch and the sugar dissolves, 3 to 4 minutes. Return the bowl to the mixer stand and beat with the whisk attachment on medium-high speed until the meringue is glossy and stiff peaks form, 4 to 6 minutes. (The meringue should hold a peak when you lift the beater.)

3 Put a dab of meringue under each corner of the parchment paper to secure it to the baking sheet. Fill a measuring cup with water.

4 Using a large soupspoon and all of the meringue, scoop 6 spoonfuls of meringue onto the prepared baking sheet, spacing them evenly. Use the back of the spoon dipped in water to spread each to a round about 3½ inches in diameter. Working from the center of each, make a well about 2½ inches in diameter. Build the walls to a height of ¾ to 1 inch. The bottoms should be

about ¼ inch thick. Continue to dip the spoon into the water as needed, to keep it from sticking to the meringue.

5 Dust the pavlovas with confectioners' sugar. Bake, rotating the baking sheet about two-thirds of the way through the baking time, until the meringues are just dry to the touch, but still white, 2 to 2½ hours. Transfer the sheet to a wire rack. Let the meringues cool completely before gently pulling them off the parchment.

6 Heat the butter in a 9- or 10-inch skillet over medium-high heat. Add the plums, nectarines, peaches, granulated sugar, and salt and cook until the fruit lets go of its juices and the skins soften, 5 to 8 minutes.

7 Place the meringues on serving plates. Spoon the warm fruit into the well of each meringue and top each with whipped cream.

TIP The lemon juice in the meringue keeps the interior of the cooked pavlovas soft.

Pumpkin Roulade

My thanks to Val Denner, a talented baker at SoNo Baking Company, for this recipe. French roulades (or jelly-roll cakes, as they're called in America) are baked in a thin layer in a jelly-roll pan, spread with frosting, and tightly rolled. You can make an entire roulade and wrap and store it in the freezer. When guests arrive unexpectedly, you can whip the roulade out of the freezer and quickly impress. (Count on about thirty minutes to thaw.) This cake is a good alternative to pumpkin pie for Thanksgiving and can be sprinkled with pumpkin seeds for an autumnal flair.

MAKES ONE 12-INCH ROLLED CAKE; SERVES 8

Roulade

- ¾ cup all-purpose flour
- 1 teaspoon baking powder
- 1 teaspoon coarse salt
- 2 teaspoons ground cinnamon
- 1 teaspoon ground ginger
- 4 large eggs, at room temperature
- 1 cup granulated sugar
- ⅔ cup canned pumpkin puree
- 1½ teaspoons freshly squeezed lemon juice (from 1 lemon)
- Finely grated zest of 1 orange
- 5 to 6 tablespoons confectioners' sugar

Orange Cream Cheese Frosting

- 6 ounces cream cheese, at room temperature
- ½ cup (1 stick) unsalted butter, at room temperature
- 2 cups confectioners' sugar
- 2 teaspoons pure vanilla extract
- 1 teaspoon finely grated orange zest

- 1 recipe Whipped Cream (page 48), or store-bought whipped cream (optional)
- ¼ cup pumpkin seeds (optional)

1. Set the oven rack in the lower third of the oven. Preheat the oven to 375°F. Spray a 17 by 12-inch rimmed baking sheet with nonstick cooking spray and line with parchment paper. Spray the top of the parchment and the sides of the pan; set aside.
2. To make the roulade: In a medium bowl, sift the flour with the baking powder, salt, cinnamon, and ginger; set aside.
3. In the bowl of a standing mixer fitted with the whisk attachment, beat the eggs on high speed until foamy, 1 to 2 minutes. With the mixer running, gradually add the sugar and beat until frothy, 2 to 3 minutes. On medium speed, beat in the pumpkin puree, lemon juice, and orange zest until blended, about 1 minute. On low speed, beat in the flour mixture until combined, scraping down the sides of the bowl with a rubber spatula halfway through, about 1 minute.
4. Pour the batter into the prepared baking sheet and spread it evenly with an offset spatula. Tap the pan on the countertop to ensure that the batter is evenly distributed and to remove air bubbles. Bake, rotating the pan about two-thirds of the way through the baking time, until the cake begins to pull away from the sides of the pan and a cake tester inserted in the center of the cake comes out clean, 15 to 20 minutes (be sure not to overbake).
5. Remove from the oven to a wire rack and let cool in the pan for 10 minutes. Sharply pat the sides of the pan to loosen the cake. Run a knife around the edges if necessary. Place a piece of parchment on top of the cake. Cover with another sheet pan

recipe continues

TIP The frosting recipe makes about ½ cup more than you need to fill the cake. Refrigerate the remainder in an airtight container for another use, or use it to decorate the roulade: Put the frosting in a piping bag fitted with a rosette tip and pipe ten equally spaced rosettes on top of the cake.

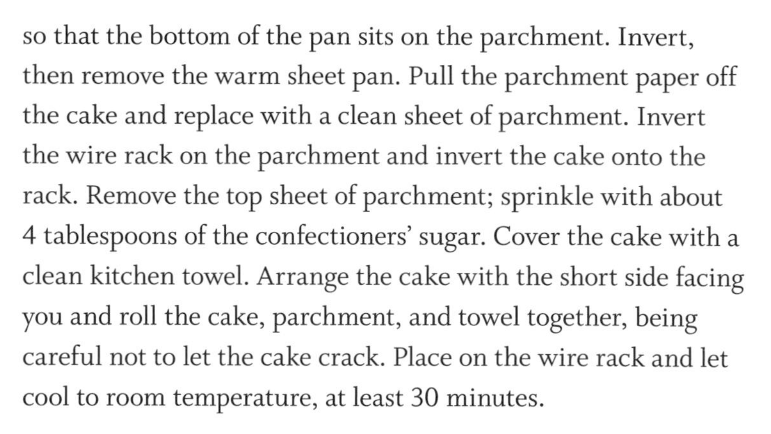

so that the bottom of the pan sits on the parchment. Invert, then remove the warm sheet pan. Pull the parchment paper off the cake and replace with a clean sheet of parchment. Invert the wire rack on the parchment and invert the cake onto the rack. Remove the top sheet of parchment; sprinkle with about 4 tablespoons of the confectioners' sugar. Cover the cake with a clean kitchen towel. Arrange the cake with the short side facing you and roll the cake, parchment, and towel together, being careful not to let the cake crack. Place on the wire rack and let cool to room temperature, at least 30 minutes.

6 To make the frosting: In the bowl of a standing mixer fitted with the paddle attachment, beat the cream cheese with the butter on medium speed until light and fluffy, 2 to 3 minutes, scraping down the bowl and paddle halfway through. On low speed, add the confectioners' sugar in three batches, beating well after each addition. Add the vanilla and orange zest and beat until smooth, light, and fluffy, 2 to 3 more minutes.

7 To fill the cake, on a work surface, overlap two pieces of plastic wrap to form a rectangle about 16 by 26 inches. Unroll the cake so that the parchment is on the bottom and the short side faces you. Remove the towel and place the cake—still atop the parchment—on the plastic wrap. Use an offset spatula to spread the cake with all but ½ cup of the cream cheese frosting. Use the parchment to help tightly roll the cake away from you into a log. Discard the parchment. Roll the filled roulade in the plastic wrap, pulling the plastic tight to shape the log into an even roll. Wrap in a second layer of overlapping sheets of plastic so that the wrapping is solid. Fold over the ends to seal. Refrigerate, seam on the bottom of the roll, for at least 2 hours, or overnight.

8 To serve, unroll the plastic wrap and discard. Place the roulade on a cutting board, seam side down. Trim the edges. Sift the remaining confectioners' sugar over the top (this will cover any cracks). Cut into 1½-inch-wide slices on an angle with a serrated knife and a sawing motion. Decorate with rosettes of whipped cream and pumpkin seeds, if you like.

Babette's Banana Éclairs

I grew up on custard-filled éclairs from the local Long Island and Brooklyn pastry shops. They were typically oversize—big enough to feed a family of four. I loved them then, and still do. When I ran into the real deal in patisseries in Paris, I was fascinated by how thin and perfectly shaped they were, and much more elegant and appetizing. I've improved on the original by adding banana, one of my favorite fruits. It's named after Elisabeth (or, Babette, as I called her), the young woman who introduced me to real French éclairs. The baked éclair shells can be frozen successfully for at least one week. Let them come to room temperature before filling. Once filled and iced, they're best eaten as soon as possible, but they may be refrigerated for up to four hours.

SERVES 12

Choux Pastry

- **½ cup (1 stick) unsalted butter**
- **¼ teaspoon coarse salt**
- **1 cup plus 2 tablespoons all-purpose flour**
- **4 to 5 large eggs (about 1 cup), at room temperature**

- **¼ recipe Chocolate Ganache (page 148)**
- **2 recipes Vanilla Pastry Cream (page 124)**
- **6 ripe but firm bananas**

1 To make the pastry: In a medium, heavy-bottomed saucepan, combine 1 cup water, the butter, and the salt and bring to a rolling boil over medium heat. Remove from the heat. Add all the flour at once and stir with a wooden spoon to incorporate. Return the pan to low heat and cook, stirring, until the dough comes together in a mass, pulls away from the sides, and leaves a film on the bottom of the pan, 2 to 3 minutes.

2 Transfer the dough to a mixer bowl and beat with the paddle attachment on low speed for 2 to 3 minutes to release excess steam. Increase the speed to medium. Add 4 eggs, one at a time, beating until fully incorporated after each addition and scraping down the sides and bottom of the bowl. Whisk the remaining egg in a small bowl, and add a little at a time, beating after each addition, until the dough is smooth and shiny, loose enough that it falls easily from the spoon but tight enough that it makes a peak when you pull the spoon away.

3 Set the oven rack in the lower third of the oven. Preheat the oven to 425°F. Cut a sheet of parchment paper to the size of a baking sheet (17 by 12 inches is standard). Arrange the parchment paper on a work surface with the long side facing you. Fold in the left and right sides to fold the sheet into thirds. Open the paper out flat. Use a dab of the choux batter in each corner to secure the paper to the baking sheet.

recipe continues

TIP The tops of the éclairs are brushed with water before baking to keep the crust moist as it expands. This prevents cracks and ensures a smooth surface for icing. Do not open the oven door during the first 25 minutes of baking. In order for the éclairs to rise effectively, the initial oven heat must be high. If you open the door and let out the heat, you risk the éclairs collapsing.

4 With a rubber spatula, scoop the dough into a pastry bag fitted with a round 1¹⁄₁₆-inch tip (such as Ateco #809). Using the folds on the parchment as a guide, pipe four curved lines of dough, between the folds, evenly spaced, one underneath the other and roughly the shape of a banana onto each third of the parchment sheet, to make 12 pastries. (Stagger the rows slightly to prevent the éclairs from spreading into one another.) Using a pastry brush, brush the tops of the éclairs with water.

5 Bake for 25 minutes without opening the oven door (see Tip). Rotate the baking sheet and reduce the oven temperature to 350°F. Continue baking until the éclairs are golden brown and feel very light for their size (because most of the moisture has evaporated), 25 to 30 more minutes. (If you're new at this, cut one open. If it's still custardy inside, it will collapse when it comes out of the oven; return to the oven for 5 more minutes.)

6 Place the sheet pan on a wire rack and allow the éclairs to cool completely, about 30 minutes.

7 Make the ganache as on page 150 and let cool for 5 minutes, stirring occasionally. Do not allow to stiffen.

8 To assemble the éclairs, transfer the pastry cream to the bowl of a standing mixer fitted with the paddle attachment. Beat on medium speed to soften. Transfer to a pastry bag fitted with a ⅝- or 9⁄16-inch plain tip (such as Ateco #808 or #807). Cut off about 1 inch from each end of the bananas so they are about the same length as the éclairs; split each banana horizontally. Slice the cooled éclairs in half lengthwise.

9 Working assembly-line fashion, pipe a line of custard in the bottom of each éclair. Top each with a banana half. Pipe a line of pastry cream on top of the bananas. Add the éclair tops and press to adhere. Place the éclairs on a baking sheet and place in the freezer for 5 minutes.

10 Transfer the ganache to a shallow oval dish large enough to dip the éclairs. Holding the éclairs from underneath, in the middle of the éclair and by your thumb, forefinger, and middle finger, dip the tops of the éclairs in the ganache, tilting them slightly to evenly cover the tops. Let the excess drip off and place, coated side up, on a wire rack set over a rimmed baking sheet. Refrigerate until the glaze is set, about 10 minutes, or transfer to an airtight container and refrigerate up to 4 hours.

Pumpkin Whoopie Pies with Cinnamon Cream

Traditional whoopie pies (with fluffy domed chocolate cakes and marshmallow filling) are a New England specialty, though they're now popular all over the country. There's not a kid in the world, including mine, who doesn't love whoopie pies; kids seem to love anything they can eat with their hands. And these are a generous size, so little ones feel like they're getting a real treat. I owe this pumpkin variation to a good friend of mine, Patrizia Jonker, whose bakery Amore, in Fairfield, Connecticut, was known for whoopie pies. When she came to work with me, Patrizia brought the recipe with her.

MAKES 8 WHOOPIE PIES

Cakes

- **1 cup all-purpose flour**
- **½ teaspoon baking soda**
- **½ teaspoon baking powder**
- **¼ teaspoon coarse salt**
- **¾ teaspoon ground cinnamon**
- **¼ teaspoon grated nutmeg**
- **¼ teaspoon ground cloves**
- **¼ cup (½ stick) unsalted butter, at room temperature**
- **¼ cup firmly packed light brown sugar**
- **¼ cup granulated sugar**
- **3 tablespoons vegetable oil**
- **1 large egg, at room temperature**
- **⅔ cup canned pumpkin puree**
- **3 tablespoons whole milk**

Cinnamon Cream

- **½ cup (1 stick) unsalted butter, at room temperature**
- **½ cup superfine sugar**
- **¼ teaspoon ground cinnamon**
- **¼ teaspoon coarse salt**
- **½ teaspoon vanilla paste (see sidebar, page 212) or pure vanilla extract**
- **2 tablespoons all-purpose flour**
- **½ cup whole milk**

1 Set the oven rack in the lower third of the oven. Preheat the oven to 400°F. Line two baking sheets with parchment paper or nonstick silicone baking mats.

2 To make the cakes: In a medium bowl, sift together the flour, baking soda, baking powder, salt, cinnamon, nutmeg, and cloves; set aside.

3 In the bowl of a standing mixer fitted with the paddle attachment, combine the butter, brown sugar, and granulated sugar and beat on medium-high speed until light and fluffy, about 2 minutes, scraping down the sides of the bowl halfway through. Beat in the oil, egg, and pumpkin puree, beating until blended after each addition. With the mixer on low speed, beat in the flour mixture in three batches, alternating with the milk.

4 Scoop 8 scoops of batter with a #40 ice cream scoop or 2 tablespoons' worth, about 2 inches apart, onto each of the prepared baking sheets. Baking one pan at a time, bake the cakes, rotating the sheet about two-thirds of the way through the baking time, until a cake tester inserted into the center of the cakes comes out clean, 8 to 10 minutes. Remove the baking sheets to cooling racks and let the cakes cool for 10 minutes. Then remove to the rack with a metal spatula and allow to cool completely.

5 To make the cinnamon cream: In the bowl of a standing mixer fitted with the paddle attachment, combine the butter, superfine sugar, cinnamon, and salt and beat until light and fluffy, and until the sugar has dissolved and is no longer gritty, 5 to 10

minutes. Scrape down the sides of the bowl about halfway through. Beat in the vanilla. Transfer to a small bowl; set aside.

6 In a small saucepan, whisk together the flour and milk until smooth. Cook over medium heat until the mixture forms a very thick paste and the flour taste has cooked out, 6 to 10 minutes. Transfer to the mixer bowl and beat until completely cool. Beat in the butter-sugar mixture on medium-high speed until light and fluffy, 4 to 5 minutes.

7 To assemble the whoopie pies: With a small spatula or butter knife, spread the flat sides of 8 of the cooled cakes with about 2 tablespoons of the cinnamon cream. Top with the remaining 8 cakes.

6

Crisps, Cobblers, and Other Fruit Spoon Desserts

Peach-Raspberry Crisp

Cherry-Almond Crisp

Nectarine-Mango Cobbler with Blackberries

Fourth of July Mixed Berry Cobbler

Mini Apple Charlottes

Spiced Strawberry-Rhubarb Brown Betty

Strawberry Fool

Buttermilk Panna Cotta with Raspberries

Lemon Pudding Cups

Elenore's Mardi Gras Apple Crepes

This chapter contains some of the homiest fruit desserts in my repertoire. They are very straightforward, require little technical skill, and are extremely easy to put together. Some of these recipes require no baking at all.

Crisps, cobblers, and brown bettys, warm from the oven, top the chapter list. These regional American favorites are basically fruit pies without the dough. The fruit is sweetened, thickened with cornstarch, and given a topping that provides textural contrast. The layer and the fruit are interchangeable. You can decide what you're in the mood for.

Choose a crisp, with or without oats, when you want a sweet, chunky streusel-like mixture. Cobblers offer a buttery, flaky, biscuit topping. The cobbler dough may be spooned directly over the fruit or cut into shapes, like biscuits, and arranged on top. A traditional "betty" is topped with a layer of buttered bread crumbs. My Spiced Strawberry-Rhubarb Brown Betty (page 207) substitutes buttered bread cubes that have been toasted for extra crunch and sweetened with cinnamon-sugar. The Mini Apple Charlottes on page 204 are a French cousin to these rustic American favorites. They feature an apple compote encased in a golden-brown crust of buttered, toasted bread slices. All these desserts are fantastic eaten warm, with a generous scoop of ice cream melting around the soft fruit.

Fruit also adapts very well to luscious spoon desserts such as puddings, mousses, and fools. Strawberry Fool (page 208) is just a fancy way of serving strawberries with whipped cream. Buttermilk Panna Cotta with Raspberries (page 211) is a light, velvety smooth custard bound with gelatin instead of egg. Lemon Pudding Cups (page 213), served warm or chilled, are the airy, magically self-layering puddings that many of us grew up with. The chapter finishes with my German mother-in-law Elenore's Mardi Gras Apple Crepes (page 215), rich with eggs and dusted with confectioners' sugar.

The crisps, cobblers, and brown bettys in this chapter were tested in both a 12 by 9-inch and a 10 by 14-inch gratin dish. Either will work. For a more elegant presentation, you can bake them in 4-inch ramekins or other individual baking dishes that hold about one cup. Bake until the fruit is bubbling around the topping and the topping is browned.

Store leftover crisp, cobblers, and brown bettys at room temperature, loosely covered with plastic wrap. Lemon puddings, fools, and unmolded panna cotta can be placed directly into a large Pyrex or Rubbermaid container with an airtight lid so each cup needn't be individually wrapped in plastic.

Most of these simple recipes make great weeknight desserts. If you are a beginning baker, this chapter is for you. If you're no longer a beginner, I hope you'll enjoy my take on these favorites from my home kitchen.

Peach-Raspberry Crisp

Raspberries taste fantastic with the cinnamon in this crisp oatmeal-streusel topping. If peaches are not at their best when you shop, nectarines, apricots, or plums make a fine substitute. I serve this with a scoop of Vanilla Gelato (page 220), Nik's Raspberry Gelato (page 222), or whipped cream (page 48).

SERVES 8

Topping

- **1 cup all-purpose flour**
- **1 cup firmly packed light brown sugar**
- **½ teaspoon coarse salt**
- **¼ teaspoon ground cinnamon**
- **½ cup (1 stick) cold unsalted butter, cut into ¼-inch cubes**
- **½ cup old-fashioned rolled oats (not instant)**

- **2 pounds fresh peaches, halved, pitted, and sliced into ½-inch-thick wedges**
- **2 (6-ounce) baskets raspberries**
- **⅓ to ½ cup sugar**
- **3 tablespoons cornstarch**
- **2 teaspoons freshly squeezed lemon juice (from 1 lemon)**
- **1 teaspoon coarse salt**

1 Set the oven rack in the lower third of the oven. Preheat the oven to 375°F. Set a 12 by 9-inch or 14 by 10-inch oval baking dish on a baking sheet lined with parchment paper or a nonstick silicone baking mat.

2 To make the topping: In a medium bowl, use a fork to stir together the flour, brown sugar, salt, and cinnamon. Add the butter and, using your fingertips, quickly work it into the dry ingredients until pea-size crumbs form. Add the oats and toss gently. Set aside in the refrigerator.

3 In a medium bowl, toss together the peaches, raspberries, sugar, cornstarch, lemon juice, and salt. Transfer to the gratin dish. Sprinkle the topping mixture evenly over the top.

4 Bake, rotating the baking sheet about two-thirds of the way through the baking time, until the juices bubble up and the topping is golden brown and very crisp, 45 to 50 minutes. Let cool for 15 minutes before serving.

Cherry-Almond Crisp

I love cherry desserts, especially when they're home-baked. The tart-sweet fruit plays well with the warm flavor of toasted almonds. This crisp can be made with fresh cherries, but frozen are infinitely easier to work with because they're pitted. Look for individually quick-frozen cherries (not cherries frozen in syrup) or pit and freeze your own.

SERVES 6 TO 8

Topping

- **½ cup sliced almonds**
- **2½ cups all-purpose flour**
- **1 cup firmly packed light brown sugar**
- **2 teaspoons ground cinnamon**
- **½ teaspoon coarse salt**
- **1 cup (2 sticks) unsalted butter**
- **¾ teaspoon almond extract**

- **2½ pounds pitted fresh or frozen cherries (page 25)**
- **⅓ cup sugar**
- **3 tablespoons cornstarch**
- **2 teaspoons freshly squeezed lemon juice (from 1 lemon)**
- **1 teaspoon coarse salt**
- **½ teaspoon almond extract**

1 Set the oven rack in the lower third of the oven. Preheat the oven to 375°F. Set a 12 by 9-inch or 14 by 10-inch oval gratin dish on a baking sheet lined with parchment paper or a nonstick silicone baking mat.

2 To make the topping: Spread the almonds over a rimmed baking sheet. Bake, stirring once, until lightly browned, 5 to 7 minutes; set aside to cool. In a large bowl, sift the flour with the brown sugar, cinnamon, and salt. Melt the butter in a small saucepan; let cool for 2 minutes. Pour the melted butter over the flour mixture. Add the almond extract. Work the mixture with your fingertips to press into large crumbs. Gently incorporate the toasted almonds with a rubber spatula; set aside.

3 In a medium bowl, toss together the cherries, sugar, cornstarch, lemon juice, salt, and almond extract. Transfer to the gratin dish. Distribute the topping mixture evenly over the top.

4 Bake, rotating the baking sheet about two-thirds of the way through the baking time, until the juices bubble up and the topping is golden brown and very crisp, 50 to 60 minutes. Let cool for 15 minutes before serving.

Nectarine-Mango Cobbler with Blackberries

I don't play much with tropical fruits outside of bananas and pineapple. I'm a classicist, I guess. But Peter, my youngest, is a mango fanatic, and I discovered that the exotic flavor of warm mangos pairs nicely with nectarines and fresh ginger. Fresh ginger can be frozen in a resealable bag. When I need it at home, I peel the required amount, let the ginger thaw enough to cut, and throw the rest back in the freezer. It will last at least several months.

SERVES 6 TO 8

- **1 pound (about 3) fresh nectarines, halved, pitted, and cut into wedges (about 3½ cups)**
- **2 pounds (about 2) fresh mangos, flesh cut off the pits, peeled, and cut into 1-inch dice**
- **1 pint fresh blackberries**
- **⅓ to ½ cup granulated sugar (depending on the ripeness of the fruit)**
- **½ teaspoon coarse salt**
- **Juice of 1 lemon (2 to 3 tablespoons)**
- **3 tablespoons cornstarch**
- **2 teaspoons grated peeled fresh ginger**

Biscuit Dough

- **1⅓ cups all-purpose flour**
- **⅓ cup granulated sugar**
- **¼ cup toasted wheat germ**
- **1½ teaspoons baking powder**
- **1 teaspoon baking soda**
- **½ teaspoon coarse salt**
- **6 tablespoons (¾ stick) cold unsalted butter, cubed**
- **⅔ cup buttermilk, plus extra for brushing**
- **3 tablespoons sanding sugar, for finishing**

1 In a large bowl, toss together the nectarines, mangos, blackberries, sugar, salt, lemon juice, cornstarch, and ginger. Transfer to a 12 by 9-inch or 14 by 10-inch oval baking dish.

2 Set the oven rack in the lower third of the oven. Preheat the oven to 375°F. Line a baking sheet with parchment paper or a nonstick silicone baking mat.

3 To make the biscuit dough: In a large bowl, whisk together the flour, sugar, wheat germ, baking powder, baking soda, and salt.

4 Working quickly so as not to warm the butter, work the butter into the flour mixture with your fingers until it resembles coarse crumbs. Add the buttermilk and fold with a rubber scraper or your hands until the buttermilk has been absorbed and there are no dry patches. Do not overwork. The dough will be wet.

5 Spoon dollops of biscuit dough on top of the fruit. Brush the dough with buttermilk and sprinkle with sanding sugar. Bake, rotating the baking sheet two-thirds of the way through the baking, until the fruit filling is bubbling and the biscuit topping is lightly browned and cooked through, 40 to 45 minutes. Let cool for 15 minutes before serving. Serve warm or at room temperature.

Fourth of July Mixed Berry Cobbler

This oversize red, white, and blue cobbler is designed to feed a Fourth of July party crowd. Crystallized ginger adds a little zing to a standard cobbler topping. Although this is a classic summer cobbler, it can be made successfully out of season with frozen berries (no need to thaw). The recipe is easily cut in half; bake it in a 9-inch deep-dish pie plate for forty to forty-five minutes. Crystallized ginger is fresh ginger that has been dried and preserved in sugar. Good-quality crystallized ginger should not be fibrous, and it should be moist and tasty enough to eat out of the bag.

SERVES 16

3⅓ cups (about 21 ounces) fresh blueberries

3⅓ cups (about 21 ounces) fresh blackberries

3⅓ cups (about 21 ounces) fresh raspberries

1 cup plus 2 tablespoons granulated sugar (depending on the ripeness of the berries)

1⅛ teaspoons coarse salt

2 teaspoons freshly squeezed lemon juice (from 1 lemon)

6 tablespoons cornstarch

Biscuit Dough

2⅔ cups all-purpose flour

⅔ cup granulated sugar

1 tablespoon baking powder

2 teaspoons baking soda

1 teaspoon coarse salt

½ cup diced crystallized ginger

12 tablespoons (1½ sticks) cold unsalted butter, cubed

½ cup buttermilk

1 tablespoon sanding sugar, for finishing

1 In a large bowl, toss together the blueberries, blackberries, raspberries, granulated sugar, salt, lemon juice, and cornstarch. Transfer to a 10 by 14-inch rectangular, ceramic baking dish.

2 Set the oven rack in the lower third of the oven. Preheat the oven to 375°F. Line a baking sheet with parchment paper or a nonstick silicone baking mat.

3 To make the biscuit dough: In a large bowl, whisk together the flour, granulated sugar, baking powder, baking soda, salt, and crystallized ginger.

4 Working quickly so as not to warm the butter, work the butter into the flour mixture with your fingers until it resembles coarse crumbs. Add 6 tablespoons of the buttermilk and fold with a rubber scraper or your hands until the buttermilk has been absorbed and there are no dry patches. Add the remaining 2 tablespoons of buttermilk as necessary (you won't use all of it; reserve what's left for brushing the dough). The dough should be dry enough to hold a shape when you cut it out.

5 Turn the dough out onto a lightly floured work surface. With lightly floured hands, pat the dough to about ¾ inch thick. Cut out twelve stars with a 3⅜-inch (measuring point to point) star cookie cutter and place them in a single layer on top of the fruit. Brush the stars with the reserved buttermilk, and sprinkle each with ¼ teaspoon of sanding sugar. Bake, rotating the baking sheet two-thirds of the way through the baking time, until the biscuit topping is lightly browned and cooked through, 60 to 65 minutes. Serve warm or at room temperature.

Mini Apple Charlottes

An apple charlotte is a classic French dessert made with a special two-handled mold lined with buttered bread and filled with apple compote. Once baked, the bread browns to a crisp, buttery casing for the apples. I've simplified things for home kitchens by baking individual charlottes in a jumbo muffin tin, which can be purchased at any supermarket.

MAKES 6 INDIVIDUAL CHARLOTTES

- **2 tablespoons plus 1 cup (2 sticks) unsalted butter**
- **4 large Granny Smith apples, peeled, cored, and cut in ½-inch dice**
- **Pinch of coarse salt**
- **1 teaspoon freshly squeezed lemon juice (from 1 lemon)**
- **¼ cup sugar**
- **Pinch of ground cinnamon**
- **¼ cup white wine or apple juice**
- **¼ cup golden raisins**
- **21 slices white bread from 2 (1-pound) loaves**
- **1 recipe Whipped Cream (page 48), or 1 pint store-bought vanilla ice cream (optional)**

1 Heat the 2 tablespoons of butter in a large skillet over high heat until melted. Add the diced apples and spread in a single layer. Sprinkle with the salt, then the lemon juice, sugar, and cinnamon. Cook, stirring or shaking the pan every now and then, until the apples are tender but not mushy and are caramelized, 8 to 10 minutes. The apples will give off their liquid first and the liquid will evaporate.

2 When the apples are cooked and the liquid has evaporated, add the wine and the raisins and stir over medium-high heat until the liquid is entirely evaporated, 3 to 5 minutes; set the compote aside.

3 In a medium saucepan, melt the remaining 1 cup of butter over medium heat. Once melted, let it bubble for 2 minutes to boil off some of the water. Transfer to a small bowl and let cool.

4 Set the oven rack in the lower third of the oven. Preheat the oven to 375°F.

5 Using a 2⅜-inch cookie cutter, or a glass of the same diameter, cut out 6 rounds of bread. Dip one side of each round in the butter, and place them, buttered sides down, in the bottom of each muffin mold. Trim the crusts from 9 mores slices of bread and cut each slice in half to make 18 rectangles. Dip one side of one rectangle in the butter and press it over the side of one of the molds, buttered side facing the metal. Repeat with 2 more bread rectangles, overlapping as needed, so the sides of the mold

recipe continues

TIP I add wine or juice to the pan with the sautéed apples and raisins to boost the flavor, pick up any caramelized browned bits on the bottom of the pan, and plump the raisins.

are completely covered. Continue this way to line the sides of the remaining five molds with buttered bread.

6 Divide the apple compote among the lined molds. Use a 3½-inch cookie cutter, or a glass of the same diameter, to cut 6 more rounds of bread. Dip one side of each round in the melted butter. Place them, buttered sides up, on top of the compote. The rounds should completely cover the sides; this will be the base of the charlottes.

7 Place the muffin pan on a baking sheet and bake, rotating the baking sheet about two-thirds of the way through the baking time, until the bread is crisp and brown, 20 to 25 minutes.

8 Remove the muffin pan from the oven. Place a wire rack on top and, with one hand (protected by an oven mitt) on the wire rack, quickly invert the muffin pan. Place the wire rack on a baking sheet and carefully remove the muffin pan. Let stand about 15 minutes before serving. Serve with whipped cream, or ice cream, if you like.

Spiced Strawberry-Rhubarb Brown Betty

I have a hard time selling rhubarb to my kids, but I fell in love with it when I was studying at the Culinary Institute of America. I love sour tastes, and rhubarb is one of the best. In the spring, when the rhubarb bounces off the ripe flavor of the strawberries, it tastes delicious against the sweet, buttery, cinnamon-spiced bread topping. The quality of the bread is important in this recipe. I like sourdough because it adds another dimension of taste. Its sturdy texture crisps up in the oven, providing a nice textural contrast to the soft filling. But any good-quality bread with texture may be substituted.

SERVES 6 TO 8

- **4 cups cubed (½-inch) sourdough bread, crusts removed**
- **1 cup sugar**
- **2½ teaspoons ground cinnamon**
- **¾ cup (1½ sticks) unsalted butter, melted, plus extra for the baking dish**
- **1 pound rhubarb, trimmed and cut crosswise into 1-inch pieces**
- **1 quart (1 pound) fresh strawberries, hulled and quartered if large, halved if small**
- **Grated zest of ½ orange**
- **2 tablespoons freshly squeezed orange juice (from 1 orange)**
- **2 tablespoons cornstarch**
- **⅛ teaspoon grated nutmeg**
- **¼ teaspoon coarse salt**

1. Set the oven rack in the lower third of the oven. Preheat the oven to 250°F. Place the bread on a rimmed baking sheet. Bake, rotating the baking sheet about two-thirds of the way through the baking time, until the cubes are crisp, about 30 minutes. Let cool completely. Transfer to a bowl.

2. Raise the oven temperature to 375°F. Line a clean baking sheet with parchment paper or a nonstick silicone mat. Place a 12 by 9-inch or 14 by 10-inch oval baking dish on top; set aside.

3. In a small bowl, stir together ½ cup of the sugar and 2 teaspoons of the cinnamon; set aside. Combine the toasted bread cubes with the melted butter in a large bowl and toss to coat. Add the cinnamon-sugar and toss; set aside.

4. In another large bowl, combine the rhubarb, strawberries, the remaining ½ of cup sugar, the orange zest and juice, the cornstarch, the remaining ½ teaspoon of cinnamon, the nutmeg, and salt and toss to coat; set aside.

5. Spread the fruit mixture over the bottom of the prepared baking dish. Top with the buttered toasted bread cubes.

6. Transfer to the prepared baking sheet and bake, rotating about two-thirds of the way through the baking time, until the topping is golden and the juices are bubbling, 60 to 70 minutes. Cover with foil if the bread cubes are getting too brown. Transfer to a wire rack and let cool for 15 minutes before serving. Serve warm.

Strawberry Fool

A fool is an old-fashioned English dessert consisting of cooked and pureed fruit plus whipped cream. I simplify things by macerating the strawberries in sugar instead of cooking them, so nothing gets in the way of the ripe berry taste. I like to serve this in pretty individual stemmed glasses or custard cups. You may prefer a large decorative bowl. Just make sure to use glass or Pyrex so you can see that gorgeous bottom layer of fruit. This is a great, early summer dessert to showcase strawberries in season. You can substitute any berry that looks good. The fool can be made up to two days in advance and refrigerated.

SERVES 4

1 pound fresh strawberries, hulled and quartered, plus 4 whole, perfect strawberries with leaves, for garnish
¼ cup granulated sugar
Pinch of coarse salt
2 tablespoons strawberry jam
1 cup heavy cream
¼ cup confectioners' sugar

1 In a medium bowl, combine the 1 pound of strawberries, the granulated sugar, and the salt and mash with a fork to release some of the juices. Cover and let macerate for 2 hours at room temperature, or overnight in the refrigerator.

2 Drain the strawberries; discard the liquid. Return them to the bowl and stir in the strawberry jam.

3 In the bowl of a mixer fitted with the whisk attachment, beat the cream with the confectioners' sugar to firm peaks.

4 Divide about one-quarter of the strawberry mixture among four 6-ounce Pyrex custard cups or stemmed glasses, or spoon into the bottom of a medium Pyrex or glass bowl. Fold the remaining strawberries into the whipped cream with a large rubber spatula. Divide the whipped cream mixture among the custard cups. Cover and refrigerate for 10 minutes.

5 Place a whole strawberry on top of each fool before serving.

Buttermilk Panna Cotta with Raspberries

A single gorgeous raspberry turns these delicate, intensely vanilla-scented custards into a beautiful summer dessert. Panna cotta—"cooked cream," in Italian—was traditionally made by cooking cream until it thickened and the flavor concentrated. I just bring the cream to a simmer (with buttermilk, for a refreshing tang), add gelatin, and chill. Think of it as a cream-based Jell-O. I like crunch, so I serve the custards on top of a crisp, orange-flavored butter cookie cut just large enough so the edges peek out from underneath the custard. (If you like, substitute a thin store-bought butter cookie, about three inches in diameter. Or serve butter cookies on the side.) You'll need six 4-ounce ramekins (measuring 2¾ inches across) and one 3-inch fluted cookie cutter.

SERVES 6

Panna Cotta

- **1 (¼-ounce) envelope (about 1 tablespoon) gelatin**
- **¾ cup buttermilk**
- **¾ cup heavy cream**
- **6 tablespoons granulated sugar**
- **½ teaspoon coarse salt**
- **1 teaspoon vanilla paste (see sidebar, page 212) or pure vanilla extract**

Cookies

- **½ recipe Orange Sugar Cut-Out Cookies (page 83), chilled**
- **1 large egg white, whisked with a fork**
- **¼ cup sanding sugar**

- **¼ recipe Whipped Cream (page 48) or good-quality store-bought whipped cream**
- **6 perfect fresh raspberries, for garnish**

1 Spray six 4-ounce ramekins lightly with nonstick cooking spray; set aside.

2 To make the panna cotta: In a small bowl, sprinkle 5 tablespoons of cold water over the gelatin and let stand for 5 minutes.

3 In a 1-quart saucepan, combine the buttermilk, cream, granulated sugar, salt, and vanilla paste, if using. Heat over medium heat until hot to the touch; do not boil. Remove from the heat. Add the gelatin and stir to dissolve.

4 Strain the mixture into a large Pyrex measuring cup and stir in the vanilla extract, if using. Divide among the prepared ramekins. Cover with plastic (do not allow the plastic to touch the custard mixture) and refrigerate at least 6 hours or overnight.

5 Set the oven rack in the lower third of the oven. Preheat the oven to 350°F. Line a baking sheet with parchment paper or a nonstick silicone baking mat.

6 To make the cookies: On a lightly floured work surface, roll the dough about ⅛ inch thick. Cut out 6 rounds with a 3-inch fluted cookie cutter. Place on the prepared baking sheet and chill for 15 minutes. Lightly brush with egg white (just enough to encourage the sugar to stick) and sprinkle each round with ¼ teaspoon sanding sugar. Bake until the edges and bottoms of

recipe continues

the cookies are lightly browned, 9 to 11 minutes. Remove the baking sheet to a wire rack to cool completely.

7 To serve, place a cooled cookie on six small serving plates. Use your fingers to gently loosen the edges of the panna cottas from the sides of the ramekins. Invert each onto a cookie. Top each with a dab of whipped cream and a raspberry.

Vanilla Paste

Vanilla paste is a viscous, concentrated vanilla flavoring made with the tiny black seeds of long, thin, black vanilla beans. In the home kitchen, I recommend the paste instead of the beans for most recipes because the paste is less expensive and more convenient, and it has a longer shelf life. Use vanilla paste in pale-colored preparations in which the tiny black seeds will show, such as in pastry creams, panna cottas, ice creams, and gelatos. Substitute 2 teaspoons vanilla paste for 1 vanilla bean. Vanilla paste may also be substituted for vanilla extract (1 teaspoon paste to 1 teaspoon extract); unlike the extract, vanilla paste will not lose its potency in hot mixtures. Vanilla paste is available at specialty stores. Refrigerate for up to several months.

Lemon Pudding Cups

A fluffy cake on the top, a saucy, lemony custard on the bottom, this has been a classic home dessert for decades and it's just as popular with my family at home. It never fails to fascinate my kids that the pudding separates during baking. The pudding is traditionally made with milk, but I substitute buttermilk for its richness and acidity. To serve it warm, put this in the oven as the family sits down for dinner, or make it ahead and serve chilled.

SERVES 6

- **3 large eggs, separated**
- **½ cup plus 2 tablespoons sugar**
- **1 tablespoon grated lemon zest (from 1 to 2 lemons)**
- **2 tablespoons all-purpose flour**
- **1 cup buttermilk**
- **¼ cup freshly squeezed lemon juice (from 2 lemons)**
- **¼ teaspoon coarse salt**
- **1 pint fresh raspberries or blackberries (optional)**

1 Set the oven rack in the lower third of the oven. Preheat the oven to 350°F. Bring water to a boil for a water bath.

2 In a large bowl, whisk the egg yolks with the ½ cup sugar and the lemon zest until blended. Whisk in the flour until smooth. Add the buttermilk, lemon juice, and salt and whisk until blended.

3 In the bowl of a standing mixer fitted with the whisk attachment, whisk the egg whites on low speed until frothy, about 1 minute. With the mixer running, gradually sprinkle in the remaining 2 tablespoons of sugar. Raise the speed to medium-high and beat the meringue until stiff peaks form, about 3 minutes. With a large rubber spatula, fold the meringue into the liquid ingredients.

4 Divide the mixture among six 6-ounce Pyrex custard cups. The mixture will come right to the tops of the cups. Place the cups in a roasting pan, place the pan in the oven, and pour in the boiling water to come about ½ inch up the sides of the cups. Bake, rotating the roasting pan about two-thirds of the way through the baking time, until the puddings are lightly browned and set, with no jiggle, 20 to 25 minutes. The puddings will soufflé, and then fall.

5 Remove the cups from the water bath with tongs. Serve with the berries on top, if you like.

Elenore's Mardi Gras Apple Crepes

These light, moist German pancakes are a delicious way to enjoy apples throughout the fall, winter, and spring. My mother-in-law, Elenore, made these apple crepes for our family on Mardi Gras night for many years. They're served right out of the pan and we'd dig in while she cooked the next one. Warm, with a dusting of confectioners' sugar, these are fabulous also for breakfast or brunch. Elenore didn't cook the apple slices as I do in step 2, but I like to soften the fruit over heat with a little butter and sugar to bring out its flavor.

MAKES 8 TO 9 PANCAKES; SERVES 4

Crepe Batter

- **3 large eggs**
- **¾ cup all-purpose flour**
- **1½ teaspoons granulated sugar**
- **⅛ teaspoon coarse salt**
- **1 cup whole milk**

- **4 to 5 tablespoons unsalted butter**
- **3 fresh, firm apples (such as Cortland, Rome, or Granny Smith), peeled, cored, and thinly sliced**
- **4½ teaspoons granulated sugar**
- **¼ teaspoon ground cinnamon**
- **⅛ teaspoon coarse salt**
- **1 to 2 tablespoons confectioners' sugar, for dusting**
- **½ cup apricot jam, for serving**

1 To make the batter: In a medium bowl, whisk the eggs to blend. Add the flour, granulated sugar, and salt and whisk to incorporate. Add the milk and whisk until smooth, 1 to 2 minutes. Set aside at room temperature.

2 Heat 3 tablespoons of the butter in a 10-inch skillet or sauté pan over medium heat. Add the sliced apples, granulated sugar, cinnamon, and salt and cook until the apples are tender but not mushy, 7 to 9 minutes; set aside.

3 In an 8-inch, slope-sided nonstick omelet pan, melt just enough butter to coat the bottom of the pan (about ½ teaspoon). Add 8 to 9 slices of cooked apple in a single layer. Add about ¼ cup of the batter, enough to coat the bottom of the pan. Tilt the pan to spread the batter and spoon batter over any exposed apples. Cook until the crepe is set and browned on the bottom, 2 to 3 minutes. Turn with a wide spatula. Cook to brown the other side, 2 to 3 minutes. Slide the crepe onto a serving plate. Dust with confectioners' sugar and spoon jam on top. Serve immediately. Continue to make the rest of the crepes.

7 Frozen Fruit Desserts

One of my earliest memories is of eating gelato—ice cream's Italian cousin—at San Marco, the pizza place around the corner from my grandparents' house. I've been a fan ever since.

My kids are, too. They like all different styles of frozen desserts: ice cream, gelato, sherbet, sorbet, semifreddo, and soufflé glacé. These preparations are delicious with seasonal fruit, and even some vegetables. Making frozen desserts is a good project for kids because it requires minimal equipment and very little actual cooking. And show me a kid (or grown-up for that matter) who *doesn't* like ice cream.

I earned my stripes in the field of frozen desserts at the Helmsley Palace Hotel in Manhattan. My first station there was ice cream and sorbets. Those first few months, I was continually panic-struck that I'd ruin the huge batches I was responsible for: fifty gallons at a time. Eventually, I mastered the techniques and became fascinated with the science.

After I sold Cousin John's Café in 1996, I was thinking aloud to one of my purveyors about my interest in gelato. "You've got to go to Italy," he said. "It's the only place to learn." So I spent a week training at Fabbri in Bologna. Fabbri is the oldest and best-respected family-owned gelato and pastry supply manufacturer in Italy. The class was in Italian—I had to take a translator—and the coursework was scientifically very complex. Correctly made gelato is a complicated balancing act between fat, sugar, nonfat milk solids, and moisture. But I had great fun there. The recipes translate well to my home kitchen and you'll enjoy making them in your home too. They are easy to make and foolproof, if you adhere to a few guidelines.

With the exception of the Lemon Soufflé Glacé (page 227) and the Hazelnut Semifreddo with Raspberries (page 218), all of the recipes in this chapter are made in a standard home ice cream freezer (see sidebar on page 230). All warm mixtures should be chilled in an ice bath before churning, to cool them as quickly as possible and prevent the growth of bacteria. Once chilled, all of the mixtures containing cream are best refrigerated, or "aged" as it's called in the industry, for twelve to twenty-four hours before churning. An overnight in the refrigerator allows the mixture to incorporate more air when it is churned, and makes for a smoother texture. The mixtures may separate in the refrigerator and must be stirred before churning. Once they hit the chilled container of the ice cream machine, the mixtures will immediately begin to freeze and won't have a chance to blend.

Frozen desserts are best eaten as soon as possible, but all of these recipes will last at least one week in the freezer.

Hazelnut Semifreddo with Raspberries

A semifreddo is a good choice for home cooks who don't own an ice cream maker. The creamy, feather-light—almost marshmallowy—mixture is frozen in a loaf pan and cut into slices for serving. When I studied with Fabbri in Bologna, I got to taste some of the best gelato flavors in the world. One of my favorite was gianduja, a chocolate-hazelnut combination that tastes like Nutella. Served with a chocolate sauce, this semifreddo mimics the delicate flavor of gianduja that I love. Cover and store leftover chocolate sauce in the refrigerator.

SERVES 8

Semifreddo

- **3 ounces (¼ cup) praline paste (see Sources, page 281), or Nutella**
- **4½ teaspoons brandy**
- **¾ cup egg yolks (about 12 eggs)**
- **½ cup sugar**
- **4½ teaspoons honey**
- **½ teaspoon coarse salt**
- **1½ cups heavy cream, very cold (see Whipped Cream, page 48)**
- **½ cup (2¼ ounces) chopped skinned hazelnuts (see page 112)**
- **6-ounce container fresh raspberries, for serving**

Chocolate Sauce

- **⅔ cup unsweetened cocoa powder**
- **8 ounces bittersweet chocolate, cut into ¼-inch pieces**
- **½ cup plus 2 tablespoons sugar**
- **¼ cup corn syrup**
- **¼ teaspoon coarse salt**

1 To make the semifreddo: Cut two pieces of plastic wrap: one 24 inches long by 12 inches wide; the second, 20 inches long by 12 inches wide. Center the longer piece lengthwise in an 8½ by 4½-inch loaf pan. Center the shorter piece of plastic wrap, overlapping and perpendicular to the first piece; set aside.

2 In a small bowl, whisk the praline paste with 3 tablespoons water and all the brandy to break up the paste and form a homogenous mixture; set aside.

3 Bring about 1 inch of water to a simmer in a medium saucepan. In the bowl of a standing mixer fitted with the whisk attachment, combine the egg yolks, sugar, honey, and salt. Place over (not in) the simmering water and heat, whisking, until the sugar has dissolved and the mixture is hot to the touch (about 140°F). Place the bowl on the mixer stand and beat at high speed for 4 to 6 minutes, until the mixture is pale yellow and holds a thick ribbon when the whisk is lifted from the bowl. Transfer to a large bowl. Wash and dry the mixer bowl and whisk. Add the cream to the bowl and beat to soft peaks; set aside.

4 Add about ½ cup of the warm egg mixture to the praline mixture and whisk to loosen. Gently fold it into the egg mixture with a rubber spatula. Fold in the whipped cream.

5 Transfer half of the semifreddo mixture to the plastic-lined loaf pan. Spread the hazelnuts evenly over the mixture. Top with the rest of the semifreddo mixture and spread to even it out. Tap the pan gently on the countertop to remove any air bubbles. Cover and freeze overnight.

6 To make the chocolate sauce: In a medium saucepan, combine the cocoa powder, chocolate, sugar, corn syrup, salt, and 1 cup water. Bring to a simmer over medium heat. Simmer, whisking, until the sugar has dissolved, the chocolate has melted, and the mixture is smooth, about 10 minutes. Place a fine strainer over a medium bowl. Strain the sauce into the bowl. Transfer to a serving pitcher.

7 To serve, use the overhanging plastic wrap to lift the semifreddo out of the loaf pan. Invert onto a serving platter or cutting board. Remove the plastic. Cut the semifreddo into eight slices and serve each on a plate with the warm chocolate sauce and the raspberries. Or present as a loaf on an attractive serving platter, decorated with berries, and pass the sauce.

Styles of Frozen Desserts

Each style has something to recommend it. Ice cream, gelato, sorbet, and sherbet are churned in a machine. Ice cream and gelato are similar: They're both made with dairy. But gelato is lighter; its butterfat content ranges between 6 and 12 percent, depending on the flavor, while the butterfat in ice cream can reach as high as 20 percent. The lower butterfat content of gelato makes for very bright and intense flavors, while ice cream tastes creamier. Sherbet is made with water and milk and sometimes egg whites. It is lighter than both gelato and ice cream. Sorbet is a mixture of pureed fruit and simple syrup, the lightest of the four.

Soufflé glacé and semifreddo are similar to ice cream, but a little airier. The mixtures are frozen in molds rather than churned in a machine. Although one is French and the other Italian, there is no difference between the two mixtures. Semifreddo is traditionally frozen in a loaf pan and served in slices, but if you like, it may be frozen in individual ramekins like the soufflé glacé.

Vanilla Gelato with Caramelized Bananas

I fell in love with the combination of frosty vanilla ice cream and warm caramelized bananas while I was living and working in New Orleans as a teenager. New Orleans restaurants are known for their flambéed desserts. All kinds of fruits are flambéed, but bananas are particularly popular—bananas flambés, bananas Foster—and I probably tasted every one of them. My version is made with gelato rather than ice cream because I wanted an intense vanilla flavor. It's an easy dessert to make at home, and the effect is always dramatic.

MAKES ABOUT 1½ QUARTS GELATO AND 4 TO 6 SERVINGS OF BANANAS

Vanilla Gelato

- **6 large egg yolks**
- **1 cup granulated sugar**
- **½ teaspoon coarse salt**
- **3 cups skim milk**
- **1 cup heavy cream**
- **2 tablespoons vanilla paste (see sidebar, page 212) or pure vanilla extract**
- **2 tablespoons light corn syrup**

Caramelized Bananas

- **¼ cup (½ stick) unsalted butter**
- **¼ cup firmly packed light brown sugar**
- **¼ teaspoon coarse salt**
- **2 ripe but firm bananas, peeled and sliced ½ inch thick**
- **2 tablespoons dark rum, or brandy (optional)**

1 Prepare an ice bath by filling a large bowl or tub with ice and water.

2 To make the gelato: In a medium, heat-proof bowl, whisk together the egg yolks, ½ cup of the granulated sugar, and the salt; set aside.

3 In a medium saucepan, combine the remaining ½ cup of sugar, the skim milk, heavy cream, and vanilla paste, if using. Bring to a simmer over medium-low heat. Whisking constantly, gradually pour the hot mixture into the egg mixture to temper it. Return the mixture to the saucepan and cook, stirring, until the custard is thick enough to coat the back of a spoon, 5 to 6 minutes. Do not boil. Remove from the heat.

4 Place a fine strainer over a medium bowl. Strain the custard into the bowl and chill completely in the ice bath. Stir in the corn syrup and vanilla extract, if using. Cover and refrigerate for 12 to 24 hours.

5 Stir the chilled custard well and transfer to an ice cream machine. Process according to manufacturer's instructions.

6 To make the caramelized bananas: In a 12-inch skillet, melt the butter with the brown sugar and salt over medium heat until bubbly. Stir to dissolve the sugar. Add the banana slices in a single layer and cook until golden brown and caramelized, 2 to 3 minutes. Turn with a small offset metal spatula or two forks. Cook for 2 to 3 minutes to brown the other side. Remove the

pan from the heat. Add the rum, if using. Return the skillet to the heat and simmer to reduce and thicken the sauce, about 2 minutes.

7 Serve the gelato in bowls with the warm banana mixture spooned over.

Nik's Raspberry Gelato

My elder son, Nik, is in his twenties now. But when he was younger, we liked to ride bikes together on the weekends. One Sunday, on our way home, we stopped off to pick a few raspberries from the bushes at the end of our block when they were at a perfect stage of ripeness. In the end, we picked so many that we had to use Nik's helmet to hold them all. We walked our bikes home and made gelato, on the spot. It became our summer tradition.

MAKES ABOUT 1 QUART

- **1 cup fresh or frozen raspberries**
- **1 tablespoon plus ½ cup sugar**
- **½ teaspoon freshly squeezed lemon juice (from 1 lemon)**
- **3 large egg yolks**
- **1 large whole egg**
- **¼ teaspoon coarse salt**
- **1½ cups skim milk**
- **½ cup heavy cream**
- **1 tablespoon light corn syrup**

TIP I leave some of the raspberry seeds in the gelato mixture. The dark specs are beautiful against the ripe red gelato. And the seeds let you know what fruit you're eating.

1. Prepare an ice bath by filling a large bowl or tub with ice and water. If using frozen raspberries, thaw overnight in the refrigerator.
2. In a medium bowl, mash the raspberries to a coarse puree with 1 tablespoon of the sugar and the lemon juice; set aside.
3. In a medium, heat-proof bowl, whisk the egg yolks with the whole egg, ¼ cup of the sugar, and the salt.
4. In a medium saucepan, combine the remaining ¼ cup of sugar, the skim milk, and the heavy cream. Bring to a simmer over medium-low heat. Whisking constantly, gradually pour the hot mixture into the egg mixture to temper it. Return the mixture to the saucepan and cook, stirring, until the custard is thick enough to coat the back of a spoon, 3 to 4 minutes. Do not boil. Remove from the heat. Place a fine strainer over a medium bowl. Strain the custard into the bowl and chill completely in the ice bath.
5. Mash the raspberry mixture through a fine sieve into a small bowl. Reserve about one-third of the seeds; discard the rest.
6. Stir the corn syrup into the chilled custard. Stir in the raspberry puree. Add the reserved raspberry seeds. Cover and chill for 12 to 24 hours.
7. Stir the custard well and transfer to an ice cream maker. Process according to the manufacturer's instructions.

Sweet Corn Ice Cream

This recipe is my answer to the question of what to do with sweet corn when it's coming out of our ears every summer in Connecticut. I pair it with slices of toasted Polenta Pound Cake (page 175). The ice cream tastes like sweetened creamed corn, with a hint of bourbon. It's wonderful against the crisp-edged cake.

MAKES ABOUT 1½ QUARTS

- **3 cups fresh or frozen corn kernels**
- **2 cups heavy cream**
- **¼ cup granulated sugar**
- **¾ cup firmly packed light brown sugar**
- **½ teaspoon coarse salt**
- **2 cups whole milk**
- **9 large egg yolks**
- **2 tablespoons bourbon**
- **2 tablespoons light corn syrup**

TIP The custard must be completely cold before you add the raspberry puree. Otherwise, the heat of the custard will diminish the vibrant color of the fruit.

1 Prepare an ice bath by filling a large bowl or tub with ice and water.

2 In a medium saucepan, combine the corn, heavy cream, granulated sugar, ¼ cup of the light brown sugar, and the salt. Bring to a boil, reduce the heat, and simmer for 10 minutes. Transfer to a blender and puree.

3 Place a fine strainer over a medium, heat-proof bowl. Strain the corn mixture into the bowl and discard the solids. Stir in the milk. Return the mixture to the saucepan and return to a boil.

4 In the same heat-proof bowl, whisk together the egg yolks and the remaining ½ cup of light brown sugar. Whisking constantly, gradually pour the corn milk into the egg mixture to temper it. Return the mixture to the saucepan and cook over medium-low heat, stirring, until the custard is thick enough to coat the back of a spoon, 5 to 6 minutes. Do not boil. Remove from the heat.

5 Place a clean fine-mesh strainer over a medium bowl. Strain the custard into the bowl and chill completely in the ice bath. Stir in the bourbon and corn syrup. Cover and refrigerate for 12 to 24 hours.

6 Stir the mixture well and transfer to an ice cream machine. Process according to the manufacturer's instructions.

Pumpkin Pie Ice Cream

This flavor is a big favorite with my kids at Thanksgiving. It tastes just like a pumpkin pie, but cold. A big scoop tastes great with pecan, apple, and pumpkin pies. Good-quality canned pumpkin puree is so readily available that I would never use fresh. And it allows us to enjoy the ice cream year-round.

MAKES ABOUT 1 QUART

- **6 large egg yolks**
- **½ cup plus 2 tablespoons firmly packed light brown sugar**
- **½ teaspoon coarse salt**
- **1 cup whole milk**
- **1 cup heavy cream**
- **1 cup pumpkin puree**
- **2 tablespoons honey**
- **½ teaspoon ground cinnamon**
- **¼ teaspoon ground ginger**
- **¼ teaspoon grated nutmeg**
- **2 tablespoons light corn syrup**

1. Prepare an ice bath by filling a large bowl or tub with ice and water.
2. In a medium, heat-proof bowl, whisk together the egg yolks, ½ cup of the sugar, and the salt; set aside.
3. In a medium saucepan, combine the remaining 2 tablespoons of sugar, the milk, heavy cream, pumpkin puree, honey, cinnamon, ginger, and nutmeg. Whisk until smooth. Bring to a simmer over medium-low heat. Whisking constantly, gradually pour the hot mixture into the egg mixture to temper it. Return the mixture to the saucepan and cook, stirring, until the custard is thick enough to coat the back of a spoon, 4 to 5 minutes. Do not boil. Remove from the heat.
4. Place a fine strainer over a medium bowl. Strain the custard into the bowl and chill completely in the ice bath. Stir in the corn syrup. Cover and refrigerate for 12 to 24 hours.
5. Stir the chilled mixture well and transfer to an ice cream machine. Process according to the manufacturer's instructions.

Strawberry Ice Cream

Ripe strawberries and cream are an unbeatable combination. This beautiful pale-pink ice cream with its contrasting chunks of red strawberry always reminds me of the Helmsley Palace Hotel in Manhattan. Strawberry was a favorite flavor when I worked there in the 1980s. We made our ice creams and sorbets fresh every day. I took home whatever was left over at the end of service. One of the German bakers taught me how to wrap the ice cream directly on top of several layers of newspaper, folded up and placed in a plastic bag so that it would stay frozen during the ride home on the Long Island Rail Road. I'd open up the bag on the kitchen table and my brothers and I would devour the ice cream right off the newspaper.

MAKES ABOUT 1½ QUARTS

- **2 cups diced hulled fresh strawberries**
- **2 tablespoons strawberry jam**
- **6 large egg yolks**
- **½ cup sugar**
- **½ teaspoon coarse salt**
- **1 cup whole milk**
- **1 cup heavy cream**
- **2 tablespoons light corn syrup**

TIP The color of berry ice creams and gelato varies with the season and the ripeness of the berry, but an overnight chilling will usually deepen the color.

1 In a medium bowl, toss the strawberries with the jam; set aside to macerate for 2 hours. Mash well with a fork.

2 Prepare an ice bath by filling a large bowl or tub with ice and water.

3 In a medium, heat-proof bowl, whisk the egg yolks with ¼ cup of the sugar, and the salt; set aside.

4 In a medium saucepan, combine the remaining ¼ cup of sugar, the milk, and heavy cream. Bring to a simmer over medium-low heat. Whisking constantly, gradually pour the hot mixture into the egg mixture to temper it. Return the mixture to the saucepan and cook, stirring, until the custard is thick enough to coat the back of a spoon, 4 to 5 minutes. Do not boil. Remove from the heat.

5 Place a fine strainer over a medium bowl. Strain the custard into the bowl and chill completely in the ice bath. Stir in the corn syrup and fold in the mashed strawberry mixture. Cover and refrigerate for 12 to 24 hours.

6 Stir the chilled mixture well and transfer to an ice cream maker. Process according to the manufacturer's instructions.

Lemon Soufflé Glacé

Soufflé glacé means "frozen soufflé," and that's exactly what these elegant frozen desserts look like. They taste like a frozen lemon chiffon cake—very light and fluffy, with a creamy, lemony flavor. The lemon is highlighted by an Italian lemon liqueur, limoncello, which is produced in southern Italy with a variety of lemon that has grown there for centuries. These soufflé glacés are perfect for a celebratory meal. You'll need six 4- or 5-ounce ramekins and two sheets of parchment paper to make a paper "collar" for each ramekin. The collars allow the mixture to extend above the edges of the ramekins. Dusted with confectioners' sugar, they look like hot dessert soufflés, right out of the oven. You can make them a day in advance and they're quite impressive looking.

SERVES 6

2 large eggs
3 large egg yolks
¼ cup granulated sugar
¼ teaspoon coarse salt
Grated zest of ½ lemon
2 tablespoons freshly squeezed lemon juice (from 1 lemon)
2 tablespoons limoncello liqueur
1 cup heavy cream, very cold (see Whipped Cream, page 48)
1 tablespoon confectioners' sugar, for dusting

TIP For this recipe, as well as the Hazelnut Semifreddo with Raspberries (page 218), it's very useful to have an extra bowl for the standing mixer so you don't have to wash a bowl while preparing the mixtures. You can beat the egg mixture in one bowl, take it off the stand, and replace it with a second bowl to hold the cream.

1 Cut 6 parchment strips 12 inches long by 5 inches wide. Fold each strip in half lengthwise. Wrap each strip around each of six 4- or 5-ounce ramekins, so that the folded edge is on top and the strip extends about 1 inch above the top of the ramekins. Overlap the ends of each strip and secure with a rubber band or a piece of kitchen string.

2 In the bowl of a standing mixer, combine the eggs, egg yolks, granulated sugar, and salt. Bring about 1 inch of water to a simmer in a medium saucepan. Place the mixer bowl over (not in) the simmering water and heat, whisking, until the mixture is hot to the touch and the sugar has dissolved.

3 Place the bowl on the mixer stand and beat with the whisk attachment on high speed until the mixture is pale yellow and thick, about 5 minutes. Add the lemon zest and juice, and the limoncello. Transfer to a medium bowl and set aside to cool.

4 Wash and dry the mixer bowl and whisk. Beat the cream to soft peaks on high speed. When the egg mixture is cool, fold in the whipped cream with a rubber spatula.

5 Scoop out about 1 cup of the mixture for each of the prepared ramekins. Cover loosely with plastic wrap and freeze overnight, or until firm.

6 To serve, remove the paper collars from the ramekins. Dust with confectioners' sugar.

Banana Sorbet

The natural consistency of ripe banana gives this unusual sorbet a nice, velvety texture, as if there were cream in it. But the flavor is pure essence of banana. It's delicious with Chocolate Sauce (page 218), topped with chopped pecans or peanuts. Very ripe bananas are essential for the flavor and texture of this sorbet. Five to six will give you a bit more puree than you need. I stir it into yogurt for Peter as an afternoon snack.

MAKES ABOUT 1½ QUARTS

1½ cups sugar
5 to 6 fully ripe bananas
1 teaspoon freshly squeezed lemon juice (from 1 lemon)
2 tablespoons light corn syrup
½ teaspoon coarse salt
2 tablespoons dark rum (optional)

1 Prepare an ice bath by filling a large bowl or tub with ice and water.

2 In a medium saucepan, combine the sugar and 1 cup water. Bring to a simmer over medium heat, whisking to dissolve the sugar. Chill in the ice bath.

3 In the bowl of a food processor, puree the bananas until smooth. Measure 2 cups; reserve the remainder for another use. Return the puree to the food processor. Add ¼ cup water and the lemon juice, and puree until smooth. Add the corn syrup, salt, the chilled syrup, and the rum, if using, and process to blend.

4 Stir the mixture well and transfer to an ice cream machine. Process according to the manufacturer's instructions.

Granny Smith Sorbet

This is one of the coolest, most refreshing desserts I know. It tastes like you're eating an apple right off the tree. I puree the apple mixture with some of the peel to give the sorbet a bright green color. The bits of peel are strained out before freezing.

MAKES ABOUT 1½ QUARTS

- **3 cups sugar**
- **4 fresh Granny Smith apples**
- **¼ cup light corn syrup**
- **2 teaspoons freshly squeezed lemon juice (from 1 lemon)**
- **1 teaspoon coarse salt**

1. Prepare an ice bath by filling a large bowl or tub with ice and water.
2. In a medium saucepan, combine the sugar with 2 cups water and bring to a simmer over medium heat, whisking to dissolve the sugar. Transfer to a bowl and chill in the ice bath.
3. Roughly peel the apples in strips, leaving some peel on the apples. Core and stem the apples, then cut them into pieces. Transfer to a blender. Add the corn syrup, lemon juice, salt, and the chilled sugar syrup. Blend until the apples are finely pureed (there will still be some texture).
4. Place a fine strainer over a medium bowl. Strain the mixture into the bowl. Discard the solids.
5. Stir the mixture well and transfer to an ice cream machine. Process according to the manufacturer's instructions.

Chocolate-Cherry Sherbet

I like to make this for my kids' birthday parties. It's my version of Ben & Jerry's Cherry Garcia; theirs combines vanilla ice cream with cherries and chocolate chunks, and mine starts with an intense bittersweet-chocolate sherbet. The dried cherries play very well with the taste of the chocolate and the kids love the mini chocolate chips.

MAKES ABOUT 1¼ QUARTS

- **¾ cup whole milk**
- **¾ cup sugar**
- **8 ounces bittersweet (60% cacao) chocolate, cut into small pieces**
- **⅔ cup unsweetened cocoa powder**
- **½ teaspoon coarse salt**
- **¼ cup light corn syrup**
- **1 cup dried cherries, plumped in boiling water (page 22) and drained**
- **½ cup mini semisweet chocolate chips**

1. Prepare an ice bath by filling a large bowl or tub with ice and water.
2. In a medium saucepan, combine 1½ cups water, the milk, sugar, chopped chocolate, cocoa powder, and salt. Bring to a simmer over medium heat, whisking to blend and melt the chocolate.
3. Place a fine strainer over a medium bowl. Strain the mixture into the bowl and chill completely in the ice bath. Stir in the corn syrup. Gently fold in the cherries and the chocolate chips.
4. Stir the mixture well and transfer to an ice cream machine. Process according to the manufacturer's instructions.

Ice Cream Machines

There are various styles of ice cream makers to choose from. I recommend one of two types of electric machines. The less expensive of the two comprises a double-walled insulated canister, which contains, between the walls, a solution that freezes below the freezing point of water. The canister is placed in the freezer overnight. Once chilled, the canister is fitted with a paddle. The ice cream mixture is poured into the canister, the canister is fit into a base with an electric motor, and the motor turns the paddle to churn the ice cream. (You can also buy a nonelectric machine that works by the same system, but the paddle must be turned periodically by hand.) The more expensive type of machine has a built-in compressor and has no canister to chill. The ice cream mixture is poured directly into the bowl of the machine.

Lemon-Buttermilk Sherbet

Bright and pleasantly sour with lemon, this is an incredibly refreshing summer dessert. The buttermilk adds extra sour zing and a little richness. This sherbet is delicious as is, but for a more special presentation, add macerated raspberries, buttery Citrus-Glazed Sablé cookies (page 89), or your favorite store-bought butter cookie. Its sourness makes this sherbet one of my favorites, but it's still a bit tart for my young children's palates.

MAKES ABOUT 1¼ QUARTS

1½ cups sugar

Zest of 2 lemons, stripped off with a vegetable peeler

½ cup freshly squeezed lemon juice (from 3 to 4 lemons)

½ teaspoon coarse salt

1 quart buttermilk

¼ cup light corn syrup

1. Prepare an ice bath by filling a large bowl or tub with ice and water.
2. In a small saucepan, combine the sugar, lemon zest and juice, and salt. Bring to a simmer over medium heat, whisking to blend and dissolve the sugar.
3. Place a fine strainer over a medium bowl. Strain the mixture into the bowl and chill completely in the ice bath. Stir in the buttermilk and corn syrup.
4. Stir the mixture well and transfer to an ice cream machine. Process according to the manufacturer's instructions.

8
Tarts, Quiches, Pastas, and More

Baked Ziti with Summer Vegetables

Classic Onion Tart

Asparagus Tart with Herbed Béchamel and Gruyère

Potato, Leek, and Shrimp Galette

Red Pepper, Fennel, and Salmon Quiche

Tomato, Smoked Mozzarella, and Pesto Pizzette

Red Pepper and Tomato Pissaladière

Spinach and Feta Turnovers

Escarole Pie

Ratatouille Hand Pies

Baked Quesadillas with Corn, Chicken, and Jalapeños

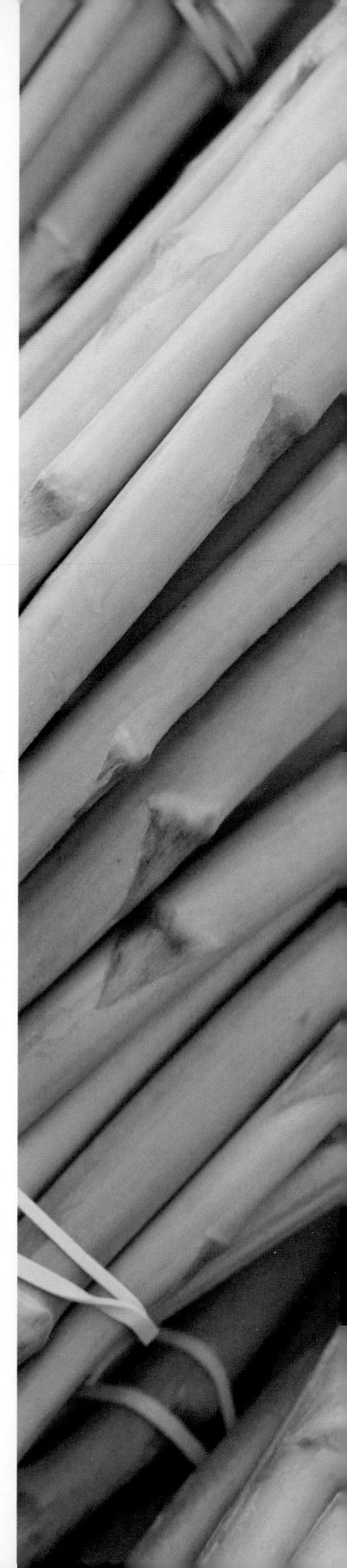

I grew up eating savory pies. One of my favorites was my grandmother Julia's Escarole Pie (page 250) flavored with garlic and Parmesan cheese. It was a welcome snack during the family's annual Fourth of July beach picnic at my uncle's house on the Long Island Sound. My grandmother cut the pie into neat squares and handed it out in the afternoon to keep us going until the big outdoor barbecue at the end of the day.

Tarts, pies, and quiches are a practical way to feed a crowd. They're also a terrific opportunity to take advantage of fresh vegetables in season. Choose whatever looks good at the farmers' market or in the produce section of the supermarket. Leftover cooked vegetables also make an excellent base for these delicious savory items.

I don't remember balking at vegetables as a kid. My sons, Nik and Peter, have always been robust eaters. My daughter Nola is more particular. But a cheesy quiche or a crisp hand pie will usually encourage her to try new things. Just don't ask her to eat a fresh tomato.

I hope the variation and versatility of the savory pies, quiches, and turnovers in this chapter inspire you. Many of these recipes were developed as hors d'oeuvres in the catering division of the SoNo Baking Company but they also make great dinner food at home. Asparagus Tart with Herbed Béchamel and Gruyère (page 239), for example, made with a rectangle of store-bought puff pastry, can be cut into elegant bite-size squares for parties or large squares for dinner. Potato, Leek, and Shrimp Galette (page 241) is an unusual style of pie baked in a crisp free-form round of cornmeal pastry. Red Pepper and Tomato Pissaladière (page 247) and my grandmother's escarole pie are rustic items made with pizza dough—homemade or store-bought, it's your choice. Kids love hand pies, almost regardless of the filling.

The smooth, rich custard in the Red Pepper, Fennel, and Salmon Quiche (page 242) is my standard quiche mixture. Vary it with any vegetable, cheese, seafood, meat, or poultry you like. Remember that all the ingredients must be completely cooked through before combining with the custard. They won't cook further in the oven.

I've included recipes for two other family favorites in this chapter: hearty Baked Ziti with Summer Vegetables (page 234) and cheesy Baked Quesadillas with Corn, Chicken, and Jalapeños (page 255). Both are big hits with my kids and I hope they will be with yours, too.

Before I worked at Martha Stewart Living Omnimedia, I wasn't an advocate of freezing. At the bakery, I'm still not. But Martha demonstrated the practicality of freezing for the home cook. Next time you make a pie or tart, roll and line a second pie shell. Wrap it well in plastic and freeze it. It doesn't take long to put together a filling and with a soup and/or green salad, you're set for dinner. With the exception of the quesadillas, which are best served hot, all of these dishes may be served warm or at room temperature.

Baked Ziti with Summer Vegetables

Baked ziti was a typical dish that my grandmother Julia made on Sundays for friends and family (the comarra, *in Italian, pronounced "gou-mah-dah" in my family's southern Italian dialect). She often sent a couple of trays home with us to get my dad through the week. All he had to do was reheat. My grandmother layered the pasta with tomato sauce and ricotta, mozzarella, and Parmesan cheeses. I've enriched the dish for my own family with roasted eggplant and squash. This was one of Nik's favorite dishes growing up. And Nola, who doesn't like tomatoes, doesn't notice them here. Baked ziti is an easy dish to make in bulk. Prepare two and stash one in the freezer for the* comarra.

SERVES 8 TO 10

- **1¼ pounds eggplant, cut into ¾-inch dice**
- **12 ounces yellow squash, cut into ¾-inch dice**
- **12 ounces zucchini, cut into ¾-inch dice**
- **¼ cup olive oil**
- **Coarse salt**

Tomato Sauce

- **3 medium garlic cloves**
- **1½ tablespoons coarse salt**
- **2 tablespoons olive oil**
- **1 medium onion, diced**
- **2 tablespoons sugar**
- **2 (28-ounce) cans crushed tomatoes in thick puree**
- **1 pound ziti**

- **1½ pounds ricotta cheese**
- **1 cup grated Parmesan cheese**
- **2 cups grated mozzarella cheese**

1. Set the oven rack in the lower third of the oven. Preheat the oven to 450°F.

2. Put the eggplant, yellow squash, and zucchini into a large bowl. Add the oil and 1 tablespoon salt. Spread in an even layer on a baking sheet and roast, stirring once, until the vegetables are tender and caramelized, about 40 minutes; set aside. Reduce the oven heat to 325°F.

3. To make the sauce: Slice the garlic on a cutting board. Add the salt and chop until the garlic is minced; the salt helps break down the garlic. In a large saucepan, add the oil, onion, and garlic mixture. Cook over medium-low heat, stirring often, until the onion is soft and translucent, about 5 minutes. Stir in the sugar. Add the tomatoes with the puree, rinsing out each can with a couple of tablespoons of water (about ¼ cup total) to catch all the tomato. Simmer, uncovered, until the sauce is slightly reduced and the taste of raw tomato is cooked out, 20 to 25 minutes; set aside.

4. Bring a large pot of heavily salted water to a boil for the pasta. Add the ziti and cook 2 minutes less than the package instructions; drain and rinse under cold running water to keep the pasta from clumping. Rinse and dry the pot; set aside.

5. Rub a 9 by 13-inch baking dish with oil. In a medium bowl, stir together the ricotta cheese and ½ cup of the Parmesan. In a large bowl, toss the ziti with 1 cup of the tomato sauce to coat.

recipe continues

TIP For the tomato sauce, starting the garlic and onion in oil at room temperature prevents scorching. Sugar balances the acidity of the tomato.

6 Spread 1 cup of the tomato sauce over the bottom of the baking dish. Add half of the ziti, using a rubber spatula to even it out. Sprinkle with half of the roasted vegetables. Dot with half of the ricotta mixture. Sprinkle with 1 cup of the mozzarella and ¼ cup of the Parmesan. Spread with 1 more cup sauce. Add the rest of the pasta and even the surface with the spatula. Sprinkle with the rest of the vegetables. Dot with the rest of the ricotta mixture. Spread with 2 more cups of the tomato sauce and sprinkle with the remaining 1 cup of mozzarella, and ¼ cup of Parmesan.

7 Place on a baking sheet and bake, uncovered, until the cheeses are melted and the interior is hot, 1 hour to 1 hour 10 minutes. Let stand for 20 minutes before serving. Heat the remaining tomato sauce in a small saucepan and serve on the side.

Classic Onion Tart

This classic Paris bistro tart is all about the onions. Long, slow cooking develops a sweet caramelized flavor that is highlighted by salty, smoky bacon. It is distinguished from its famous cousin, Quiche Lorraine, by the absence of cheese and by a minimal amount of custard. Serve this with a salad of soft lettuces such as Bibb and Boston.

MAKES ONE 9½- OR 10-INCH TART; SERVES 8 TO 10

- **4 ounces bacon (preferably thick-cut slab), cut into ⅓- to ½-inch dice (about ⅓ cup)**
- **2 tablespoons unsalted butter**
- **4 large onions (3¾ pounds), thinly sliced**
- **Coarse salt and freshly ground black pepper**
- **1 teaspoon chopped fresh thyme**
- **2 tablespoons all-purpose flour**
- **½ recipe Pâte Brisée (page 110), chilled**
- **2 large eggs**
- **1 large egg yolk**
- **½ cup heavy cream**
- **⅛ teaspoon grated nutmeg**

TIP When cooking onions, if you notice a lot of brown caramelization building up in the bottom of the pan, add about 1 tablespoon water to the pan. Do this as necessary throughout the cooking. This will prevent the bottom of the pan from burning and will allow for maximum caramelization.

1 Cook the bacon in a Dutch oven over medium-low heat until the fat is rendered and the bacon is lightly browned, about 8 minutes. Remove the bacon with a slotted spoon; set aside. Discard the bacon fat. Add the butter to the pan and melt. Add the onions, 1½ teaspoons salt, and ¼ teaspoon pepper. Cook, stirring, until the onions are very soft, sweet, and lightly browned, about 1 hour. Reduce the heat if the onions begin to stick. Stir in the thyme, flour, and bacon. Transfer to a large bowl and let cool completely, at least 30 minutes.

2 On a lightly floured work surface, roll dough to a 12½- to 13-inch round, about ⅛ inch thick. Fit dough into a 9½- to 10-inch-round, 1½-inch-deep tart pan with a removable bottom (or ceramic tart pan) and trim dough so that it comes slightly above the rim of the tart pan. The dough will just fit, with little or no excess. Chill in the refrigerator until firm, about 30 minutes.

3 Set the oven rack in the lower third of the oven. Preheat the oven to 450°F.

4 In a medium bowl, whisk the eggs and egg yolk to combine. Add the cream, nutmeg, ½ teaspoon salt, and ¼ teaspoon pepper and whisk to blend.

5 Place the chilled tart shell on a baking sheet. Spread the cooled onion mixture over the bottom; do not pack it down. Place the baking sheet in the oven, and carefully pour the custard mixture into the tart shell. Reduce the oven temperature to 425°F. Bake until the crust is golden brown and the custard is just set (a knife inserted into the center of the tart will come out clean), 40 to 45 minutes.

6 Let cool on a wire rack for at least 10 minutes.

Asparagus Tart with Herbed Béchamel and Gruyère

Peter, my younger son, is such a big fan of asparagus that I dream up ways to serve it as often as I can when it comes into season in the spring. This rectangular tart is an elegant and unusual way to enjoy asparagus. Serve it for dinner, as part of a brunch buffet, or as a first course for a party. Cut into small squares, it makes an attractive party hors d'oeuvre. Swap out the Gruyère cheese with a white Cheddar or fontina, if you like.

SERVES 6

Béchamel Sauce

- **½ tablespoon unsalted butter, plus extra for dotting**
- **2¼ teaspoons all-purpose flour**
- **½ cup whole milk**
- **Coarse salt and freshly ground black pepper**
- **Pinch of grated nutmeg**
- **½ teaspoon chopped fresh thyme, or ¼ teaspoon dried**
- **¼ cup (about ¾ ounce) grated Gruyère, white Cheddar, or fontina cheese**

- **Coarse salt**
- **1 bunch medium asparagus, trimmed to 6-inch stalks**
- **1 sheet good-quality store-bought puff pastry such as Dufour brand, thawed, if necessary, in the refrigerator**
- **1 large egg beaten with a pinch of coarse salt, for egg wash**
- **¾ cup (about 2¾ ounces) grated Gruyère cheese**

1 To make the béchamel sauce: Melt the butter in a medium heavy-bottomed saucepan. Whisk in the flour and cook, stirring constantly, until the paste cooks and bubbles a bit, about 2 minutes. Do not allow the paste to brown. Whisk in the milk. Bring to a boil, whisking constantly as the sauce thickens. Add ¼ teaspoon salt, ⅛ teaspoon pepper, the nutmeg, and the thyme. Reduce the heat and cook, whisking constantly, for 1 minute. Stir in the grated cheese. Remove the sauce from the heat. Dot with butter to prevent a skin from forming and let cool.

2 Meanwhile, bring a large sauté pan of salted water to a boil. Add the trimmed asparagus and cook until just tender, 8 to 9 minutes. Drain and cool under cold running water; set aside.

3 Line a baking sheet with parchment paper or a nonstick silicone baking mat. On a lightly floured work surface, gently roll the puff pastry sheet to an 11 by 14-inch rectangle, ⅛ inch thick. With a ruler and a pizza cutter, trim to an 8 by 12-inch rectangle. Place on the prepared baking sheet. Score a 1-inch border on all four sides, stopping 1 inch short of each corner so that a 6 by 10-inch rectangle is marked inside the larger rectangle of dough.

4 Set the oven rack in the lower third of the oven. Preheat the oven to 425°F.

recipe continues

5 Brush the pastry borders with egg wash. Spread the béchamel over the inner rectangle of pastry. (Do not allow the béchamel to cover the score marks or border; it will hinder the pastry from rising.) Arrange the asparagus evenly over the top in a single layer, ¼ to ½ inch apart, completely covering the béchamel. Sprinkle the grated cheese evenly over the top.

6 Bake, rotating the baking sheet about two-thirds of the way through the baking time, until the pastry is golden brown and puffed and the cheese is melted and bubbly, 20 to 25 minutes.

7 Let cool on a wire rack for 10 minutes before serving. Cut crosswise into eight equal pieces, or into 12 squares for hors d'oeuvres.

Potato, Leek, and Shrimp Galette

A galette (also called a crostata in Italy) is a round free-form pastry baked on a baking sheet. The combination of potato and leek is classic and appeals to my love of French cuisine. It tastes delicious with the shrimp, which contribute a beautiful pink color to the mix. I like to use small fingerling potatoes for this. The skin is thin enough that the potatoes needn't be peeled and the flesh is smooth and tender. The topping of sliced potatoes protects the shrimp from drying out while it steams in the fragrant juices from the leeks. My son Peter plucks the shrimp out first, then eats the rest of the galette. Serve this warm any time of the year.

MAKES ONE 7- TO 8-INCH GALETTE; SERVES 8

- **½ pound fingerling potatoes, washed but not peeled**
- **Coarse salt and freshly ground black pepper**
- **2 tablespoons olive oil**
- **1 leek, trimmed of dark green parts, split in half lengthwise, cut crosswise ¼ inch thick, and rinsed thoroughly**
- **1 teaspoon chopped fresh dill**
- **1 tablespoon all-purpose flour**
- **½ recipe Cornmeal Pastry Dough (page 126), chilled**
- **1 pound medium shrimp, peeled, deveined, rinsed, and patted dry**
- **1 large egg beaten with a pinch of coarse salt, for egg wash**

1. In a medium saucepan, cover the potatoes with cold salted water. Bring to a simmer and cook until just tender, about 20 minutes. Drain; let cool. Cut lengthwise into ¼-inch-thick slices; set aside.
2. In a small skillet, heat 1 tablespoon of the olive oil over medium heat. Add the chopped leek, ¼ teaspoon salt, and a pinch of pepper. Cook, stirring, until softened, 5 to 7 minutes. Stir in the dill and the flour; set aside to cool.
3. Set the oven rack in the lower third of the oven. Preheat the oven to 425°F. Line a baking sheet with parchment paper or a nonstick silicone baking mat.
4. On a lightly floured work surface, roll out the dough to ⅛ inch thick, and cut a 12-inch round with a pizza cutter. Place on the prepared baking sheet. Spread the cooled leeks over the center of the dough, allowing a 2- to 2½-inch border. Arrange the shrimp on top of the leeks. Cover with the potato slices. Sprinkle with ⅛ teaspoon salt and a big pinch of pepper. Drizzle with the remaining 1 tablespoon of olive oil. Fold the edges of the dough in toward the center to make a 2-inch border of dough all around. Brush the dough with egg wash.
5. Bake the galette for 20 minutes. Reduce the oven temperature to 375°F. Rotate the baking sheet and continue baking until the crust is golden brown and the shrimp are cooked through, 25 to 30 more minutes.
6. Let cool on a wire rack for 10 minutes before serving.

Red Pepper, Fennel, and Salmon Quiche

I love the sweet anise taste of fresh fennel. It's particularly delicious sautéed with red bell pepper strips and paired with fresh salmon in this Mediterranean-inspired quiche. I'll sometimes vary this recipe for Peter by substituting half a bunch of medium asparagus for the fennel and red pepper. Use the top third of the asparagus only, and cut into 1-inch pieces. Cook in boiling salted water until tender, one to two minutes; drain and cool under cold running water. Layer the asparagus into the tart in step 7 in place of the cooked vegetables. Add the rest of the cheese and the custard mixture and bake as in the recipe below.

MAKES ONE 9½- OR 10-INCH QUICHE; SERVES 8 TO 10

Fennel-Seed Pâte à Foncer

- 1 teaspoon fennel seeds
- 1 large egg yolk
- ¼ cup ice water (see page 110)
- 2 cups all-purpose flour
- 1 tablespoon sugar
- 2 teaspoons coarse salt
- ½ cup (1 stick) cold unsalted butter

- ½ pound boneless, skinless salmon fillet, ¾ to 1 inch thick
- 2 teaspoons plus 2 tablespoons olive oil
- Coarse salt and freshly ground black pepper
- 2 red bell peppers, stemmed, cored, seeded, and thinly sliced
- 2 medium fennel bulbs, trimmed, quartered lengthwise, cored, and thinly sliced
- 4 large eggs
- 2 large egg yolks
- 1 cup whole milk
- 1 cup heavy cream
- 2 tablespoons chopped flat-leaf parsley
- ⅔ cup (about 3 ounces) grated fontina cheese

1 To make the pastry: Put the fennel seeds in a resealable plastic bag and crush with a rolling pin. Then follow the directions for making a standard Pâte à Foncer (page 118), but add the crushed fennel seeds to the bowl of the food processor with the flour, sugar, and salt, then add the butter and the egg mixture. Chill for 30 minutes.

2 On a lightly floured work surface, roll the dough to a 12½- to 13-inch round, about ⅛ inch thick. Fit the dough into a 1½-inch-deep, 9½- to 10-inch round ceramic baking dish or tart pan with a removable bottom and trim the dough so that it comes slightly above the rim of the tart pan. The dough will just fit, with little or no excess. Chill in the refrigerator until firm, about 30 minutes.

3 Set the oven rack in the lower third of the oven. Preheat the oven to 450°F.

4 Rub the salmon with 2 teaspoons of the olive oil and sprinkle with ¼ teaspoon salt and ¼ teaspoon pepper. Roast on an oiled baking sheet until the salmon flakes easily with a fork and is no longer translucent in the center, 10 to 12 minutes. Let cool. Leave the oven on.

5 Meanwhile, in a large sauté pan, heat the remaining 2 tablespoons of oil over medium-low heat. Add the bell pepper and fennel slices, season with 1½ teaspoons salt and ¼ teaspoon pepper, and cook until tender, 15 to 20 minutes. Reduce the heat to low if the vegetables begin to brown. Let cool.

6 In a medium bowl, whisk the eggs and egg yolks to combine. Add the milk and cream and whisk to blend. Whisk in the parsley and season with 1 teaspoon salt and ¼ teaspoon pepper.

7 Place the chilled tart shell on a baking sheet. Break up the salmon in large flakes over the bottom. Sprinkle with about half of the grated cheese. Add the cooked vegetables in an even layer. Place the baking sheet in the oven, and carefully pour the custard mixture into the tart shell. Evenly sprinkle with the remaining cheese. Reduce the oven temperature to 425°F. Bake, rotating the baking sheet about two-thirds of the way through the baking time, until the crust is golden brown and the custard is just set (a knife inserted into the center of the pie will come out clean), 40 to 45 minutes.

8 Let cool on a wire rack for at least 10 minutes.

Tomato, Smoked Mozzarella, and Pesto Pizzette

Late August through September, the air at Connecticut farmers' markets is heavy with the spicy scent of basil. And wherever you look it's tomatoes and more tomatoes—all sizes, shapes, and colors. The farmer across from us at Wooster Square in New Haven showcases eight varieties of heirloom tomatoes with names like Striped German, Brandy Wine, and Eva Purple Ball. When tomatoes are so ripe and gorgeous, I want to treat them minimally. This tart embellishes them with a smear of pesto and a light sprinkle of smoked mozzarella—nothing to get in the way of that fabulous meaty tomato flavor. If you have a pizza stone, preheat it in the oven and bake the tart on top of it to help cook the bottom of the crust.

MAKES ONE 9-INCH TART; SERVES 6 TO 8

- **½ recipe Pâte Brisée (page 110), chilled**
- **2 tablespoons pesto, store-bought**
- **1 to 2 large, ripe red or yellow beefsteak tomatoes, cored and sliced ¼ inch thick**
- **½ cup (2½ ounces) grated smoked mozzarella cheese**
- **1 tablespoon olive oil, plus more for drizzling**
- **Freshly ground black pepper**
- **5 fresh basil leaves, cut into thin strips, for garnish**

1 On a lightly floured work surface, roll out the dough to a 12-inch round about ⅛ inch thick. Fit it into a 9-inch fluted tart pan with a removable bottom and trim the dough so that it comes slightly above the rim of the pan. Then press the excess dough against the sharp edge of the rim with your fingers to cut it level with the pan. Chill until firm, about 30 minutes.

2 Set the oven rack in the lower third of the oven. Preheat the oven to 425°F.

3 Spread the bottom of the tart shell with the pesto. Shingle the tomato slices over the pesto in a circle, overlapping the edges by about ½ inch. Place one slice in the center. Sprinkle all over with the mozzarella. Drizzle with the olive oil and sprinkle with ¼ teaspoon pepper.

4 Bake on a sheet pan until the crust is golden brown, the cheese is melted, and the tomatoes are soft but still hold their shape, 25 to 30 minutes. Let cool for 15 minutes on a wire rack. Sprinkle with the slivered basil and drizzle with olive oil. Serve warm or at room temperature.

Red Pepper and Tomato Pissaladière

A pissaladière is a robust pizza from southern France. It's traditionally topped with onions, Niçoise olives, and anchovies. I add bell pepper and tomatoes because I love the combination. My kids like the bell pepper, but not the anchovies, so I omit anchovies on half the pizza. Because this pizza relies on plum tomatoes it's a great year-round lunch or dinner option. Make your own olive dough, or knead one cup of olives into one pound of store-bought pizza dough. Serve with a green salad.

SERVES 12

Olive Dough

- **¾ cup warm water**
- **½ teaspoon sugar**
- **1 teaspoon active dry yeast**
- **1¾ cups all-purpose flour, plus extra for kneading**
- **1 teaspoon coarse salt**
- **1 tablespoon olive oil**
- **1 cup pitted Niçoise olives**

Topping

- **2 pounds ripe plum tomatoes**
- **¼ cup olive oil**
- **1 tablespoon chopped garlic (about 2 cloves)**
- **½ teaspoon crushed red pepper flakes**
- **1 large onion, thinly sliced**
- **Coarse salt**
- **1 red bell pepper, stemmed, cored, seeded, and thinly sliced**
- **1 yellow bell pepper, stemmed, cored, seeded, and thinly sliced**
- **Two (2-ounce) containers anchovies preserved in oil, drained (24 halves)**
- **12 Niçoise olives, pitted**
- **¼ cup chopped flat-leaf parsley (optional)**

1 To make the dough: In a small bowl, combine ¼ cup of the warm water, the sugar, and the yeast and let stand until frothy, about 5 minutes. In a large bowl, stir together the flour and salt. When the yeast has proofed, add it to the flour mixture along with the remaining ½ cup of warm water and the oil, and stir together.

2 Turn the dough out onto a lightly floured surface and knead by successively scooping the dough up from underneath with a metal or plastic bench scraper and pressing down with the palm of the other hand. As the gluten develops, the flour absorbs moisture; as you work it, the dough will pull together into a ball and become less tacky. Knead for 5 to 7 minutes, or until the dough is smooth, springy, and still a little tacky. (Avoid adding flour.) Knead in the olives.

3 Place the dough into a large, lightly oiled bowl. Turn the dough to coat with the oil, cover with oiled plastic wrap, and let stand for about 1½ hours, or until the volume increases by 1½ to 2 times.

4 Lightly oil a baking sheet. Turn the dough out onto the sheet and press it out to cover the surface. Press against the side of the baking sheet to make a lip. Prick the dough all over with a fork. Cover with plastic wrap and set aside in a warm place (at least 70°F) to rise until puffy, 30 to 40 minutes.

recipe continues

5 Meanwhile, to make the topping: Cut the tomatoes in quarters lengthwise. Using a spoon, scoop out and discard the pulp and seeds. Cut the meat of the tomato lengthwise into thin strips; set aside.

6 In a large sauté pan, heat the olive oil over medium-low heat. Add the garlic and red pepper flakes and cook until fragrant, about 2 minutes. Add the onion and ¾ teaspoon salt. Cook until the onion is wilted, 7 to 10 minutes. Add the red and yellow bell peppers and ½ teaspoon salt and cook until the peppers are wilted and lightly browned, 12 to 15 minutes. Add the tomatoes and cook until all of the vegetables are soft but the tomatoes still hold their shape, 5 to 7 more minutes. Let cool completely to room temperature.

7 Set the oven rack in the lower third of the oven. Preheat the oven to 425°F.

8 Strew the vegetable mixture loosely over the tart dough as if you were making a pizza (do not press it down). Crisscross the anchovies on top of the vegetables (three X's across, by four X's down) and place an olive at the center of each crossing. The dough will deflate, so cover it with plastic wrap and let it rise again until puffy, 15 to 20 minutes.

9 Bake, rotating the pan about two-thirds of the way through the baking time, until the crust is crisp and golden brown, 35 to 40 minutes. Remove from the oven and immediately slide the tart off the pan onto a wire rack. Sprinkle all over with the parsley, if you like. Cut into 12 squares and serve warm or at room temperature.

Spinach and Feta Turnovers

My kids love foods they can pick up and eat with their hands. So although Nik is the only one of my kids who is fond of spinach on its own, everybody is happy to eat it when it's mixed with feta cheese and folded into turnovers.

MAKES 12 TURNOVERS

Oregano Pâte Brisée

- **2¼ cups all-purpose flour**
- **2 teaspoons sugar**
- **1 teaspoon coarse salt**
- **2 teaspoons coarsely chopped fresh oregano or marjoram**
- **1 cup (2 sticks) cold unsalted butter, cut into small pieces**
- **¼ cup ice water (see page 110)**

- **2 pounds baby spinach**
- **Coarse salt and freshly ground black pepper**
- **1⅓ cups (about 7 ounces) crumbled feta cheese**
- **1 egg beaten with a pinch of coarse salt, for egg wash**

TIP Make sure to squeeze out the spinach very well so that it doesn't soak the pastry.

1 To make the pastry dough: Follow the directions for making a standard Pâte Brisée (page 110), but pulse the chopped oregano into the flour, sugar, and salt mixture, then add the butter and ice water. Chill for 30 minutes.

2 Put the spinach in a large pot and sprinkle with 2 teaspoons salt. Cover and place over medium-low heat. Cook, stirring halfway through the cooking time, until wilted, 8 to 10 minutes. Drain well in a colander, pressing with the back of a spoon to remove liquid. Let cool, then squeeze between your hands to remove more water. Transfer to a medium bowl and fold in feta with a rubber spatula. Season with ¼ teaspoon pepper.

3 Set the oven rack in the lower third of the oven. Preheat the oven to 425°F. Line a baking sheet with parchment or a nonstick silicone baking mat; set aside.

4 On a lightly floured work surface, roll out one disk of the dough to an 11 by 16-inch rectangle, about ⅛ inch thick. With a large knife, trim to a 10 by 15-inch rectangle. Use a pizza cutter and a ruler to cut six 5-inch squares. Brush 2 adjacent edges of each square with egg wash. Divide the filling among the 12 pastry squares, placing it into the center of each square. Pick up the 2 dough edges that have not been egg-washed, and fold the dough diagonally over the filling to form a triangle. Press to seal. Crimp the edges using the floured tines of a fork. Place on the prepared baking sheet. Brush all over with egg wash. Sprinkle the tops with a pinch of coarse salt, and cut vents with the points of kitchen scissors to allow the steam to escape.

5 Bake until the turnovers are golden brown and crisp, 20 to 25 minutes. Remove to a wire rack to cool for 10 minutes.

6 Repeat to cut, fill, and bake the remaining 6 turnovers.

Escarole Pie

This classic, southern Italian double-crust pie is one of my grandmother Julia's recipes. Baked between two thin, crisp layers of pizza dough, the delicious bitter flavor of the escarole is balanced by the sweet raisins, the savory, salty Parmesan, and the heat of the pepper. This is spicy; if you like a milder flavor, reduce the red pepper flakes to ¼ teaspoon. My grandmother made her pies in 9 by 13-inch Pyrex baking dishes that held six to seven heads of escarole each. My brothers and I went through that as a snack. For my family, I get by with about half the amount of escarole in a 9½-inch round pie dish. Make your own dough, or buy a one-pound bag of pre-made pizza dough at the supermarket.

MAKES ONE 9½-INCH PIE; SERVES 6

- **⅓ cup olive oil**
- **2 garlic cloves, thinly sliced**
- **½ teaspoon crushed red pepper flakes**
- **4 heads (about 4¼ pounds total) escarole, heads and tail ends trimmed, leaves cut into 1-inch pieces, washed well, and drained (page 27)**
- **Coarse salt**
- **1 cup grated Parmesan cheese (3 ounces)**
- **⅓ cup golden raisins**
- **Freshly ground black pepper**
- **½ recipe Pizza Dough (page 269), proofed, or 1 pound store-bought dough**
- **1 egg lightly beaten with a pinch of coarse salt, for egg wash**

1 Divide the oil, garlic, and red pepper flakes between two very large pots. Place over medium-low heat and cook, stirring often, until the garlic turns golden brown, 3 to 5 minutes. Add half the escarole and 1 teaspoon salt to each pot. Stir to coat with the oil. Raise the heat to high and cook, stirring often, until the escarole is soft and wilted, 10 to 15 minutes. The escarole will give off water. Drain well in a colander, pressing with the back of a spoon to get out every bit of liquid. Discard the liquid. Let cool, then squeeze the escarole between your hands to remove more water; transfer to a large bowl. With a rubber spatula, fold in the Parmesan, raisins, and ⅛ teaspoon black pepper.

2 Set the oven rack in the lower third of the oven. Preheat the oven to 375°F. Brush a 9½-inch Pyrex deep dish pie pan with olive oil.

3 Turn the dough out onto a lightly floured work surface and cut in half. Roll one half to a 12-inch round, about ⅛ inch thick, and fit it into the pie pan. There will be about 1 inch of overhang. Brush the edges with egg wash. Fill with the escarole mixture and smooth the top. Roll the second half of the dough ⅛ inch thick and cut a 1-inch hole in the center. (A pastry tip or small knife works well for this.) Set the dough round on top of the escarole. Trim the dough to within about ⅛ inch of the edge of the pie pan. Pinch the edges to seal.

4 Brush the top crust with egg wash. Bake on a baking sheet, rotating the sheet about two-thirds of the way through the baking time, until the pastry is cooked through and golden brown, top and bottom, 90 minutes. Let stand for 10 minutes on a wire rack before cutting, or cool completely and serve at room temperature.

Ratatouille Hand Pies

Ratatouille, a mellow Mediterranean stew starring eggplant, summer squash, tomato, and onion, is one of my all-time favorite vegetarian dishes. These vegetables were traditionally a late summer–early fall crop but most are available year-round now. I take full advantage of that fact to make these crisp hand pies as often as I can. Even people who don't like eggplant love these turnovers. As soon as I get them off the baking sheet, they magically disappear.

MAKES 24

- **6 tablespoons olive oil**
- **1 small eggplant, trimmed and cut into ⅓- to ½-inch dice**
- **Coarse salt**
- **1 zucchini, trimmed and cut into ⅓- to ½-inch dice**
- **1 yellow squash, trimmed and cut into ⅓- to ½-inch dice**
- **1 red bell pepper, stemmed, seeded, and cut into ⅓- to ½-inch dice**
- **1 cup diced (⅓- to ½-inch) onion (about 1 small onion)**
- **2 garlic cloves, minced**
- **1¼ cups seeded, diced tomatoes, or good-quality canned diced, drained tomatoes (from a 28-ounce can)**
- **2 teaspoons chopped fresh thyme**
- **1 bay leaf**
- **Freshly ground black pepper**
- **3 (14-ounce) sheets good-quality store-bought puff pastry such as Dufour brand, thawed 2 to 3 hours in the refrigerator, if frozen**
- **1 large egg beaten with a pinch of coarse salt, for egg wash**

1 Set the oven rack in the lower third of the oven. Preheat the oven to 350°F.

2 In a large skillet, heat 2 tablespoons of the olive oil over medium-high heat. Add the eggplant, sprinkle with ½ teaspoon salt, and cook until the eggplant begins to color, 4 to 5 minutes. Transfer to a rimmed baking sheet. Add 2 more tablespoons of oil to the pan. Add the zucchini and yellow squash and sprinkle with ½ teaspoon salt. Cook until the vegetables begin to color, about 5 minutes. Transfer to the baking sheet with the eggplant. Add the remaining 2 tablespoons of oil to the pan. Add the bell pepper, onion, garlic, diced tomatoes, and ½ teaspoon salt. Cook until the vegetables soften, about 4 minutes; transfer to the baking sheet.

3 Add the thyme, bay leaf, and ¼ teaspoon pepper and stir to blend. Cover with aluminum foil and bake for 20 minutes. Uncover and bake until the vegetables are very soft and the flavors have melded, 20 more minutes. Transfer to a large bowl and let cool completely to room temperature, about 30 minutes. Discard the bay leaf.

4 Preheat the oven to 425°F. Line two baking sheets with parchment paper or a nonstick silicone baking mat.

5 On a lightly floured work surface, roll out one sheet of dough to a 12 by 12-inch square, about ⅛ inch thick. Use a pizza cutter and a ruler to cut nine 4-inch squares. Brush 2 adjacent edges of each square with egg wash. Scoop 2 tablespoons of filling into the center of each square. Pick up the 2 dough edges that have

not been egg-washed, and fold the dough diagonally over the filling to form a triangle. Press to seal. Crimp the edges with the floured tines of a fork. Place on the prepared baking sheet. Brush all over with egg wash. Cut vents to allow the steam to escape.

6 Bake, rotating the sheet about two-thirds of the way through the baking time, until the turnovers are golden brown and crisp and the filling is beginning to bubble up through the vents, 16 to 18 minutes. Remove to a wire rack to cool for 10 minutes before serving.

7 Repeat to cut, fill, and bake the remaining 2 sheets of puff pastry, cutting only six squares from the third sheet (there will not be enough filling for more). If the dough gets too warm while you're working, chill for 5 minutes, then continue working. (Brush the leftover pastry with melted butter, sprinkle with cinnamon-sugar, cut into squares, and bake on an ungreased baking sheet at 425°F until puffed and golden, 10 to 12 minutes.)

TIP To seed fresh tomatoes, cut in half through the equator (rather than the stem end). Use a finger to scoop out the seeds and pulp; discard. Or squeeze each half, cut side down, over the sink to squeeze out the seeds and pulp.

Baked Quesadillas with Corn, Chicken, and Jalapeños

Although only in middle school, my daughter Nola is becoming a serious athlete. She plays lacrosse, field hockey, and softball and she's teaching her young brother to play lacrosse. With her after-school sports schedule, it's often difficult to make time for dinner. These quesadillas are quick and nourishing. I like the combination of roasted chicken, creamy avocado, and corn for the summer. But quesadillas are a terrific way to use up leftovers, anytime. Vary this recipe with pork, steak, or chicken, leftover cooked vegetables, and other cheeses such as sharp cheddar and fontina. Just make sure the vegetables are not too wet or they will soak the tortillas. Quesadillas are a good way to feed a variety of vegetables to kids.

SERVES 4 TO 6

- **2 tablespoons olive oil, plus extra for brushing**
- **½ cup chopped onion**
- **Coarse salt**
- **1 jalapeño pepper, ribs and seeds removed, chopped**
- **Kernels from 1 ear corn (page 26), or ½ cup frozen corn kernels**
- **2 teaspoons chopped fresh thyme**
- **Four 8-inch flour tortillas**
- **2 cups grated Monterey Jack cheese**
- **2 firmly packed cups (about 14 ounces) shredded roasted chicken breast**
- **1 ripe but firm avocado, halved, pitted, peeled (page 20), and cut into ½-inch cubes**
- **Sour cream, for serving**

1. In a medium skillet, add the olive oil, onion, and ½ teaspoon salt. Place over medium-low heat and cook until the onion is softened, 5 to 7 minutes. Add the jalapeño, corn kernels, and thyme and cook until the corn is warmed through, 6 to 8 minutes; set aside.
2. Set the oven rack in the lower third of the oven. Preheat the oven to 425°F. Coat a baking sheet with olive oil.
3. Generously brush 2 of the tortillas with olive oil. Invert the tortillas, oiled sides down, side by side on the prepared baking sheet. Sprinkle each with ½ cup grated cheese, then 1 cup of the shredded chicken, half of the corn mixture, half of the avocado, and ½ cup cheese. Top each with a second tortilla.
4. Cover the quesadillas with a sheet of parchment paper, then a baking sheet on top and a weight, such as a 5-pound bag of sugar for 10 minutes.
5. Remove the weight, baking sheet, and parchment. Brush the tortillas with oil. Bake, flipping the quesadillas about halfway through the baking time, until the cheese is melted and bubbling and the tortillas are lightly browned, 15 to 20 minutes. Cut into wedges and serve with the sour cream.

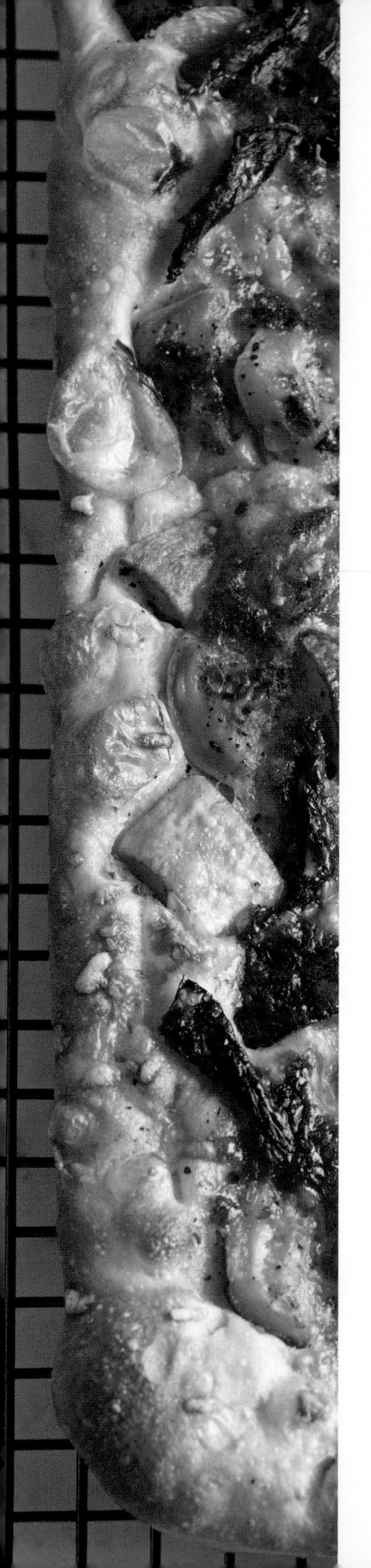

9

Focaccia and Pizza on the Grill

Friday night was pizza night in my family. We ate focaccia, too, although it was called "Sicilian pizza" in our neighborhood. Mario's Pizzeria, around the corner from our house, offered it alongside of their thin-crust Neapolitan-style pizza.

Pizza and focaccia are fantastic vehicles for fresh produce of all kinds, fruit included. I use them as an excuse to get my kids to try different vegetables and cheeses. For both pizza and focaccia, it's important to use low-moisture toppings so that the bread doesn't get soaked. Vegetables are roasted, then drained, to remove as much moisture as possible. Loaf mozzarella is better than fresh because it contains less water. But if you do use fresh mozzarella, press out some of the moisture as described on page 271.

Focaccia toppings can be as simple as a scattering of cooked onion (see page 260). I'm encouraging my younger children to appreciate roasted butternut squash (see page 266), but they still like green and yellow summer squash better. These mild-tasting squash are at their best paired with mozzarella, sun-dried tomatoes, and Grana Padano cheese (see page 264). Focaccia with Mushrooms and Fontina (page 258) remains an adult pleasure but both children like cherry-grape focaccia with cinnamon (see page 263) because the fruit topping turns the bread into a sweet, open-faced summer pie.

I still go out for pizza with my family. Nola and Peter always get the Santa Margherita, topped with fresh tomato and mozzarella. I order mine topped with arugula, thin-sliced prosciutto, and shaved Parmesan cheese (see page 274 for my "Salad Pizza" variation). But we have fun making pizza at home, too. Home ovens don't work as well as commercial ovens for pizza because they're not hot enough. Grilling is a great solution. I love the simplicity: no need for an oven, and you're working outside. For urbanites who may not have access to a grill, I've devised a method for cooking pizza in a 500°F oven on an inverted baking sheet to produce the best pizza I've ever tasted from a home oven.

I've included several of my family's favorite pizzas in this chapter, including two unusual dessert pizzas: Grilled Pizza with Mascarpone and Stone Fruit (page 273), and Grilled Pizza with Bananas, Nutella, and Chocolate (page 279). Each topping recipe yields enough for four pizzas and the recipes halve easily so that you can make two toppings and get two different pizzas out of one recipe of dough. I encourage you to mix and match: You can swap cheeses and herbs, and the focaccia toppings work well for pizzas. My kids love to help, particularly with the grilling, and especially when Nutella and chocolate are involved.

Over the years I've become adept at stretching the pizza dough between my hands to place on the grill. For this book, we came up with an easier technique. The dough is rolled into oblongs and placed on parchment sheets inverted onto the grill. You'll find it foolproof.

Focaccia with Mushrooms and Fontina

Of my children, only Nik has learned to appreciate the delicate, woodsy flavor of mushrooms. I love them, sautéed or roasted in olive oil with onions and fresh thyme. I search out different varieties at farmers' markets to serve as a side dish, or in omelets and quiches, and to top this sumptuous focaccia. White button, cremini, portobello, and shiitake mushrooms are almost always available in supermarkets these days, but if you come across other varieties wherever you shop, add them to the mix. I recommend Danish in lieu of Italian fontina because it's firmer and easier to grate.

MAKES APPROXIMATELY 1 DOZEN SQUARES

1 recipe Focaccia Dough (page 266)

½ cup olive oil, plus extra for the bowl

Topping

3 pounds assorted mushrooms such as button, cremini, shiitake, portobello, oyster, chanterelle, or hen of the woods, stems trimmed (shiitake stems removed)

5 tablespoons olive oil, plus extra for drizzling

Coarse salt and freshly ground black pepper

1½ medium onions, thinly sliced

6 ounces (about 1½ cups) grated Danish fontina cheese

1½ teaspoons chopped fresh thyme leaves

1 Make the focaccia dough through the first rise (step 2).

2 Set one oven rack in the lower third of the oven and a second rack in the center. Preheat the oven to 425°F.

3 To make the topping: Quarter or halve the mushrooms, depending on size, to yield 1-inch pieces. In a large bowl, toss the mushrooms with 3 tablespoons of the olive oil, 1½ teaspoons salt, and ¼ teaspoon pepper. Spread over two 17 by 12-inch rimmed baking sheets. Roast for 7 minutes. Divide the onion slices among the baking sheets, stir to combine, and continue roasting until the mushrooms are tender and the onions are caramelized, about 10 more minutes. Drain in a colander; set aside. Turn off the oven.

4 Wipe off one of the baking sheets and coat with nonstick cooking spray. Add the ½ cup olive oil. Use the plastic scraper to turn the dough out onto the oiled baking sheet. Flip the dough so that the oiled side is up. Press the dough out to the edges of the pan with your fingertips until the dough fills the baking sheet and is dimpled all over. If the dough contracts, set it aside for 10 minutes to relax, and try again. Cover with oiled plastic wrap and let rise until puffy and increased about 1½ times in bulk, 30 to 45 minutes.

5 Preheat the oven to 450°F.

6 Scatter the mushroom mixture over the dough. Sprinkle with the grated cheese, and the remaining 2 tablespoons of olive oil. The dough will have deflated somewhat; set aside to rise again for 20 minutes.

7 Bake in the lower third of the oven, rotating the sheet about two-thirds of the way through the baking time, until the focaccia is evenly golden on top and bottom, about 30 minutes. Immediately slide the focaccia onto a wire rack. Drizzle lightly with olive oil and sprinkle with the thyme. Cut into squares and serve warm or at room temperature.

Olive Focaccia with Caramelized Onions

This focaccia is similar to those I ate in Italy when I was learning to make focaccia there in the 1990s. I adapted the basic dough by adding olives. They're delicious against the natural sweetness of slow-cooked red onion and the rich, salty flavor of pecorino cheese. I recommend Greek Kalamata olives for this dough. Most supermarkets carry them, they're a substantial size, and they're already pitted. Large green ceriola olives would be delicious in this recipe, too. Basically, use anything you like except the canned black olives that your kids like to stick on the ends of their fingers.

MAKES TWO 8- OR 9-INCH ROUNDS; SERVES 6 TO 8

Olive Focaccia Dough

1¾ cups warm (105° to 110°F) water

1½ teaspoons active dry yeast

3½ cups plus 2 tablespoons all-purpose flour

1½ tablespoons coarse salt

¼ cup olive oil, plus extra for the bowl

½ cup (about 3 ounces) pitted, halved Kalamata olives

Topping

2 large onions, thinly sliced

5 tablespoons olive oil, plus extra for drizzling

Coarse salt and freshly ground black pepper

⅔ cup (about 2½ ounces) grated pecorino cheese

2 tablespoons chopped flat-leaf parsley

1 To make the dough: In a small bowl, combine ¼ cup of the warm water with the yeast and let proof for about 5 minutes.

2 In a large bowl, stir together the flour and salt and make a well in the center. When the yeast has proofed, pour it into the well along with 2 tablespoons of the oil and the remaining 1½ cups of warm water. Using a plastic pastry scraper, gradually pull the flour into the wet ingredients, folding to mix, until a very wet dough forms. Then knead the dough in the bowl for 5 minutes by folding the dough over on itself with the plastic pastry scraper while you turn the bowl. Gently knead in the olives. Scrape the dough out onto a clean work surface; wash and dry the bowl. Smear the bottom of the bowl with olive oil. Scrape up the dough with the plastic scraper, return it to the bowl, and turn to coat with the oil. Cover with an oiled sheet of plastic wrap. Let stand in a warm place (at least 70°F) for about 1½ hours, or until the volume increases by 1½ times.

3 Set the oven rack in the lower third of the oven. Preheat the oven to 425°F.

4 To make the topping: In a large bowl, toss the onions with 3 tablespoons of the olive oil, ½ teaspoon salt, and ¼ teaspoon pepper. Spread over a rimmed baking sheet and roast, tossing the onions halfway through, until the onions are soft, sweet, and beginning to brown, 15 to 20 minutes; set aside. Turn off the oven.

5 Use the plastic scraper to turn the dough out onto a lightly floured surface and to cut it in half.

6 Coat each of two 8- or 9-inch cake pans with nonstick cooking spray. Add 1 tablespoon of the remaining olive oil to each pan. Gently shape each piece of dough into a round. Put one piece of dough in each pan, smoothest side down, and coat with the oil. Turn the dough over so that the smooth side faces up. With your fingertips, push the dough out toward the edges of the cake pan, creating dimples and bubbles, until the dough fills the pan and is dimpled all over. If the dough contracts, set it aside for 10 minutes to allow it to rest, and try again. Cover with oiled plastic wrap and let rise until puffy and increased about 1½ times in bulk, 30 to 40 minutes.

7 Preheat the oven to 450°F.

8 Spread half of the onion topping over each focaccia round. Sprinkle each with ⅓ cup of the cheese. The dough will have deflated somewhat; set aside to rise again for 20 minutes.

9 Drizzle each focaccia with 1 tablespoon of the remaining oil. Bake, rotating the pans about two-thirds of the way through the baking time, until the focaccia is evenly golden on top and bottom, 30 to 35 minutes. Remove the focaccias from the pans with a knife or offset spatula and let cool on a wire rack. Sprinkle with the parsley and drizzle with more oil. Cut into wedges and serve warm or at room temperature.

Sweet Cinnamon Focaccia with Cherries and Grapes

I've been making a sweet, cinnamon-scented focaccia with dried fruit for years. It's a favorite with my kids, who clamor for it for breakfast. This is an adaptation of that recipe topped with fresh fruit and sanding sugar. It's a treat for breakfast but you may also like to make it for dessert as an open-faced fruit pie with a great, yeasty crust. The addition of sugar in the dough makes it softer and less crispy.

MAKES APPROXIMATELY 1 DOZEN SQUARES

- **1 recipe Focaccia Dough (page 266)**
- **½ cup granulated sugar**
- **1 teaspoon ground cinnamon**
- **½ cup olive oil**

Topping

- **1 cup pitted, halved fresh cherries**
- **1 cup halved fresh red grapes**
- **1 cup halved fresh green grapes**
- **2 tablespoons olive oil**
- **3 tablespoons sanding sugar**

1. Make the focaccia dough through the first rise (step 2), adding the granulated sugar and cinnamon to the dough with the flour and salt in step 2.
2. To make the topping: In a large bowl, toss the cherries and red and green grapes with the olive oil.
3. Coat a 17 by 12-inch rimmed baking sheet with nonstick cooking spray. Add the ½ cup of olive oil. Use a plastic scraper to turn the dough out onto the oiled baking sheet. Flip the dough so that the oiled side is up. Press the dough out to the edges of the pan with your fingertips until the dough fills the baking sheet and is dimpled all over. If the dough contracts, set it aside for 10 minutes to relax, and try again. Cover with oiled plastic wrap and let rise until puffy and increased about 1½ times in bulk, 30 to 45 minutes.
4. Set the oven rack in the lower third of the oven. Preheat the oven to 450°F.
5. Scatter the fruit over the dough and sprinkle with the sanding sugar. The dough will have deflated somewhat; set aside to rise again for 20 minutes.
6. Bake, rotating the sheet about two-thirds of the way through the baking time, until the focaccia is evenly golden on top and bottom, about 30 minutes. Immediately slide the focaccia onto a wire rack. Cut into squares and serve warm or at room temperature.

Cheese Focaccia with Summer Squash

In Connecticut, yellow and green squash (or zucchini) are plentiful during the summer months. Every food market carries them, including the farm stand down the road. A double roasting—once on a baking sheet and again on top of the focaccia—pulls out most of the water so you really taste the subtle sweet flavor of the squash (see photo, page 256). Grana Padano is a hard cow's-milk grating cheese, similar to Parmesan and often less expensive. Try it if you can find it. Otherwise, substitute Parmesan.

MAKES APPROXIMATELY 1 DOZEN SQUARES

1 recipe Focaccia Dough (page 266)

½ cup olive oil, plus extra for the bowl

Topping

½ cup (about 2 ounces) thinly sliced sun-dried tomatoes

2 large zucchini (about 1½ pounds), trimmed and cut into 1-inch cubes

2 large yellow squash (about 1½ pounds), trimmed and cut into 1-inch cubes

5 tablespoons olive oil, plus extra for drizzling

Coarse salt and freshly ground black pepper

1 tablespoon chopped marjoram or oregano

1 cup (4 ounces) grated loaf mozzarella cheese

½ cup (2 ounces) grated Grana Padano or Parmesan cheese

1 Make the focaccia dough through the first rise (step 2).

2 Set the oven rack in the lower third of the oven. Preheat the oven to 425°F.

3 To make the topping: Bring about 1 cup water to a boil. Pour it over the sun-dried tomatoes in a small heat-proof bowl and plump for 5 minutes. Drain; set aside.

4 In a large bowl, toss the zucchini and yellow squash with 3 tablespoons of the olive oil, 2 teaspoons salt, ¼ teaspoon pepper, and the marjoram. Transfer to a 17 by 12-inch rimmed baking sheet. Roast, tossing the squash with a spatula about halfway through the cooking, until tender, 20 to 25 minutes. Drain in a colander. Stir in the sun-dried tomatoes. Turn off the oven.

5 Wipe off the baking sheet and coat with nonstick cooking spray. Add ½ cup olive oil. Use a plastic scraper to turn the dough out onto the oiled baking sheet. Flip the dough so that the oiled side is up. Press the dough out to the edges of the pan with your fingertips until the dough fills the baking sheet and is dimpled all over. If the dough contracts, set it aside for 10 minutes to relax, and try again. Cover with oiled plastic wrap and let rise until puffy and increased about 1½ times in bulk, 30 to 45 minutes.

6 Preheat the oven to 450°F.

7 Scatter the squash mixture over the dough. Sprinkle with the grated mozzarella and Grana Padano cheeses. Drizzle with the remaining 2 tablespoons of oil. The dough will have deflated somewhat; set aside to rise again for 20 minutes.

8 Bake, rotating the sheet about two-thirds of the way through the baking time, until the focaccia is evenly golden on top and bottom, about 30 minutes. Immediately slide the focaccia onto a wire rack. Drizzle with oil. Cut into squares and serve warm or at room temperature.

Sun-Dried Tomatoes

I steep sun-dried tomatoes in boiling water for about 5 minutes to soften them and remove any added sugar. Sun-dried tomatoes are sold packaged in plastic or packed in olive oil. I prefer to buy them dried, then I steep them and marinate in my favorite good-quality olive oil with herbs and sometimes with capers.

Focaccia with Butternut Squash and Ricotta Salata

I perfected the art of making focaccia in Bologna during a two-week class with Margherita and Valeria Simili in the early 1990s. They were a real comedy act. One sister speaks English, the other only speaks Italian. I felt like I was back in the basement of my grandmother's house, where my aunt and her two sisters used to banter back and forth as they cooked, each insistent that hers was the correct recipe or method. The focaccia I learned to make in Italy were fairly simple—a sprinkle of herbs and coarse sea salt was standard. I adapted the techniques I learned there for this focaccia with sweet, caramelized roasted butternut squash. This makes a gorgeous fall supper served with a tossed green salad.

MAKES APPROXIMATELY 1 DOZEN SQUARES

Focaccia Dough

- **1¾ cups warm (105° to 110°F) water**
- **1½ teaspoons active dry yeast**
- **3½ cups plus 2 tablespoons all-purpose flour**
- **4½ teaspoons coarse salt**
- **2 tablespoons plus ½ cup olive oil**

Topping

- **1½ large butternut squash, halved lengthwise, seeded, peeled (page 29), and cut into 1-inch cubes (about 10 cups)**
- **5 tablespoons olive oil, plus extra for drizzling**
- **Coarse salt and freshly ground black pepper**
- **8 shallots, peeled and thickly sliced**
- **1 tablespoon chopped fresh sage, rosemary, or thyme**
- **6 ounces ricotta salata cheese, crumbled (about 1½ cups) or shaved with a vegetable peeler**

1 To make the dough: In a small bowl, combine ¼ cup of the warm water with the yeast and let proof for about 5 minutes.

2 In a very large bowl, stir together all the flour and salt and make a well in the center. When the yeast has proofed, pour it into the well along with the remaining 1½ cups water and 2 tablespoons of the oil, setting aside the remaining ½ cup of oil. Using a plastic pastry scraper, gradually pull the flour into the yeast mixture, folding to mix, until a very wet dough forms. Then knead the dough in the bowl for 5 minutes by folding the dough over itself with the plastic pastry scraper while you turn the bowl. Scrape the dough out onto a clean work surface; wash and dry the bowl. Smear the bottom of the bowl with olive oil. Scrape up the dough with the plastic scraper, return it to the bowl, and turn to coat with the oil. Cover with an oiled sheet of plastic wrap. Let stand in a warm place (at least 70°F) for about 1½ hours, or until the volume increases by 1½ times.

3 Set the oven rack in the lower third of the oven. Preheat the oven to 425°F.

4 To make the topping: Put the cubed squash in a large bowl. Add 3 tablespoons of the oil, 2 teaspoons salt, and ¼ teaspoon pepper and toss to coat the vegetables with the oil. Spread in an

recipe continues

even layer over two 17 by 12-inch rimmed baking sheets and roast for 15 minutes, stirring once about halfway through the roasting. Divide the shallots between the sheet pans and stir to combine. Continue roasting, stirring the mixture once during roasting, until the vegetables are tender and caramelized, 5 to 7 more minutes. Transfer to a large bowl or platter to cool. Turn off the oven.

5 Wipe off one of the baking sheets and spray with nonstick cooking spray. Add the reserved ½ cup of oil. Use the plastic scraper to turn the dough out onto the oiled baking sheet. Flip the dough so that the oiled side is up. Press the dough out to the edges of the pan with your fingertips until the dough fills the baking sheet and is dimpled all over. If the dough contracts, set it aside for 10 minutes to relax, and try again. Cover with oiled plastic wrap and let rise until puffy and increased about 1½ times in bulk, 30 to 45 minutes.

6 Preheat the oven to 450°F.

7 Scatter the squash mixture over the dough. Sprinkle with the sage. Drizzle with the remaining 2 tablespoons olive oil. The dough will have deflated somewhat; set it aside to rise again for 20 minutes.

8 Bake, rotating the sheet about two-thirds of the way through the baking time, until the focaccia is evenly golden on top and bottom, about 30 minutes. Immediately slide the focaccia onto a wire rack. Scatter the cheese over the top. Drizzle lightly with oil. Cut into squares and serve warm or at room temperature.

Grilled Pizza Margherita

I'm always amused that my daughter Nola, who won't touch a fresh tomato, shares her younger brother's penchant for this pizza. Whether we're at the neighborhood pizzeria or cooking in our backyard, this traditional red-sauce pizza with basil and fresh mozzarella cheese is their *pizza. I usually make half this topping recipe, enough for the two of them, and make a second topping for the adults. Everybody's happy. Use my tomato sauce or your favorite store-bought brand.*

MAKES 4 PIZZAS; SERVES 6 TO 8

Pizza Dough

- **2 packets rapid-rise active dry yeast or active dry yeast (1 tablespoon plus 2½ teaspoons)**
- **1½ cups warm water**
- **3 tablespoons olive oil, plus ½ cup for grilling and brushing**
- **4 cups all-purpose flour**
- **1 tablespoon coarse salt**

Topping

- **2 cups Tomato Sauce (page 234), or store-bought tomato sauce**
- **1 pound fresh mozzarella, torn into large, thin pieces by hand and weighted, or grated loaf mozzarella (see Tip, page 271)**
- **1 cup fresh basil leaves**
- **Coarse salt and freshly ground black pepper**

1 To make the dough: Combine the yeast and the warm water in a 2-cup measuring cup. Add 2½ tablespoons of the oil and let proof for about 5 minutes.

2 In the bowl of a food processor, combine the flour and salt and pulse to mix. Add the yeast mixture through the feed tube while pulsing and pulse until the dough comes together. Turn it out onto a lightly floured work surface. It comes out of the machine a little ragged, but as you knead it, it will come together very quickly. You want to get a nice rocking motion, folding the dough over and pushing it down, folding it over and pushing it down. Knead for 2 to 3 minutes, until the dough is smooth and satiny.

3 Put the remaining ½ tablespoon of oil in a large bowl. Put the dough in the bowl, smooth side down, and turn the dough in the bowl to coat with the oil. Cover with an oiled sheet of plastic wrap and let stand in a warm place (at least 70°F) for about 1 hour, or until the volume is increased by about 1½ times. Punch it down by folding the edges of the dough in toward the center. Use the dough immediately, or flip it over in the bowl, cover with plastic, and refrigerate.

4 When the dough has risen, light a gas or charcoal grill to medium (about 300°F). Line the backs of two baking sheets with parchment paper.

recipe continues

5 Turn the dough out onto a lightly floured work surface and cut into 4 pieces. Roll 2 pieces to 11 by 8-inch oblongs and place on the back of one of the parchment-lined baking sheets. Roll the remaining 2 pieces to 11 by 8-inch oblongs and place on the back of the second parchment-lined baking sheet. Let rest for a few minutes.

6 Brush the dough pieces with olive oil. Cover each pair with another sheet of parchment paper. Invert another baking sheet on top. Flip the baking sheets. Remove the top sheet pan and parchment. Brush the dough with olive oil (both sides of each will now be oiled). Cut each sheet of parchment down the middle, separating the dough pieces.

7 Pick up one piece of parchment by opposite corners and flip the dough onto one half of the grill. Peel off the parchment; discard. If your grill is large enough, repeat to flip a second piece of dough onto the grill; otherwise, grill one pizza at a time. Grill until lightly browned on the bottoms, 2 to 3 minutes. Flip with tongs; the crusts will be stiff. Grill until the crusts are lightly browned on the other side, 2 to 3 minutes. Remove with tongs to the back of the baking sheet. Repeat to grill the remaining crusts.

8 If using a gas grill, turn it to low (250°F). If using a charcoal grill, lower the heat by dispersing some of the coals to the edges of the grill. With a rubber spatula, spread the grilled crusts with tomato sauce to within about ½ inch of the edges. Top with a layer of mozzarella and scatter basil leaves over. Season with salt and pepper. Slide two of the pizzas back onto the grill with a wide spatula. Cover and cook until the cheese melts, 5 to 8 minutes. With the tongs, slide the pizzas onto the back of the baking sheet or onto a cutting board. Repeat to grill the remaining 2 pizzas.

9 Brush the edges of the pizzas with oil. Cut the pizzas crosswise into 6 or 8 pieces and serve.

TIP To remove some of the moisture in fresh mozzarella (it will pool on the pizzas as they cook), double a layer of paper towels and place on a plate. Tear the mozzarella into large, thin pieces and arrange in a single layer on the paper towels. Cover with another layer of paper toweling and a plate. Weight the plate with cans. Let stand for at least 15 minutes to press out the moisture.

Grilled Chicken-and-Eggplant Parmesan Pizza

My adult son, Nik, has been to Italy several times already and he cooks Italian food in his own home. Eggplant Parmesan was one of his favorite dinners as a child, along with pizza. So I put together this combination for him one fall evening. Nik has been running his own household for a few years now but he's happy to eat this when he comes home for a visit. This hearty pizza is a great way to make use of leftover roasted chicken.

MAKES 4 PIZZAS; SERVES 6 TO 8

- **1 recipe Pizza Dough (page 269)**
- **½ cup olive oil, for grilling and brushing**

Topping

- **1 large eggplant (1¼ pounds), trimmed, halved lengthwise, and cut into thin (¼-inch-thick) half-moons**
- **¼ cup olive oil**
- **Coarse salt and freshly ground black pepper**
- **2 cups Tomato Sauce (page 234)**
- **1 whole breast (about 1 pound) rotisserie chicken, shredded into large chunks (about 3 cups)**
- **2 cups ricotta cheese**
- **3 cups (12 ounces) grated loaf mozzarella cheese**
- **½ cup (about 2 ounces) grated Parmesan cheese**

1. Make the pizza dough through the first rise (step 3).
2. Preheat a gas or charcoal grill to medium.
3. To make the topping: Place the eggplant slices on a baking sheet. Drizzle with the olive oil. Sprinkle with 1 teaspoon salt and ¼ teaspoon pepper. Toss with both hands or a spatula to coat. Transfer to the grill and cook in a single layer until tender and marked, turning halfway through with tongs, about 5 minutes total. Remove to a medium platter; set aside.
4. Roll and grill 4 oblong pieces of pizza dough (through step 7 on page 271). Reduce the grill temperature to low (about 250°F).
5. With a rubber spatula, spread each of the cooked crusts with ½ cup of the tomato sauce to within about ½ inch of the edges. Top each with a single layer of eggplant slices—6 to 8 half-moons. Scatter ¾ cup of the shredded chicken over the pizza. Dot each with about ½ cup of the ricotta cheese, in dollops. Then sprinkle each with ¾ cup of the grated mozzarella and 2 tablespoons of the Parmesan. Slide 2 of the pizzas back onto the grill with a wide spatula. Cover and cook until the cheeses are melted, 5 to 8 minutes. With the tongs, slide the pizzas back onto the back of the baking sheet, or onto a cutting board. Repeat to grill the remaining 2 pizzas.
6. Brush the edges of the pizzas with oil. Cut the pizzas crosswise into 6 or 8 pieces and serve.

Grilled Pizza with Mascarpone and Summer Fruit

Grilled pizza makes a surprisingly great dessert. I'll often make a half-recipe of savory topping and a half-recipe of dessert topping—this one or the banana, Nutella, and chocolate topping on page 279. We like having pizza for dinner and dessert. The grill is on anyway! The colors of the plums are beautiful on this pizza. Cooking the plums turns the skins deep purple and the interiors orange, like the apricots. Add a little grated lemon zest to the cheese, if you like.

MAKES 4 PIZZAS; SERVES 8

- **1 recipe Pizza Dough (page 269)**
- **½ cup olive oil, for grilling and brushing**

Topping

- **2 (8-ounce) containers mascarpone cheese (see sidebar, page 60)**
- **5 tablespoons sugar**
- **2 tablespoons vanilla paste (see sidebar, page 212) or pure vanilla extract**
- **2 tablespoons unsalted butter**
- **4 fresh black plums, halved, pitted, and sliced**
- **4 fresh apricots, halved, pitted, and sliced**
- **Pinch of coarse salt**
- **1 pint fresh blackberries (optional)**

TIP Sautéing makes less-than-perfect fruit sweeter and juicier. But if the fruit is ripe and the quality good, raw plums and apricots work beautifully in this recipe.

1 Make the pizza dough through the first rise (step 3).

2 To make the topping: In a medium bowl, stir together the mascarpone, 3 tablespoons of the sugar, and the vanilla; set aside.

3 In a large skillet, melt the butter over medium-high heat. Add the remaining 2 tablespoons of sugar. Add the plum and apricot slices in a single layer. Sprinkle with salt and cook, shaking the pan (don't stir) to toss and turn the slices until the fruit is wilted and the color of the skins starts to bleed and intensify, 7 to 10 minutes. The skillet should remain fairly dry. If the fruit throws off a lot of moisture, turn up the heat. Set aside.

4 Preheat a gas or charcoal grill to medium (300°F).

5 Roll, brush, and grill 4 oblong pieces of pizza dough (through step 7 on page 271).

6 Spread the warm crusts with the flavored mascarpone. Scatter the cooked fruit and blackberries, if using, over the top.

7 Brush the edges of the pizzas with oil. Cut the pizzas crosswise into 8 pieces and serve.

Salad Pizza

I owe the inspiration for this recipe to my good friend Michael Lauretano, who owns Pizza Lauretano, an authentic Neapolitan brick-oven pizzeria in Bethel, Connecticut. I've been taking my family there since it opened. My daughter Nola loves Michael's Pizza Margherita, and my son Peter eats anything Michael makes. Every time I go I try a different pizza, and they're all delicious. But I keep coming back to this one. The arugula is crisp and spicy and the prosciutto is soft and salty. It's an incredible combination.

MAKES 4 PIZZAS; SERVES 6 TO 8

- **1 recipe Pizza Dough (page 269)**
- **½ cup olive oil, for grilling and brushing**

Topping

- **8 firmly packed cups arugula**
- **2 pints (4 cups) cherry tomatoes, stemmed and halved**
- **1 pound fresh goat cheese**
- **Balsamic vinegar**
- **Olive oil**
- **Coarse salt and freshly ground black pepper**
- **20 thin slices prosciutto**

TIP Rapid-rise yeast will give you a fine dough in less than thirty minutes—just about the time you need to prepare the topping.

1. Make the pizza dough through the first rise (step 3).
2. Preheat a gas or charcoal grill to medium.
3. Roll, brush, and grill 4 oblong pieces of pizza dough (through step 7 on page 271). Reduce the grill temperature to low (about 250°F).
4. To make the topping: Combine the arugula and tomatoes in a large bowl; set aside.
5. Break the goat cheese into pieces over the grilled crusts. Slide 2 of the pizzas back onto the grill with a wide spatula. Cover and cook until the cheese melts, 5 to 8 minutes. With the tongs, slide the pizzas back onto the back of the baking sheet or onto a cutting board. Repeat to grill the remaining 2 pizzas.
6. Drizzle the arugula mixture with 2 teaspoons vinegar and 2 tablespoons oil. Season lightly with salt and pepper, and toss. Top the grilled crusts with the arugula mixture and drape with the prosciutto slices. Drizzle all over with more vinegar and olive oil.
7. Brush the edges of the pizza with oil. Cut the pizzas crosswise into 6 or 8 pieces and serve.

Grilled Pizza with Figs and Ricotta

Cheese brings out the sweet, luscious flavor of figs in the savory pizza. I like to cut it in small squares if I'm serving it as an appetizer, but cut into larger pieces, it's an excellent dinner pizza. Fresh goat or blue cheese works well in place of the ricotta.

MAKES 4 OBLONG PIZZAS; SERVES 6 TO 8

- **1 recipe Pizza Dough (page 269)**
- **½ cup olive oil, for grilling and brushing**

Topping

- **2 tablespoons olive oil**
- **2 large onions, thinly sliced**
- **Coarse salt and freshly ground black pepper**
- **1 teaspoon sugar**
- **1 teaspoon chopped fresh thyme**
- **2 cups ricotta cheese**
- **4 ounces (about 1⅓ cups) freshly grated pecorino cheese (pre-grated will not work)**
- **2 to 3 tablespoons whole milk, as needed**
- **24 fresh figs (about 1 pint), quartered lengthwise**

TIP Let the dough relax for a few minutes on the board after you roll it out so that it doesn't jump back at you when you place it on the grill.

1. Make the pizza dough through the first rise (step 3).
2. To make the topping: In a large sauté pan, heat the oil over high heat. Add the onions, 1½ teaspoons salt, and the sugar and cook, stirring often, until the onions are well caramelized and tender, 10 to 12 minutes. Stir in the thyme; set aside.
3. In a medium bowl, stir together the ricotta and about half of the pecorino. Season to taste with salt and pepper. Add the milk, as needed, to make a smearable consistency; set aside.
4. Preheat a gas or charcoal grill to medium (about 300°F). Line the backs of two baking sheets with parchment paper.
5. Roll, brush, and grill 4 oblong pieces of pizza dough (through step 9 on page 271).
6. If using a gas grill, turn it to low (250°F). With a rubber spatula, smear the cooked pizza crusts with the ricotta mixture to within about ½ inch of the edges. Scatter the onions over the cheese. Arrange 24 fig quarters in a single layer, cut sides up, over each pizza. Sprinkle each with ⅛ teaspoon coarse salt, a pinch of pepper, and the rest of the grated pecorino. Slide 2 of the pizzas back onto the grill with a wide spatula. Cover and cook until the figs are warmed through and the cheeses are melted, 5 to 8 minutes. With the tongs, slide the pizzas back onto the back of the baking sheet, or onto a cutting board. Repeat to grill the remaining 2 pizzas.
7. Brush the edges of the pizzas with olive oil. Cut the pizzas crosswise into 6 pieces and serve hot.

Oven-Baked Pizza

If you don't have a grill, I recommend the following steps to produce the very best thin-crust pizzas in your home oven using an inverted baking sheet as a pizza stone. In step 5, it's useful to have a second pair of hands to stabilize the hot sheet pan while you slide the pizza onto it.

1 Make the pizza dough on page 269 through step 3.

2 While the dough proofs, set the oven rack in the lowest position. Preheat the oven to 500°F. Heat an inverted 17 by 12-inch rimmed baking sheet in the oven for 1 hour.

3 Prepare the desired toppings.

4 Cut the dough in half; set one half aside, covered with plastic. On a sheet of lightly floured parchment, roll the second dough half to the size of the parchment sheet. Pinch the edges of the dough between your thumb and forefinger to build up the sides of the pizza by about 1/2 inch. Transfer the dough, on the parchment, to a rimless (or overturned rimmed) baking sheet. Brush the dough all over with olive oil.

5 Remove the hot, inverted baking sheet from the oven and place on the stovetop. Transfer the dough, on the parchment, to the inverted baking sheet. Return the inverted baking sheet to the oven and bake the pizza until the dough begins to crisp and lose its wet shine and blond color, 4 to 5 minutes.

6 Remove the inverted baking sheet from the oven and slide the pizza onto a cool inverted baking sheet. Return the hot baking sheet to the oven to heat. Spread the pizza crust with toppings. Brush the edges with olive oil. Then repeat step 5 to return the pizza crust to the oven. Bake until the toppings are warmed through and any cheese is melted, 9 to 10 minutes.

7 Grasp a corner of the parchment paper and use a spatula to slide the pizza onto a cutting board and cut into 12 squares. Return the inverted sheet pan to the oven to keep it hot while you repeat to prepare and bake the second pizza.

Grilled Pizza with Bananas, Nutella, and Chocolate

My son Peter was very happy with the Banana–Chocolate Chip Cupcakes with Nutella frosting (page 150) that we made for his fourth birthday party. So I came up with this dessert pizza one evening recently with him in mind. The bananas soften on top of the Nutella and everything melts together into a delicious, warm muddle.

MAKES 4 PIZZAS; SERVES 8

- **1 recipe Pizza Dough (page 269)**
- **½ cup olive oil, for grilling and brushing**

Topping

- **1⅓ cups Nutella**
- **8 small ripe bananas, cut on a diagonal ⅓ inch thick**
- **½ cup mini marshmallows (optional)**
- **1 cup chopped hazelnuts or pecans**
- **4 ounces bittersweet chocolate**

1 Make the pizza dough through the first rise (step 3).

2 Preheat a gas or charcoal grill to medium (300°F).

3 Roll, brush, and grill 4 oblong pieces of pizza dough (through step 7 on page 271). Reduce the grill temperature to low (about 250°F).

4 With a rubber scraper, spread each grilled crust with about ⅓ cup Nutella. Arrange the banana slices in a single layer on top. Press the marshmallows, if using, into the Nutella alongside the bananas. Slide 2 of the pizzas back onto the grill with a wide spatula. Cover and cook until the bananas and Nutella are warmed through, 5 to 8 minutes. With the tongs, slide the pizzas back onto the back of the baking sheet, or onto a cutting board. Repeat to grill the remaining 2 pizzas.

5 Brush the edges of the pizzas with oil. Sprinkle the pizzas with the nuts and use a vegetable peeler to shred chocolate over the tops. Cut the pizzas crosswise into 8 pieces and serve.

ACKNOWLEDGMENTS There are so many people I wish to thank for their help with this book. Thanks to my agent, Coleen O'Shea, who helped me and the book at every turn. My good friend the writer Stephanie Lyness kept me calm while she teased out story and creativity. Valerie Denner meticulously tested and retested my recipes, in a home kitchen with regular home baking equipment, and then tested them again. Val, I can't begin to thank you for your dedication. You are truly one of a kind! (And thank *you*, Bob Denner, for never saying no to all that work she did for me!)

A very big thank-you to the terrific team at Clarkson Potter, especially my editor Emily Takoudes, Lauren Shakely, Doris Cooper, and Hilary Sims for trusting me to share more of my story and recipes with our fans, customers, and television viewers. To Ben Fink: I can't thank you enough for your incredible patience and beautiful photography in the midst of a crazy week of concrete and construction at the bakery. You are a true professional. Thanks go to Francis Palmer, Karen Salsgiver, and Simon Pearce for the beautiful pottery, wonderful linens, and gorgeous glass that grace our photos. Thank you to my erstwhile mother-in-law, Elenore Bronzo, for her "prop house"; your Stangl Pottery lives on.

To my professional mentors, Rick Steffann, Martha Stewart, and Jeffrey Hamelman, who are responsible for my success. And to my bakery staff: thank you Fran, Patti, Chris Houle, Chris Gargone, Andres, Felix, Walter, Roberto, Keith, Ignacio, Deysi, and Matt-the-chef. Thank you to my counter people, especially Juan and Rene and, of course, Izzy: You guys rock and always make me look better. Thanks to Aimee Barricelli for her dedicated bookkeeping. A special thanks to Ed Schriver for his gentle way of saying "things are going to change around here" and then doing it himself: I love you Ed.

To my three children, Nikolai, Nola, and little Peter, you guys are the biggest reason I work so hard. And thanks to their mothers, because ours are three of the most amazing children on the planet. And last but not ever forgotten, a loving thank-you to my parents, Joseph and Mary Ann, who never had a chance to see my accomplishments. I love and miss you.

SOURCES

Amazon.com
www.amazon.com
Baking and pastry equipment, tools, specialty flours, chestnut paste, mascarpone, and vanilla paste.

The Baker's Catalogue/ King Arthur Flour
135 Route 5 South
P.O. Box 1010
Norwich, VT 05055
800-827-6836
www.kingarthurflour.com
Baking and pastry equipment, tools, specialty flours, praline paste, vanilla paste, and other specialty ingredients.

Bridge Kitchenware
563 Eagle Rock Avenue
Roseland, NJ 07068
973-287-6163
www.bridgekitchenware.com
Kitchen tools, bakeware, and decorating equipment.

J B Prince
36 East 31st Street
New York, NY 10016
800-473-0577
www.jbprince.com
Baking and pastry equipment, and tools.

Nielsen-Massey Vanillas, Inc.
1550 Shields Drive
Waukegan, IL 60085-8307
800-525-PURE (7873)
www.nielsenmassey.com
Extracts, orange blossom water, rose water, and vanilla paste.

Sur La Table
800-243-0852
www.surlatable.com
Bakeware, molds, nonstick silicone baking mats, and specialty tools and appliances.

Williams-Sonoma
877-812-6235
www.williams-sonoma.com
Bakeware, molds, nonstick silicone baking mats, and specialty tools and appliances.

Index

Note: Page references in *italics* refer to recipe photographs.

D

E

F

G

H

I

K

L

M

N

O

P

V

W

Z